Reckless Misfortune

MERCER UNIVERSITY PRESS

Endowed by

TOM WATSON BROWN
and
THE WATSON-BROWN FOUNDATION, INC.

Reckless Misfortune

The Century We Inherited

from the First World War

CHRISTOPHER BLAKE

MERCER UNIVERSITY PRESS
Macon, Georgia

MUP/ H1009

© 2021 by Mercer University Press
Published by Mercer University Press
1501 Mercer University Drive
Macon, Georgia 31207
All rights reserved

25 24 23 22 21   5 4 3 2 1

Books published by Mercer University Press are printed on acid-free paper
that meets the requirements of the American National Standard for
Information Sciences—Permanence of Paper for Printed Library Materials.

Printed and bound in the United States.

This book is set in Adobe Caslon Pro.

Cover/jacket design by Burt&Burt.

ISBN   978-0-88146-804-5
Cataloging-in-Publication Data is available from the Library of Congress

In gratitude to the several generations of my family whom I have

known and loved.

CONTENTS

ACKNOWLEDGMENTS

Many people have encouraged me in different ways in the writing of this book, and to each I owe much gratitude. Here I wish to identify those who have especially inspired me in some important way.

My father, Peter Blake, and my sister, Carolyn Dickins, inquired frequently on the book's status and gently nudged me to keep working. I deeply appreciate having had the opportunity to talk with them about its progress.

Several friends and colleagues in Georgia have read parts of the manuscript and offered valuable advice. I owe gratitude to the members of my Palaver Club, who listened to me reading excerpts and provided helpful comments. My thanks also are extended to my personal friends Dr. Neil Cullinan, former professor of political science at Fort Valley State University, and Rev. Dr. R. Kirby Godsey, former president and now chancellor of Mercer University. They stimulated further reflections on the contents of the book.

Detailed and valuable academic feedback was offered by Dr. Barbara Donovan, professor of political science at Wesleyan College, who helped clarify key concepts of Central European history and politics.

At my place of work, Middle Georgia State University, my colleagues were wonderfully tolerant and supportive during the project, especially my executive assistant, Ms. Carey Wimberly, and my chief of staff, Ms. Ember Bishop Bentley. Additionally, my former intern Ms. Calabria Turner performed great service in referencing of the work. I also thank the library staff of Ms. Tamatha Lambert, Ms. Abbie Holmes and Mr. Mark Ensley for their advice and help with the creation of the Index, as well as Prof. Lauren Cater for her editing of the audio version.

Finally, my wife and best friend, Melody, was patient, encouraging, and engaged throughout the project. I would not have completed it without her steadfast support and her patiently listening and commenting on many excerpts from each chapter. I cannot express how grateful I am for her belief in this project.

These and other persons were critical in my completing the book. To them all, I say, simply, thank you.

PREFACE

It has been given several names, such as the Great War, World War I, the First World War, the 1914–1918 War, and even, to some, the War of Imperialism.

That fact alone suggests that a war of such enormity and uniqueness has not been perceived in the same way by all people over the hundred years-plus since it occurred. Different generations have discerned in that early twentieth-century conflict varied aspects of human history and have chosen a name that works best for the circumstances of their generation and population. Clearly, the use of the term "first" or "one" implies the existence of a subsequent event, that being the Second World War in this case. Conversely, the term "great" suggests an event of singularity, which indeed was the Great War's estimation in the minds of people until the terrible start of the Second World War. Throughout this book, varying names and titles are used for the global conflict of the years 1914 to 1918, as well as the simple term "the war," both to convey something of the perspective each title suggests for different peoples and for literary style and effect.

Not only did that calamitous event gain different names, but it also left the world with some uncertainty and confusion about the dates of its duration and, particularly, its conclusion. Many small war memorials dot the landscape of Europe and the United States, recording the war as having occurred between 1914 and 1918 or 1919. In the United States, it is remembered as having occurred from 1917 to 1919. In Russian history, it ran from 1914 to 1917. About its beginning, there is less confusion. The war is generally recognized as having begun on Tuesday, July 28th, 1914, with the declaration by Austria-Hungary of a state of war with Serbia, with the other nations of Europe rushing into the conflict over the next week. When and how the conflict ended is less clear.

If there is some opaqueness about its duration, that condition relates also to the tragic scale of suffering and death caused by the First World War. Current estimates are that nearly ten million military combatants died fighting in the conflict, with about another twenty million military casualties. That figure, however, does not properly circumscribe the scale of the tragic impact on human life. For the first time in history, millions of civilians perished in the conflict, with some estimates suggesting marginally more than those who died in the fighting. To compound matters further, the deaths did not end with the Armistice of November 11th, 1918, but continued apace with both military and civilian populations. At the time of this book's writing, the world is facing the onslaught of the coronavirus COVID-19. A similar pandemic occurred from 1918 to 1919 with the global impact of a deadly influenza virus, named for posterity as the Spanish influenza because the Madrid press first reported its arrival. Like COVID-19, it spared no nations or populations, with President Woodrow Wilson even suffering its effects. Clearly, the Spanish flu was directly aided by the depleted strength and health of the peoples and nations of the world because of the debilitating effect of the war. By the time the Spanish flu ended, half a billion people had contracted it, and somewhere between fifty and one hundred million had succumbed to its symptoms. That pandemic killed probably three times as many people as the direct fighting of the Great War. Aside from the Spanish influenza, several military conflicts continued into the 1920s directly because of the Great War and the way it ended.

These observations are merely the external surface facts of a deeper issue regarding the nature and complexity of the First World War. The war was a shocking and seismic event of great magnitude in its unprecedented destruction and its radical alteration of the course of global history. It was and is a vast scar on the canvas of human history. Yet, paradoxically, while it is mesmerizing to some peoples and nations, it is often overlooked and ignored by others. The First World War is indeed a conundrum in these and other respects. Its origins, experiences, and consequences have raised as many questions as answers that have not been fully resolved by the passage of time. For example, its occurrence was shocking to all and made little sense in terms of the trajectory and events of the nineteenth century. Yet when war finally occurred, most Europeans and their leaders oddly claimed to have anticipated beforehand the likelihood of a broad European conflict, even if that prospect had not been pondered seriously or believed with conviction. Indeed, by the start of the twentieth century, Europe had been benefiting from an era of peace over several decades that had not existed in earlier centuries. In this sense, what was about to occur in the summer of 1914 did not make sense in the context of its times. As Margaret MacMillan aptly described in the title of her book,[1] the First World War was indeed the "war that ended peace." Similarly, its consequences produced forces and events that were completely new and unpredictable, shaping the future of the twentieth century with unfamiliar ideas and odd realities that were not part of the original rationale or motivation for its outset in that hot European summer of 1914.

The First World War does not thus possess a clear element, rationale, or story that neatly delivers to us a logical explanation of its causes, its unfolding, and its legacy to history. It has been viewed with different lenses by various nations and subsequent generations, and in making sense of it, those peoples have altered the courses of their own histories and destinies. The Cambridge University historian David Reynolds calls this the "long shadow"[2] of the First World War, casting its effect across the decades. Because of its impact and complexity, it is both one of the most significant events of all modern history and still an enduring enigma. It does not provide us a definitive and convincing resolution of its raison d'etre or a clear value proposition of its heritage. Instead, it invites those of us who have lived in its shadow for one hundred years to look back into its

---

[1] Margaret MacMillan, *The Road to 1914–The War That Ended Peace* (Random House, 2014).
[2] David Reynolds, *The Long Shadow: The Great War and the Twentieth Century* (New York: Simon & Schuster, 2013).

odd causes, its traumatic horrors, and its ominous consequences like a complex novel invites us to understand different characters, or a piece of art invites us to perceive varied themes, moods, and hues. And, like a work of art or literature, two different beholders do not necessarily agree on the event or experience. This quality of the Great War has allowed successive generations and nations to see stories in it that illuminate their lives and histories and then to choose their futures, for good or bad, based in part on those stories. Both the shadows and the illuminations from that war have darkened and enlightened our human family's path over the past century.

This enigmatic and intangible quality of the First World War makes it a subject of rich and fertile soil for the historian, the artist, the observer, the philosopher, the novelist, the storyteller, and the poet, among others. It has provided vast material of worth to different peoples and schools of thought for more than four generations. That recognition of its value proposition has prevailed more strongly in the consciousness of the European and Commonwealth nations, and less so in the United States, outside of academia or the military. This presence or absence of consciousness, in turn, has affected how each generation has understood its history, its development, and its options. Today, we have no access to living memory of the war. There is no person left alive to ask about that cataclysmic time or the details of that experience. The fact that it occurred more than a century ago means that while it no longer resides in any living personal memory, it is nonetheless recent enough to have shaped our past century in ways that still condition our current human reality. With the passing of Florence Green, in 2012, at the age of 110, the world said farewell to the Great War's final veteran. Florence had worked, with the status of an enlisted soldier, at the cafeteria of a London airfield in 1918. In a war that had so few enlisted women, her passing as the last veteran of the conflict was ironic and noteworthy. The Allied nations of Britain and France held grand state funerals when their final veterans passed away, and in so doing bade a solemn farewell to all human memory of the war. From that point on, the First World War could only be reviewed as history and no longer as memory.

Of course, most of us experience this transition from memory to history in our own family lives. Our direct relationship with older family members is inevitably lost when they die, but their lives remain both in our cognition and our interpretation of their lives and significance. In short, they continue to affect the evolving story of ourselves and our families, even from the grave. Successively, we all experience some version of this transition until we ourselves become memory and story in the lives of our future family members, remembered—we hope benignly—by those subsequent generations. Our DNA-conscious world is also now easily able to access through medical technology the specific genetic legacy we inherit from our ancestors. The effect and impact of a dead ancestor on our own lives does not thus disappear with his or her physical passing. Their former life continues to inform us and our family's physical, psychological, emotional, economic, and domestic conditions. This transgenerational connectivity and consciousness are typically at their most powerful over three generations, or seventy-five years. Many persons have direct and frequent transgenerational experience between the previous generation (parents), the current generation (siblings), and the immediate subsequent generation (children). Beyond that three-generational range, direct communication begins to weaken, first with the grandparent-grandchildren degree of separation, and further still with the generation occupied by great-grandparents and great-grandchildren. By that further generational interval, connectivity has weakened considerably in the experience of most Westerners. In this longitudinal framework, the gap in time between four generations means that knowledge of experience and connections across those generations is tenuous at best. This does not mean, however, that previous generations do not influence the current one. Whether we perceive it or not, the past reaches daily into our presence and our present, and shapes how we think and behave.

This book applies that principle to a global event of four generations past. It examines how a war of unfathomable magnitude affected each subsequent generation of the human family. It was a war that reached directly into individual families, inflicting excruciating pain, and, for the first time in history, affected the global family itself. My own family knew its experiences and consequences; both of my grandfathers and at least one other family member participated in the conflict. One died there, one was an official casualty, and one returned externally unscathed but inwardly altered. Those experiences certainly changed my family history. If that happened for one family, how much more for millions of families across the world?

The answer to this question is the story of our century. This story only makes sense if we see how the First World War affected humanity across the decades, whether we are mesmerized by it or ignorant of what happened. The First World War caused great strife and inestimable changes to the people of the world and to the trajectory of human life. It shaped the lives, despairs, hopes, and aspirations of millions, who then shaped them similarly for their children. The war upended nations and continents and propelled them in utterly new directions over the past one hundred years, creating a world that we inherited and inhabit as the fourth generation after its time. We are free to choose what we do with this inheritance, but we are also very much molded by its legacy and its stipulations. What did the Great War deliver to us over the past century, and what lessons can we learn from it for those generations to come?

Reckless Misfortune

PART ONE

CALAMITY

1

UNTO THE FOURTH GENERATION

Five years to the day after the assassination of Archduke Franz Ferdinand of Austria-Hungary, the First World War formally concluded with the Treaty of Versailles on June 28th, 1919. At the time of the war's conclusion, it was commonly referred to as the "war to end all wars." That phrase was an adaptation of the title of an article, "The War That Will End War," penned by the famous author H. G. Wells at the war's outset in 1914 and adopted later by President Woodrow Wilson as part of his reasoning for American involvement in the war. The phrase "the war to end all wars" was globally popular for its hope that the human family would never revisit the kind of vast suffering and misery that were emblematic of the First World War. Dwarfing all previous conflicts in terms of breadth of destruction and loss, the ten million dead combatants, twelve million military casualties, seven million dead citizens, eight million civilian casualties, and tens of millions who further succumbed to the Spanish influenza left the world's survivors with a shattering grief. Any future reenactment of such a dreadful conflict seemed utterly unimaginable and intolerable after such monumental tragedy. To make sense of such vast and questionably pointless slaughter was only possible with the belief that somehow this scale of suffering was the final sacrifice on the altar of human hubris. Hope dictated that we would emerge as a human community into a new way of thinking and acting, in which war was banished and replaced by something different. Perhaps, finally, swords would be beaten into plowshares and spears into pruning hooks, as expressed in the book of Isaiah. Subsequent history, of course, showed the vanity and failure of this hope, and much of this book explores how that naïve dream of a peaceful future was shattered by the century that followed the "war to end all wars."

One hundred years after this epochal event, between 2014 and 2018, the British people and their government raised edifices and hosted a remarkable series of ceremonies and events to commemorate the centennial of what is familiar as the Great War in the United Kingdom. Similar commemorations were held by other Commonwealth nations as well as the main combatant nations of Europe, particularly on the Allied side. At the start of the British commemorations in 2014, an extraordinary display was created in the moat around the Tower of London. Handcrafted red ceramic poppies, about four inches in diameter, were attached to metal rods and individually placed into the grass of the moat. The exhibition, entitled "Blood Swept Lands and Seas of Red," featured more than 888,000 poppies, each symbolizing one of the combat dead of the First World War from Britain and its empire. Equally impressive during the four years of commemorations were the black, metal silhouettes of a British infantry soldier that were placed around the country in parks, roadways, shopping malls, and other places. These six-foot, two-dimensional silhouettes were intended to surprise viewers as part of an exhibition titled "There, But Not There." As the centennial of the First World War approached, the British—both young and old—appeared to be reverentially enthralled as they recalled a generation that had gone to war and either not returned or returned as different people, one hundred years earlier.

I experienced a growing interest in the nature and significance of the First World War in my adolescence and early adulthood. This was the result both of my grandfathers' enlistments in the war and the several visits I made to the Western Front of Flanders (*Vlaanderen*, in native Flemish), the agricultural region of Belgium and France that literally bogged down the opposing Central powers and Allied armies in mud and clay, a hallmark theme of the trenches of the First World War. As a resident of the United Kingdom, my awareness of the First World War was part of a strong, shared cultural consciousness of British identity and history that was—and is—pervasive and enduring.

For most Americans living in the current era, this embedded cultural memory of the First World War would be unfamiliar and perceived as a distinctly British, European (especially France), and Commonwealth (e.g., Canada, Australia) phenomenon. The Europeans, and especially the victors of Britain and France, have indeed preserved a nostalgia for the Great War that is present in a multitude of symbols, places, memorials, and anniversaries that are part of Western European culture. For the Germans, this has been challenging, since the issue of war guilt is a burdensome and defining element of both the history and the story of the First World War. But for many Americans, the Great War is akin to the later mid-century Korean War, both often termed as "forgotten wars" and denuded in perceived meaning and legacy. A recent and highly visible illustration of this under-recognition of the First World War was evident during the Allied centennial commemoration of the Armistice in Paris, in November 2018. As the ceremony concluded, the weather turned to rain, prompting President Donald Trump to cancel his scheduled visit to the nearby American military cemetery at Meuse-Argonne, the resting place of fifteen thousand dead Americans from one of the deadliest battles in US history.

Other narratives of military conflict, on the other hand, have dominated and prevailed in the US. For example, the United States' pivotal role in the Second World War, its decade-long engagement and subsequent anguish about the Vietnam War, and its incomplete engagements, more recently, in Afghanistan and Iraq have collectively overshadowed the role of the US in the first global conflict that occurred in the second decade of the twentieth century. This is statistically odd and myopic, and some collateral context illustrates this point. In the later Second World War, the United States suffered four hundred thousand military fatalities, a figure marginally higher than the British cost, but considerably lower than the multi-million fatality figures suffered by other major fighting nations such

5

as Germany, Japan, and the USSR. The size of the American casualty figure does, though, account for an enduring public narrative of the importance and cost of the Second World War, especially when combined with its epic theme of freedom versus tyranny, with the United States delivering that welcome victory. The narrative of both the tragic price of that war and the success of its outcome for the cause of democracy has underpinned the Allied interpretation of World War II since 1945. For the Russians, a similar but individualized narrative was developed and nurtured as its specific national story, clear in the name given by Russians to the conflict as the "Great Patriotic War."

In short, the past three generations of Americans have articulated a persuasive, strong, and enduring narrative that understands its national engagement in the Second World War, and the heroic loss of some four hundred thousand of its young men, as a story about saving democracy from totalitarianism. What surprises many Americans is learning the significance of the sacrificial cost borne by its young fighting men one generation earlier, in the First World War in 1917, and discovering that the rationale for American engagement was little different in 1917 from what it was in 1941, including, in both cases, a considerable reluctance to participate. While active engagement on the battlefields of the First World War was limited for American troops to the months between September 1917 and November 1918, in those thirteen months America lost nearly twice as many dead as it did in the twelve combat years of the Vietnam War. The Battle of Meuse-Argonne remains the costliest battle in terms of the number of military dead and casualties in all US history, and the battle was a capstone event that helped successfully conclude the Great War. Yet many Americans know little of Meuse-Argonne and do not relate to its historic significance, which is not the case for, say, Gettysburg or the Alamo or Bunker Hill or Normandy. In short, America's role in the First World War was not an inexpensive or painless one. In terms of its history at that time, it was seismic, even though today many have little knowledge of that earthquake or its consequences.

Why has one major historical event become enshrined as an enduring element of a national narrative while another similarly influential event is lost or weak within that narrative? The answer may reside in how our own stories—individual and communal—serve a number of purposes that assist us in constructing a functioning mental map of reality, and how this reality is fashioned and informed by our own role and purpose. History is both a study of past events and the stories we tell of the past. The First World War is a story that is not well relayed or heard in America, which contrasts with the esteemed account and view of the war belonging to its northern Canadian neighbors. This is an omission of some significance, since the story of the Great War still shapes our world, our ideas, and our actions globally today, including in the United States. For the US, it is as if we find our geopolitical world one of great complexity, but we have forgotten a dreadful event and formative part of the journey that has led us to our present reality. By forgetting that such events over time are connected and pivotal, we risk seeing them as isolated occurrences with little context, power, influence, or symbolism. Their rich impact and potency are less visible to us and we lose their plot. They may become merely interesting rather than essential. History, in this latter context, is an optional vacation trip to our subjective interior, intriguing for a couple of weeks, but unimportant once we return from our vacation to the real world.

This risk should be carefully avoided, since it threatens the evolution of our identities and our ways of thinking and does not provide an adequate road map to the future, both for us as individuals and societies. An example from most religions, that of a pilgrimage, might help explain this importance. A pilgrimage provides for a faith community a powerful motif and a recurrent ritual that enables it to engage repeatedly with a key past event and its significance, and then repeat the connection across successive generations through reenactment. A pilgrimage—such as the Hajj to Makkah, or the Via Dolorosa to the Holy Sepulchre—also essentially requires both the journey and destination to be experienced by the pilgrim. Process and outcome are thus corequisite. In the case of a pilgrimage, the sacred event of the past (e.g., the Crucifixion of Jesus) is transcended into the current life and faith of the individual via the act of pilgrimage, thus creating a sacred narrative of past, present, and future for the faith community. This belief, experience, and action is then taught as core attributes of the religion to the next generation of the faithful. A pilgrimage thus enables the faithful to make sense of their present community, cherish past events, sustain essential stories, reinforce core values, and inform future choices and actions over successive generations. Religion, in short, requires each generation of the faithful to grasp a transcendent view of history, uniting past, present, and future in an overarching narrative. The pilgrimage is an example of this general approach, which religion appears to do rather well.

Secular historical narratives of nations and communities similarly work to illuminate and perpetuate a shared understanding of past events and their present meaning, delivering, in effect, both an understanding of the route from past to present, as well as a map to the future destination, or destiny, of the community for each successive generation. The power of the past, in this respect, lies as much forward as backward in sustaining this narrative. When done well, each generation perceives the thread and meaning of the narrative over time. When done poorly, key past events may become diminished in the collective memory, and the narrative becomes blind to their influence. In terms of the First World War, this appears more of a risk in the United States than in Europe and the Commonwealth nations. This is both ironic and unfortunate since the twentieth century was, in many ways, the American century, and it was this very war that gave the nation its premier status. That first world war held the ensuing decades hostage to its nature and consequences in ways that were absorbed into the global geopolitical environment across each generation. Today, a century later, it is valuable for the nations of the world, and especially the former combatant nations, to reconsider how World War I has shaped their national destinies and narratives, and how it can still enlighten future options politically, nationally, and globally in the light of its outcomes. World

War I was a tragic pivot point that pushed humanity onto a new trajectory that we still follow. It gave humanity a plot and narrative of universal significance in which we participate, knowingly or unknowingly. The recent centennial commemorations have helped us think afresh, and maybe, for the first time in some places, to consider how we got here.

The war's centennial tributes show how history can be very personal and powerful and not solely the obscure interest of academia. Elsewhere I have written of family members who were drawn into the "war to end all wars." Genealogy is an instructive personal tool for exploring the nature of the past and helping to connect us existentially to a time and place now gone. The repetition of family life and its genealogical stories—the fact that most of us grow up and give birth to a new generation—is the major conduit of historic events and perceptions of identity in the lives of each successive generation. A century is made up of four human generations, each accounting for twenty-five years, and each generation is critical in transmitting forward its understanding of the past and its stories. "Unto the fourth generation" is a term found in the biblical book of Deuteronomy, reminding us that our actions reap consequences even unto the fourth generation of the future. Our personal generational map generally provides us clear guidance on our lives through a seventy-five-year window that triangulates strongly from grandparents to grandchildren, helping us know better why and how we perceive, live, and act. The First World War was a reality that was similarly handed down to subsequent generations, particularly in Europe and often literally within the family. For many (great-) grandfathers and (great-) grandmothers, the Great War was the reckless misfortune forced on them in 1914, and which miserably resumed twenty-five years later in the Second World War. That second war was, as we shall see, the product of the former, its next generation and its offspring. Today, we stand one century from the First World War, and that generational connectivity is strained and diminishing with the passage of time. The (grand) parent generation that lived and fought in the Second World War is losing four hundred American veterans every day, and by 2045, exactly one hundred years after its cessation, it is anticipated that its final veteran will have died. At that time, all living human memory of that second global conflict will also have disappeared forever.

The argument here is that the "shadow" of the First World War, to use David Reynolds's term, is strongly present but poorly observed at this twenty-first-century point in our history. The seventy-five-year tri-generational connectivity disappeared decades ago for the First World War and is now disappearing quickly with the aging of the popularly described Greatest Generation of the Second World War. But the effect of both these wars remains deep in our DNA, unto the fourth generation. Indeed, our capacity to perceive events and their meaning strongly over a seventy-five-year horizon is a generational triangulation that shows us our place on a journey through time and tells us the story of our identity, reminding us that we are not simply fixed in an immediate "now." Like a triangle that has no directional beginning or end, we also live both forward and backward, reviewing and revisiting the themes and experiences of our (grand) parents and (grand) children with new insights, emotions, explanations, and connections. We also plan our futures and have dreams for our children so that our story can continue onward through the lives of the next generation. While this generational triangulation is alive and active, we can discern the tapestry and its story with strong visibility, like white light on the past. But as the seventy-five-year triangle extends "unto a fourth generation," the picture becomes more fractured and obscure. Today, we live in that fourth generation from the First World War, at a time beyond the experiences and stories of those who experienced firsthand the years between 1914 and 1918. As such, we find it harder to see the war's role and influence. We have no white light available and rely, instead, to use the same metaphor, on ultraviolet illumination, which can only identify specific objects under certain limits and conditions.

This is the challenge of the time and place we inhabit now. During the twentieth century our generational triangulation allowed us to discern the plot, to find the connection, to hear the echoes, and to perceive the tapestry of what was the length and breadth of that century, including the enormity of the First World War. Today, we live when the passage of the years means it is harder to see how that century's events shaped our lives, with no capacity to draw on the experiences and memories of the actual generation who endured its misfortunes between 1914 and 1918. The United States, which found its place as the world's preeminent superpower by the end of the twentieth century, has not yet understood well how the First World War sent it down this pathway. Other combatant nations see the twentieth-century tapestry with a more discerning eye, appropriately regarding the first global war as fundamental and far-reaching. Without that "weaving of a tapestry," however, the events of the past may be wrongly seen as random and disassociated, not even capable of creating a mosaic, let alone a tapestry. The risk today is that the First World War may only be perceived as a distant event and relegated to the file of "gone and forgotten," of interest only to the academy. This would be an historic folly. We live now as the fourth generation from the 1914–1918 War. To understand well our own story and our current reality, we need to reach back and gain a stronger understanding of the global cataclysm that occurred one hundred years, or four generations, ago and track how it bequeathed great consequences, including considerable misfortunes, to subsequent generations. We are, in short, here and now in large part because of what happened there and then.

This book contends that the story of the First World War is still around us even as we approach the end of the first quarter of the twenty-first century. We do not find our identity as people and societies simply by staring into the mirror of our immediate now. Rather, we gain a better understanding of our identity if we understand our journey through time and space as a shared human story. In that story, humanity's choices and actions are shaped—but not predestined—by our communal past experiences, which then influence—but not determine—the future story as it develops across successive generations. In the case of the all-enveloping event and suffering

11

that was the First World War, we did not just send our own familial (great-) grandfathers to fight over there. Effectively, all humanity sent the millions of its (great-) grandfathers to the conflict. The tragedy left no one unscathed. The disease infected all the organs. The planet groaned. Because of that universality, the generational triangulation of the past century has ensured that the whole global family has been shaped by the war's awful legacy for more than one hundred years. The First World War, and its attendant second, is indeed still beating in the human heart today, and continues to transmit its DNA to each generation. Ours is the fourth generation, so we have the more challenging task of understanding how that first war changed forever the story of where and who we are, since we no longer have access to the men and women who knew firsthand its devastating nature. Yet by undertaking this task, we can discern how that war shaped a century which has delivered to us our national identities, our political systems, our scientific advances, our belief systems, and our visions of our destinies. We are part of a tapestry across time in which the threads unite us with the best and the worst of our shared human past.

We start to weave the threads of this tapestry at that very point and place when the guns grew silent and the yearned-for hope for peace and the healing of deep wounds began after four years and four months of total and vile war. Yet while the hopes of peace soared as the guns quieted, this past century shows us that in the extinguishing of the flames of the First World War, the sparks of future incendiary events were born, the afterglow of which can still be felt today.

2

AN OMINOUS DAWN, A PERILOUS DUSK

The hauntingly tragic occasion and symbolically loaded location was, in fact, an unassuming clearing deep in a quiet northern European forest. The railway siding in the Forest of Compiegne was utterly unremarkable and indeed could—and should—have been a place the world would readily forget. But this was a place where ghosts of the past and visions of the future would assume demonic proportions. The forest siding was intentionally secluded, and a railway carriage as unassuming a venue as one could imagine, but its significance was seismic for ensuing human history. At local French time of 5:00 A.M. on the 11th of November 1918, representatives of the main protagonists of the First World War (Russia aside) met and signed an armistice. This small gathering and its action concluded all hostilities six hours later and augured a process of international negotiations that eight months later, in June 1919, would yield a peace treaty at historic Versailles, the most significant of the treaties emanating from the war. Unbeknownst to the parties in the forest clearing and at the later assemblies in the grand palace of Versailles, the Armistice would also trigger a process destined to hold the world hostage to its misfortunes for the next one hundred years. And one moment in human time would assume the status of, and become eponymous thereafter as, the eleventh hour of the eleventh day of the eleventh month.

The Armistice was the rapture the world had longed for, concluding a conflict that had taken the lives of tens of millions, and its four years—from 1914 to 1918—had utterly dwarfed all previous human wars in its colossal nature. This colossus not only overshadowed earlier conflicts but would also cast forward a legacy to darken the rest of the century. If the famed children's tale of Jack and the Beanstalk had imagined an actual place for the bean and its stalk, the Forest of Compiegne would have been an apt setting, for what came from that place was havoc in the world thereafter of the kind wreaked by the fable's giant. Unlike the fairytale, though, the colossus that set forth from Compiegne caused not only the spilling of the blood of Englishmen, but the blood of most nations from across the globe.

The humble choice of a railway carriage for the Armistice signing rather than the grand French HQ in nearby Senlis was chosen by Marshal Ferdinand Foch, supreme Allied commander, out of respect for the sensibilities of both victor and vanquished. Haunted by the French capitulation forty-five years before in the Franco-Prussian War, and the more recent devastation of Senlis by German artillery in the 1914 Battle of the Marne, Foch felt a less emotional location would be fitting. Equally worried that the Armistice would be portrayed publicly as a humiliating surrender—which to Germany was unthinkable—the German delegation agreed that a private location was both dignified and protective of its interests.

But history has a way of upending the best-laid plans, and the Railway Carriage of Compiegne is a telling example. While carriage 2419D of the Wagon-Lits Company never journeyed passengers again to the towns of northern France, that same carriage has figuratively traveled the globe and across a century since hosting that early dawn Armistice signing. Unremarkable in terms of transportation, the rail carriage's symbolic power lay in its shaping of the mythology of the twentieth century. Just twenty-five years later, Nazi leader and architect of the even more devastating Second World War, Adolf Hitler, used the same wagon 2419D and its secluded siding in the Forest of Compiegne to force France to sign its surrender to Germany and the Third Reich. How sweet, in 1940, must have been the savor of revenge to Hitler and his cronies in their vindictive reenactment of the 1918 Armistice, with the tables turned.

Today, a replica of the original carriage still stands as a symbolic message to the world, but this time its enduring symbolism is designed to entreaty union rather than division. The original carriage was either destroyed by the retreating SS in 1945 or obliterated in an air raid. Either way, in 1950 the Wagon-Lits Company donated another version of the carriage that sits in the Armistice Museum, overlaying the original rail tracks in the forest. During the First World War centennial commemorations in 2018, another German chancellor, Angela Merkel, visited the rail carriage at the museum, accompanying French president Emmanuel Macron. Their visit stood to remind the world of the friendship and union of former warring nations in a peaceful European Union. In remembering the horrors of the past, and especially the twentieth century, the European siblings of France and Germany were at last reunited.

That centennial harmony, however, bore nothing in common with the original 11-11-11 Armistice and its attendant Treaty of Versailles, which became the moment of a new trajectory for the human family. The two German leaders of Adolf Hitler and Angela Merkel, who separately visited carriage 2419D or its replica, are both related heirs and descendants of ideas that were born of the Great War. The First World War annihilated the old world order and its nineteenth-century dynasties that had governed the great powers of Europe within a single enlarged royal family. In its place, new peoples and ideas emerged, not like the living descendants of Queen Victoria of Saxe-Coburg and her royal grandchildren, who had plunged the world into chaos in 1914. Instead, a new family of ideas was conceived at Compiegne that was equally sustaining of the destructive jealousies, rivalries, personalities, and ambitions that reside within every biological family and that had run deep in the royal bloodline of the cousins King George V, Kaiser Wilhelm II, and Czar Nicholas II. The First World War's offspring were not only manifested as flesh and blood but more perniciously as mind and soul, becoming the great enduring ideological forces of the twentieth and twenty-first centuries. These systems of thought are typically described as nationalism, Communism, and democracy, and those names still apply, but they are also known by other faces and behaviors. We as people are comfortable with fluidity in our appearances and identities, and skilled at adapting them to changing circumstances. This is also how history evolved globally, with fluid ideologies and identities coming together as a result of the First World War. As Queen Victoria's family were individuals yet also shaped by their common DNA, so these new forces that grew from the ashes of the war would be intertwined, codependent and sometimes hard to distinguish. They would rail against each other, even as they appeared and behaved and talked so much like each other. In the Old Testament story, the mark of Cain was the curse that he alone incurred through his fratricide, but without his victim brother Abel, Cain's identity and destiny would have been lost to Hebrew tradition. Brothers are, after all, intimately related, even when they wish they were not, and the family of ideas and events of the past century are similarly related and interdependent, much to the chagrin of their apologists. The voices and faces that shape our twenty-first-century world, such as those of Angela Merkel and Emmanuel Macron, are deeply indebted to the events and experiences of their national ancestors whose destinies were dangerously redirected on that fateful November morning just over one hundred years ago.

The choices at the time for waging the war, and then the choices made at its conclusion, can be seen with hindsight as both reckless and far-reaching into the future. But why reckless, and how was the First World War a misfortune outside of its own time and limits? We typically associate recklessness with an abandonment of reason and care, perhaps even define it as a set of impulsive actions that destabilize our norms. While the causes of the First World War have long been debated, what is clear is that there was a logic and reason to its genesis, and it was not simply some freak accident that appeared from nowhere. To understand its destabilizing qualities, we must look back much further than 1914, to a nineteenth-century world order that was born out of another conflict. For while the world was plunged into a new and terrifying trajectory in July of 1914, and the nations of Europe surprised by their own suicidal actions, the conditions of war had long been in place, awaiting a catalyst that would trigger the catastrophe. Whether the arrogance of the nineteenth century was more reckless than the stupidity of the Serbian crisis of July 1914 is a moot point. Both the decades prior to the First World War and the long summer days of 1914 assumed a naivety and stupidity that falsely convinced all that what was being pursued was just, reasonable, necessary, and in the long-term interests of humanity, or at least in the short-term interests of each of the great powers of Europe and their populations, whose identities and lives were bound so closely to their leaders.

In this model, bad judgment is invisible until it is too late. With consistent self-assurance, and despite powerful evidence, we humans can stubbornly cling to the notion of our immortality as we watch loved ones die, we are confident in our personal progress as disruption assails us, we choose to believe our next action will bring resolution as we remain fixed with inertia, and we believe our leaders will strengthen our democracy as chaos and divisions multiply. And perhaps we should exercise this self-assurance, for it is better to hope than to despair. We swim at the surface of "hundred thousand fathoms of nothingness," as the philosopher Soren Kierkegaard once noted, but at least we swim until we drown. It is almost as if the First World War was an impossible reality that could never come to fruition—a drowning of all humanity into a hundred thousand fathoms—until the world plunged under the surface and never returned to the same horizon. In short, no one really believed it could happen, even as they prepared for war. None of the protagonists seriously considered their world upended until it was too late. Even Kaiser Wilhelm II was so convinced that war would not happen that he left for his annual yachting vacation in the Baltic Sea in early July of that fateful summer. Going on holiday was the only sane, reasonable, and proper thing to do. Going to war would be insane. Only at the time of the world sinking into its abyss did the realization finally dawn that something very dangerous and unfortunate was indeed taking place. The week before Britain entered the war, on 4th August 1914, after the Germans ignored Britain's ultimatum for a German withdrawal from neutral Belgium, Foreign Secretary Sir Edward Grey spoke one of the best-known phrases of the twentieth century as he and a colleague looked out from his office in Whitehall as the lights came on with the onset of a London dusk: "The lamps are going out all over Europe, and we shall not see them lit again in our lifetime."[1] His intuitive sense of dread was an ominous portent of inconceivable tragedy, showing an awareness of an impending disaster utterly at odds with a world of twentieth-century progress and prosperity. His words were so prescient and symbolic that during the centennial commemorations of 2014, the British government asked its people to light a candle and place it by a window in their homes at dusk as a ritual to undo the mistakes of the past and to bring light to the gathering gloom in Europe.

Such sentimental hindsight in Britain's centennial commemorations obscures the recklessness of the actions of that July 1914, which Winston Churchill described in his memoirs as "a drama never surpassed."[2] One week after his dusk musings, in declaring Britain's decision to enter the war, Grey announced in the House of Commons that the peace of Europe could not be preserved and that Britain must not "run away from those obligations of honor and interest." With fatalistic acceptance, he announced, "We are going to suffer terribly in this war, whether we are in it or whether we stand aside." For the ten million who died fighting the war, the "we" was personal and terminal, whereas for Grey it provided an epochal context for his published memoirs years later.[3] What prompted this fatalism was a capacity to oscillate between poor decision-making and

---

[1] John Alfred Spender, *Life, Journalism and Politics*, vol. 1 (New York: F. A. Stokes, Co., 1927) 14–15.
[2] Cited in Max Hastings, *Catastrophe 1914: Europe Goes to War* (New York: First Vintage Books, 2013).
[3] Edward Grey, *Twenty-Five Years, 1892–1916* (New York: F. A. Stokes, Co., 1927).

fortune, or rather misfortune. The war's recklessness was born out of a century of belief in balance, order, and rationality. But it was not simply this that caused the world to destroy its stability and order; ironically, it was the internal logic of that order that fashioned and finally propelled a world order into rash behavior and entropic disequilibrium in 1914, particularly reflected by the thirst of its leading nations for both empire and military equality. In short, the First World War was not simply an accident or insane behavior by the ruling classes and monarchs of Europe. It had reason to occur, built steadily in the halls of European government over the preceding years. Moreover, its agonies produced a set of outcomes that continued to provide and sustain ongoing misfortunes, conditions, and consequences which held the following century hostage. In this way of thinking, the First World War did not end. It instead revived and retold its causes, pains, and effects in new ways, places, events, and peoples just as the DNA of a family is handed on in new ways, places, events, and peoples.

The summer of 1914 was thus a unique drama, as Churchill noted, in which the players had no idea of the play's dreadful conclusion. Grey's mournful dusk in Whitehall and his pained statesmanship a week later in the House of Commons were inseparable and a revealing example of this dangerous confusion of choice and destiny. Very quickly in late July and early August, the suffering that was to befall the Continent was guaranteed and bound to the British (and the Germans, Russians, Austro-Hungarians, Italians, French, and others). By arguing that there was no choice, each nation exercised its choice to enter the deadly fray. Either way, it was seen at the time as a lose-lose situation, evident when Grey declared in the House of Commons that Britain could not "run away from those obligations of honor and interest." He argued that the three reasons for entering the war were to save Britain's good name, to save her empire, and, finally, to preserve freedom in the face of tyranny. Notions of honorable name and empire were intricately bound to a cherished history, while the principle of preserving freedom provided greater justification than self-interest alone and perpetuated

19

the determination and logic of all combatant nations in the miserable years ahead. For the British army, "King and Country" was the call that demanded the ultimate sacrifice, and for the Germans it was virtually the same—"For God and Fatherland." So, Grey and the government and its citizens thus made the choice for war. And while it was a choice that left Britain and its empire simultaneously resolute in the rightness of its cause and uneasy about its process, the logic of its development provided no way out, no U-turn, and no traction for diplomacy. This might have been a political nightmare for the monarchs, prime ministers, and officers of state of the combatant nations. For the soldiers, whether regular or volunteer, it was an even worse existential reality. With stoic wit and irony, the "Tommies" (the nickname given to all British soldiers) summed up the paradox of the trench hell they endured with satirical and cheerful songs they sang together that were more revealing and honest than the dispatch boxes of the Whitehall Civil Service back in London. By 1915, one year after the slaughter had already taken the lives of 250,000 British troops, they collectively sang to themselves the reason that they were there amidst the guns and in the mud of Flanders Fields. To the tune of Auld Lang Syne, every Tommy knew why he was in that hellish place, and by the millions they would sing, "We're 'Ere Because We're 'Ere Because We're 'Ere Because We're 'Ere...," and repeat. The circuitous and self-fulfilling absurdity was clear to them. The song had no ending and neither, seemingly, did the war, as it dragged on year after year from that unhappy summer of 1914.

In this way, the recklessness of the war was in the nature of the decisions—the modus operandi of the argument—to move inexorably toward conflict and monumental suffering, built on former history and current conditions, and producing in its wake catastrophic results that then shaped history, conditions, and ideas for the future. Viewed thus, the First World War was not an accident. It was not a superstition of evil magically arriving in the world, like a malicious giant descending to earth to wreak mayhem. It was not one man's or one nation's stupidity and the decision of the others not to tolerate that stupidity. It was something else. It was one of the greatest examples in modern history of the biblical mythology of Eden and of Paradise Lost, showing with global enormity that we have the capacity for choice and that our choice has consequences, even deadly ones that change our fortunes and options forever. Our choice—reckless or other—will shape our future—our fortune or our misfortune.

The early twentieth-century philosopher and poet George Santayana left for us to rue his much-paraphrased aphorism, "Those who cannot remember the past are condemned to repeat it." This claim is powerful and regularly heralded by undergraduate students of history as a warning of our future perils if we neglect our history. But there is an irony here. Sometimes history—sometimes remembering and revisiting our past and its course—incentivizes us to perpetuate the very same dangers of our past, of resuming the same wars, of reengaging in the same hatreds, of persisting the same feuds, and of repeating the same patterns of destruction wrought by our (grand) fathers—more fathers than mothers, I suspect. The wheel of life and suffering, Buddhism reminds us, is indeed cyclical and not linear. The crisis of July 1914 asked a generation of Europeans to make choices based on their understanding of themselves and their past, and then to live with the consequences of how those choices would change their futures. And it sent millions of young men on foot and ships and railways to a war of cataclysmic suffering and consequences. Four and a half years later, in November 1918, a small gathering of powerful men met with the intent of bringing closure to the vast loss that was the First World War, and a small set of decisions would again set the world on a new trajectory in the stillness of a Belgium forest dawn. The railway carriage in the Armistice Museum on the rail tracks in the Forest of Compiegne symbolizes and reminds each successive generation of the potency of the connectedness of past, present, and future, both for good and for evil. The signatories to the Armistice unknowingly handed down a

century-defining legacy even as they thought they were simply concluding a terrible chapter in human conflict.

Of course, the opposing armies who had been facing each other
for four years in the trenches of the Western Front already knew the
dread that returned with each dusk and dawn. With the daily rising
and setting of the sun, both sides were alternately exposed and made
vulnerable by the brilliant rays of light during sunrise and sunset,
illuminating one side while shrouding the other. The British and
French dreaded the daily rising of the sun in the East, especially on
cloudless days, revealing their locations to the Germans. And the
Germans feared the Western sunset, when the same pattern was reversed. In the four years and four months between Foreign Secretary
Grey's perilous dusk in 1914 and the generals' ominous dawn in
1918, the ordinary men of Europe endured the deadly misfortunes
of war, twice a day, for 1,500 days, with the fearful dusks and dawns
of the sun's rising and setting.

3

A WORLD OF PROGRESS AND ORDER: REDUX

The subdued and private Armistice in the quiet of the forest dawn was followed eight months later by a noisy and public Treaty at Versailles in full display, and these critical events provided the concluding bookend to the First World War. The Treaty of Versailles took place around one hundred years after another seismic European treaty, that in Vienna, which concluded and resolved the chaos of the eighteenth-century revolutionary wars and the dominance of the Napoleonic era in Europe, with its risk of despotism. Today, our world lives about one hundred years beyond Versailles and two hundred years after Vienna. These critical events for European and world history, one century apart, appear to us as grand corrections, attempts to hit an historical "reset" button, and wrestle back order, normalcy, and control from the forces of randomness, instability, and turmoil. Can peoples do this? Certainly, it appears that we as individuals and as organizations generally hold on to this optimistic view of our individual and collective chances at finding peace, prosperity, and stability. Each nation-state appears to express its confidence in progress, security, and strength, even when such ideals may be in contradiction or lead nation-states into direct conflict with each other. War aside, we as humans prize the ideals of peace and love, and we live our lives for the most part in pursuit of them.

Less than ten years ago, the European Union was somewhat surprisingly awarded the Nobel Peace Prize "for over six decades [of having] contributed to the advancement of peace and reconciliation, democracy and human rights in Europe."[1] Here we have a case of a continental system of government being rewarded for its securing peace after centuries of hatred and warfare. It is fortunate, however, that the award was given in 2012, and not four years later when the United Kingdom was declaring Brexit and the EU was riven by factionalism and the rise of anti-immigrant and extremist forces. How the celebration changed so quickly into a hangover is too recent to understand well, but it is a contemporary example of this oscillation between societal endurance and disruption. This repetition of periods of upheaval followed by rebuilding, with the expectation of stable periods in between, is characteristic of societies and evidently a pattern we see in Western history over the past couple of centuries. A dialectical pattern of order, disorder, and reorder also appears to have some veracity in reviewing the place and timing of the First World War within European history. For while this book focuses primarily on how the First World War affected subsequent behavior and thinking for the following century, it is also significant that the origins of the First World War emerged from a time of similar belief in progress and stability, which Vienna had sought to create after the turmoil that was spawned at the end of the eighteenth century. To that end, Vienna succeeded considerably (despite a short-lived period of revolutionary zeal in 1848) in establishing a century of European stability regarding the parameters and borders of national identity, the sustainability of political organizations, and a working framework for international diplomacy. The Congress of Vienna established agreed-upon principles and processes for the governance of Europe, successfully articulating a vision for how Europe should work, what principles it should adopt, and which to exclude. Vienna gave Europe both a vision and a strategy for its future across the nineteenth century. In this context, the First World War appears as the tragic key moment of the collapse of a long-standing and all-encompassing international order. Triggered by the archduke's June

---

[1] https://europa.eu/european-union/about-eu/history/2010-to-day/2012/ eu-nobel_en

28th assassination, its causes were more complicated than one after-noon's act of terrorism in Sarajevo.

If history shows examples of entropic collapse after periods of renewal—a sort of reversal of the proverbial phoenix rising from the ashes—the First World War stands as a pivotal one. Its outcomes must be viewed not in isolation but within this broader continuum of entropic and harmonizing forces across the generations. The work of one popular American thinker helps explain this broader context. Two decades ago, Neil Postman, an acclaimed academic in the emerging field of media ecology at New York University, pub-lished a remarkable book, *Building a Bridge to the Eighteenth Century*. In this work, Postman, who died shortly thereafter, argued that the dawning twenty-first century would be a period of disruption. This, he asserted, was paralleled in history by a tumultuous period of up-heaval in the late eighteenth century, which finally produced a pe-riod of sustained stability and progress in the nineteenth century, a sort of calm after the storm. Postman viewed our current digital rev-olution as akin to the earlier upheaval and not to the later progress, fearing that the early decades of the twenty-first century would ex-perience considerable disequilibrium, with public life and systems in disarray.

If we take the gist of Postman's argument, the 1815 Congress of Vienna was a classic event of resolution of the previous chaos and the dawn of a new era of optimism and growth: the start of the calm after the storm, so to speak. Out of the disequilibrium of the late eighteenth century there would emerge powerful and enduring sys-tems of governance, such as the American republic and modern France, and a new framework established for intracontinental diplo-macy and alliances. Critically, Postman claimed that the chaos prior to these institutions needed great enlightened minds and leaders, such as Locke, Rousseau, and Jefferson, to enable society to transi-tion through the upheaval. In short, chaos was the temporary grow-ing pain of a new world shaped by the genius minds of the founding fathers of those revolutions. The old orders, the dying "ancien re-gimes," had collapsed in 1776 and 1789 respectively, and there was indeed turmoil for a generation, but the seeds of a better world had been sown for the world to reap. Today, a new generation of thinkers is needed, so Postman argued, to secure our twenty-first century similarly against random hyperreality and societal instability, ever-present in Twitter-feed chaos, "fake news," Cambridge Analytica, and Russian interference in US elections. He termed this destructive condition as "technopoly" and called for modern minds and prophets of humanity to help chart the way through the chaos, and deliver to our times the kinds of resolutions we see in historic examples of great enduring significance such as the 1787 US Constitution or the 1815 Congress of Vienna. To Postman, those necessary leaders and thinkers were still absent at the time of his life and work.

Elsewhere, Postman claimed our technological obsession meant we are at risk of "amusing ourselves to death," the title he gave to his most famous work. For him, the indulgent city of Las Vegas was a vast symbol of a broader cultural illness. Whether his analysis of our epistemological crisis was accurate is not of relevance here. What is relevant is that if Postman was right about a chaos-order continuum, then the First World War fits into a pattern or sequence of events that are both shaped by previous events—fortunes or misfortunes—and by the key protagonists and thinkers of their day—with their wisdom or recklessness. Taking the view that 1815 Vienna was a moment of resolution, we can then see the emergence of nineteenth-century systems of governance and thinking, celebrated, for example, in the Great Exhibition of 1851, as illustrative of this shared sense of human progress. Similarly, the American republic's civil war and its long march to civil rights stands as testimony to a nation that was shaped after upheaval by an enduring and uniquely successful Constitution with a moral vision. Postman was labeled in his time as a romantic and conservative, but in truth he was a radical whose ideas posed a devastating critique of what we can see as the emergent Facebook-Google-Apple "technopoly."

If this sense of historical chaos (entropy) and order (negentropy) has validity, it sheds a far-reaching light on how the collapse of the European house of cards in June 1914 led to the chaos of the First

World War. Moreover, it helps explain how that war critically did not resolve itself or its chaos, but disastrously reordered it subsequently with increased potency and deadly energy. A war of such magnitude required an even grander resolution than the one Europe had achieved back in 1815. The failure of the First World War to conquer its demons is examined in the next chapter. But the fact that the war occurred one hundred years after the Congress of Vienna is testimony to the endurance and effectiveness of Vienna in shaping out of eighteenth-century turmoil a nineteenth century of order and progress, while, ironically, also providing its subsequent fourth generation with the resources, alliances, and tensions for abandoning that order and choosing calamity instead. Exactly a century—four generations—after Vienna, the peace and prosperity that it had bequeathed to Europe was abandoned with terrifying disregard in the rush to war in the summer of 1914. What occurred though was not random, but rather chosen by its protagonists and prompted by the very success, power, and ego that the nineteenth century had delivered to the nations of Europe. In this sense, Europe became a victim of its own success in 1914. Complacent about its good life, Europe perversely decided to throw it all away. The heralded story of nineteenth-century European success, born of Vienna, gave early twentieth-century Europeans the knowledge and tools for their own self-destruction.

The status of Vienna was certainly understood from the moment the congress adjourned as one of historic importance and legacy. This is evident even in the elegant architecture that Europe has chosen for its cities, buildings, and monuments. For example, Windsor Castle, the longest-serving royal palace in British history and weekend residence of the monarch, illustrates this reverence for the achievements of Vienna. A guided tour of the castle takes the visitor through stately rooms and along hallways of opulent magnificence, detailing intricately several centuries of royal and imperial power. On the way to the state rooms and to various exhibition halls about Queen Elizabeth's wardrobe and recent royal weddings, there is an enormous hall lined with formal portraits of imposing nine-teenth-century figures. Approximately fifty yards in length and thirty yards wide, with arched ceiling buttresses that frame numer-ous skylights, this magnificent room was constructed to showcase the towering figures of its time. Known from its creation as the Wa-terloo Chamber, its construction began even while the Napoleonic Wars were in their final throes. The Waterloo Chamber was in-tended as a great manifesto to a new future after a generation of war born from the upheaval of the French Revolution. The eighteenth century had unleashed those revolutionary impulses, the result of which was continental conflict between the archrivals of France and Britain in a struggle to determine the mastery of Europe for the coming nineteenth century. The Waterloo Chamber is an edifice designed to remind us that ideas and individuals can have enduring significance. This vast room was built to convey what the diplomats at Vienna were crafting, namely that the nineteenth century would honor not France's revolution, but instead the British victors' ideals of reason and order, precisely to prevent a recurrence of the disrup-tion that Napoleon Bonaparte had inflicted upon Europe.

Indeed, the Waterloo Chamber was specifically constructed as a celebration of the Duke of Wellington's victory over Napoleon in June 1815 in what is now Belgium, effectively bringing twenty-five years of conflict to an end. That Battle of Waterloo, recognized to-day more commonly as the name of a primary rail station in London, concluded the Napoleonic era and the transformation of France from autocracy through revolution to a new modern order. The Wa-terloo Chamber is a testament to the creation of a new order for Europe. The room has been described as a "who's who" of the nine-teenth century's great and good, from monarchs to generals to statesmen who, in the Congress of Vienna, would build that new continental system as a grand corrective, or "reset" button, to the Bonaparte system. That aim—built by Vienna's diplomats across traditions, languages, political systems, and religions—would be a bulwark against tyranny and a guarantee of peace across the Conti-nent. The fact that the Anglican monarch would permit the portrait of Pope Pius VII to be hung in a royal palace, as recognition of the pope's imprisonment and resistance to Napoleon, shows the Vienna commitment to European cooperation and mutuality. Of course, the portrait of the Duke of Wellington has prize place in the Waterloo Chamber as a reminder that British military supremacy would be the bedrock of that future cooperation. Indeed, the fact that it was given the name of Waterloo and not named the "Vienna" Chamber, or similar, indicates it was clearly intended to celebrate English military primacy over Napoleon and the triumph of refined noble peerage (Wellington) over a common Corsican invalid (Napoleon). Interestingly, the room also holds the largest seamless carpet in the world, woven by prisoners of the Agra prison in India on the Golden Jubilee of Queen Victoria in 1894.

The Waterloo Chamber was being built even while the Congress of Vienna was assembling under the chairmanship of Prince Klemens von Metternich, Austria's foreign minister. The war had not officially ended, and Napoleon had escaped the Isle of Elba to force one final climactic battle on the field at Waterloo in Belgium. His perseverance and sheer daring meant he would keep on fighting for French glory even as the British, Austrians, Russians, and Prussians convened in Vienna to bring wayward France to heel. Critically, for Britain's future perception and relationship with Europe, by naming it the Waterloo Chamber and adorning its walls with the image of the duke, the mythology of sacrifice in continental Europe would achieve permanent and prominent status in British cultural consciousness. That same consciousness, implicit on the walls of the Waterloo Chamber, fueled the Great War a century later that would drag not just Europe but all the world's continents into its calamity.

The narrative of English sacrifice had already emerged centuries prior to Waterloo in Britain's fraught relationship with continental Europe. Since the Battle of Agincourt exactly four hundred years before Waterloo, when Henry V's English army crushed Charles VI's French forces, the English had nurtured an enduring sense of the threat of Europe. If the Norman Conquest of England in 1066 and the assumption of the English throne under French Plantagenet

29

control had defined the power structure of the Middle Ages, Agincourt was the moment of the great English corrective. The battle heralded the dawn of new military technology in the first use of the longbow by the English infantry, and its outcome brought the Hundred Years' War to a victorious conclusion for the English and the end of French hegemony. In this historical narrative, Waterloo then signified a reestablishment of peace and security for England, and for the Continent, with Britain and the powers of Europe at its helm in respectful cooperation, and France again on her knees. The spirit of Agincourt was the backdrop in the British understanding of Vienna. Indeed, British literature, in the form of Shakespeare's *Henry V*, has forever enshrined Agincourt within the psyche of each generation of English students. That enduring tradition inspired popular sentiment in 1914 in the clamor for war and was evident in the poetic romanticism of Rupert Brooke's celebrated work "The Soldier," with its clear nod to earlier historic struggles and its leitmotif of a foreign field that is forever England, by virtue of England's sacrifices:

THE SOLDIER

If I should die, think only this of me:
That there's some corner of a foreign field
That is forever England. There shall be
In that rich earth a richer dust concealed;
A dust whom England bore, shaped, made aware,
Gave, once, her flowers to love, her ways to roam,
A body of England's, breathing English air,
Washed by the rivers, blest by suns of home.
—Rupert Brooke (1887–1915)

In this view of English history, Brooke repeated, poetically, a theme of England's glorious struggles that Waterloo so evocatively enunciated and that Agincourt premised. It evinced a notion of an English omnipresence on European soil that was dreamlike, tragic, and noble. And in Brooke's poem it did not matter if the Soldier was an infantryman at Agincourt or Waterloo or the Somme. He was the same soldier whose dying enshrined his place and time under the eternal banner and sanctity of the flag of Albion. Indeed, Brooke's poem expressed a perennial, context-free vision in which the field that was forever England was both temporal and eternal, and not limited to one specific location, event, or battle. His poem expressed a transcendence to English sacrifice in Europe that was not bound by Agincourt, Waterloo, the Somme, or anywhere else. His poem thus communicated in words what the Waterloo Chamber communicated in appearance, that of an English destiny to secure peace and prosperity for the good of all through heroic self-sacrifice. For Brooke, the same English destiny was required four generations after Napoleonic terror in a new European war, where foreign fields—again, mainly in France—would be the final resting place of unimaginable numbers of sacrificial English dead.

For the combatant nations of the First World War, the same goal of an enduring peace with a balance of power drove them, in 1914, into a conflict of unprecedented scale with an eventual outcome that bore little resemblance to the peace dividend that Vienna had delivered in 1815. For if Vienna had succeeded in building a lasting framework for European diplomacy and stability, what came out of the First World War was a framework that spawned further chaos, instability, and hatred. At Vienna, the "Big Five" of Britain, Russia, Prussia, Austria, and vanquished France achieved a symmetry of power that could provide lasting stability and ensure that no one state could easily strive for the mastery of Europe. The architects of Vienna, if they could have anticipated such a world, would have approved a similar logic that surfaced 150 years later in the theory of nuclear arms deterrence, known as "mutually assured destruction." In this balancing act, old land boundaries would have to be sacrificed and each major power "rightsized" in political and military power to ensure restraint on the ambitions of all parties. While not democratically inclined, the signatories at Vienna knew that a rush to victory for one meant chaos for the rest, and so complementarity was essential. Except for vanquished France. No one had a problem with punishing France for its excess, and so in the final treaty, France lost her former territorial gains. Vienna permitted special alliances and treaties among ratifying nations, but these were always subservient to the greater goal of stability of the status quo to ensure that Europe would not throw itself again into revolutionary oblivion and conflict. Order, predictability, and rationality were the themes and goals—the modus operandi—of what the architects of Vienna wanted to establish for the century that lay ahead. And when this modus operandi so spectacularly failed after a century of peace in 1914, Europe marched off to war believing it could and should restore it once again for the twentieth century.

This book is not about how the confident hope and controlled order that had held together after Vienna fell tragically and comprehensively apart in 1914. From a European perspective, Margaret MacMillan's splendid work, and winner of the 2014 Book of the Year for International Affairs, *The War That Ended Peace*, charts the terrifying collapse. For readers interested in the American involvement, Michael Neiberg's *The Path to War* gives an excellent account of how the United States ended up "over there." Our concern here is less about what precipitated the collapse of the house of cards in 1914 than it is about how the house had been built and what foundations underpinned it during the century prior to its collapse. In this context, the First World War exemplified a shocking European and global abandonment of the hopes of progress that underlay the entire fabric of the nineteenth century, an era that had emerged from the shadows of Napoleonic chaos, despotism, and war, and had constructed an enduring framework for Europe's advancement. This was a century that exuded confidence and possibility and appeared impregnable. In this way, the sinking of the Titanic in 1912 was a shocking loss both literally and figuratively, accounting for the tragic death of 1,500 souls as well as the end of the dream in the invincibility of nineteenth-century progress.

The First World War needs to be understood in this context of chaos and order. Its ending was to assume greater significance for the rest of the century than its beginning, as it sought to find a new order from the anguish of its four years and four months. If the metaphor from Greek folklore were to be realized, the First World War provided such a mountain of ashes that a very powerful phoenix would need to rise in order to redeem that agony. In reviewing the war within this context of episodic confusion and chaos, followed by an attempt by the world's powers to build a new order, we find the clues to understanding our past century. Those who convened at Versailles in 1919 thought they were going to achieve the same goal of securing humanity's future as their great-grandfathers had done at Vienna. What kind of world would the Versailles negotiators reassemble, and would their creation attain the stability and longevity that Vienna accomplished for the nineteenth century? In this way, our past century has been defined less by the rationale and causes of the beginning of the calamity in 1914, and more by the plans and devices that were created to prevent a recurrence of that calamity by the power brokers of Versailles.

The Treaty of Versailles attempted to recreate the performance of Vienna: a Vienna "redux," in current vernacular, just a short six hundred miles and a distant one hundred years from the Alps to Paris. In this redux event at Versailles, the levers of power would again be pulled in the hope of creating a similar framework of stability, where the hatred and suffering of the past five years would yield to nobler tempers of security and peace. The calamity of the First World War surely called for a new and enduring calm for Europe as its legacy, one that would be worth honoring in another chamber within a grand European palace. In this context, the Treaty of Versailles would set the tone for another one hundred years. But its tone, far from being calming, would become harsh and discordant very quickly.

To that treaty we now turn.

4

A DISAGREEABLE AGREEMENT

Four days before the signatures were finally inscribed on the treaty document that was forever to be associated with grand Versailles, *The London Times* published on its front page, in enormous type, just three unpunctuated words: "GERMANY WILL SIGN." The stark nature of that expression, and its domination of the *Times'* front page on June 24th, 1919,[1] speaks to a bewilderingly complex set of facts, emotions, reliefs, and (dis)beliefs that the preceding eight months had conjured up onto the world stage, leading to this "do or die" moment of decision for Germany. The Germans did, in fact, sign four days later, but even in agreeing to the terms of the treaty, and confronted by the Allied threat of the resumption of hostilities if they refused, Germany had no appetite for honoring what it was impelled to accept with both a literal and figurative gun held to its head.

If the black-and-white images of crowds celebrating Armistice Day in the Allied capitals show jubilation and a renewed spirit of joy, the images that speak to us a century later from the halls of Versailles could not be more contrasting. The photographs show somber-looking men seated in rows by long tables, individually scribing their signatures, conveying to us imagery evocative of judicial courts, disciplinary hearings, and funeral parlors. And so, the main and greatest treaty ending the First World War (subsequent treaties were completed with other Central powers in the coming months)

---

[1] "Germans Agree to Sign," *The* (London) *Times* (24 June 1919) 13.

replaced the cheers and laughter of the Armistice with more sonorous lamentations and ominous warnings.

The treaty itself was titled presciently. The first part of the title described in perfunctory fashion and objective simplicity the nature of the document: "The Treaty of Peace between the Allied and Associated Powers and Germany." Maybe the document's title should have stopped there, but it did not. With a heavy reminder of old wounds and alliances, and an ominous hint of prescient fear of what was to occur twenty years later, the second part of the title gazed into a crystal ball: "And the Treaty between France and Great Britain Respecting Assistance to France in the Event of Unprovoked Aggression by Germany." The deal was done; a sigh of relief would be felt across the world. Now the scenes became more reminiscent of Armistice jubilation, with church bells ringing (on a Saturday), naval salutes, and spontaneous crowds gathering to celebrate again in the victors' capitals. Almost as if to conclude a busy work week and prepare for the upcoming one, President Woodrow Wilson and his recent spouse, First Lady Edith, departed to their ship promptly to set sail for America, and everyone else went their separate ways. At last, the Allied armies still occupying the Rhineland following the Armistice could afford to relax and truly believe they were finally going home.

If *The London Times'* headline was blunt, brooding, and minimalist, the New York daily paper, *The Evening World*, conveyed a bustling, back-to-business message the same day that the ink dried on the treaty. On the cluttered front page, packed with news, reactions, events, and actions, all springing from Versailles, the paper's headline exclaimed: "Wilson Leaves Paris; Sails Sunday; Germans Pledged to Act in Good Faith."[2] Then the paper variously detailed all the reactions, including Wilson's message to the nation, presumably conceived en route by train from the former battlefields to his ship at Le Havre or Cherbourg, thus intriguingly echoing a similar,

---

[2] "Wilson Leaves Paris; Sails Sunday; Germans Pledge to Act in Good Faith," *The Evening World* (28 June 1919).

though reversed, presidential journey toward a battlefield, that undertaken fifty-six years earlier by Abraham Lincoln as he penned on a train to Gettysburg his immortalized 272-word address. *The Evening World* understood well the president's experience and understanding of what had just transpired, for its pages reported the bipolar tensions that Wilson had sought to reconcile in the eight months from the carriage at La Compiegne to the palace at Versailles. *The Evening World*, on that fateful day of June 28th, 1919, faithfully captured the prevailing reality that Woodrow Wilson had faced in France and would still plague him on his return to the United States.

The second headline on the paper's busy front page detailed the Wilson perspective in literary sound-bites that, with the benefit of hindsight, reveal the internal paradox, irreconcilable goals, and inherent inefficacy that was to become the legacy of Versailles. Below the primary headline of the day, the one including Wilson's sailing itinerary, we read that the president reported to the world that the "Treaty [was] Severe on Germany but Imposes Nothing She Cannot Do." Here we have an extraordinary executive summary of the balancing act Wilson had been forced to perform. Faced with inevitable pressures, Wilson capitulated to his Allied colleagues and watched the crafting of a treaty that at its core was designed to punish Germany. But Wilson—the former professor and recent president of Princeton University, as well as a leading founder of modern progressivism—had to save face to the world, because this punitive outcome from Versailles had little to do with the goals of self-enlightenment he had hoped the end of the war would bring about. In truth, though, Wilson was putting on a brave face when he stated he believed that the terms of the treaty were feasible for Germany, thereby making it appear he endorsed the Allied party line. Yet the hollowness of that claim seemed almost tangibly manifested in the hollow physical appearance of the beleaguered and exhausted man now returning to the US as its much-absent president. *The Evening World* went on to explain that Wilson concluded his message with the hope of a new dawn—the same idealism he had used to reverse political course and drag the United States eventually into the deadly fray of the First World War earlier in April 1917. As *The Evening World* reported, President Wilson was more publicly optimistic than others about the long-term prospects for Versailles. For Wilson, the treaty still offered the world "fairness and a charter for a New World and [that] ends the rule of Selfish Groups." The term "Selfish Groups" is odd and understated, but Wilson was by then at odds with events and understated in every way possible. The ship awaited its esteemed passengers, and Wilson and the first lady eagerly departed the maelstrom that was European geopolitics in order to seek the security of the United States and home, just twenty-four hours after the treaty was signed.

In truth, Woodrow Wilson's fate, as well as his ponderous and deflated mood as he and Edith sailed west down the English Channel and out into the Atlantic, were intricately connected to the nature and outcome of Versailles. Versailles became the play that was forever written as the deadliest war in history stumbled to its conclusion, and Versailles became the script that was intended to explain that stumble. It was this script that Wilson had hoped to pen and to preserve, and for him, his presidency at home and his statesmanship abroad hinged on whether he could be the one to write it. He had furthermore raised the stakes enormously because of his extraordinary and personal investment in the Paris peace process. At a time when domestic pressures were intense, Wilson was absent from the United States and residing in Paris for several weeks in the early part of 1919. Committing his personal presence to the peace process, which included thirty-two nations but excluded Germany, he was the de facto chief negotiator for the US delegation while becoming the first sitting president to visit Europe. His inner circle of American advisors included Secretary of State Lansing and Colonel Edward House, a trusted confidante. He also called upon Republican former diplomat Henry White, and for military advice, General Tasker Bliss. This group was accompanied by many secondary advisors, but critically the president chose not to invite to Paris any congressional Republicans. This proved a major early blunder with consequences for later years, especially since the 1918 midterm elections had strengthened Republican resolve and their policy differences with the Democratic president. By omitting Republicans from the process, and by ensconcing himself for a prolonged period across the Atlantic and out of Washington, Wilson was developing adversaries and critics both at home as well as abroad. In fairness to Wilson, while he controlled his conduct and company during the Paris peace process, he, like all negotiators at Versailles and politicians of the Western capitals, was victim to the fate of how the war ended. These statesmen could make their choices within the peace process, but the war itself had handed them, collectively, some given conditions—events and facts that could not be undone or ignored. In particular, the way the actual combat of the First World War ended was something of critical determination and one that restricted the Paris negotiators.

Some recap of that final gasp of hostility is instructive. In the spring of 1918, just barely one year before Versailles, the Germans had virtually won the war. The massive spring offensive (*Kaiserschlacht*, or Kaiser's Battle) began the day of the spring equinox and was so vast, fast, and effective that by early April, the Western Front had virtually disappeared. German resolve for a final grand assault was prompted by the new peace agreement with Bolshevik Russia and withdrawal of Russian troops after the October 1917 revolution, and the prospect of a million American troops arriving in France after a painfully slow initial mobilization of American forces. General Erich Ludendorff thus decided to launch a full assault with all resources with the aim of a final, decisive breakthrough and shock victory for Germany. His gamble nearly paid off. The German army, schooled by storm trooper tactics employed so brilliantly by, among others, a young Captain Erwin Rommel, future *Wehrmacht Reichsmarschall* and Desert Fox, moved forward at such speed that within two weeks Paris and the channel ports were almost within reach. Employing howitzer cannons, the Germans bombed Paris from only forty miles away, launching the first-ever manmade object—a bomb—propelled into space, such was the enormity of the propulsion from the huge howitzers. That first-ever object in space rushed back to earth, falling on a Parisian church school and killing numerous children. One hundred years later to the week, more advanced propulsion technology launched NASA's TESS vehicle on top of the SpaceX Falcon 9 rocket to explore distant exoplanets.

Back on earth in early 1918, the Germans were within a whisker of winning the war, but they managed to snatch defeat from the jaws of victory, in large part to their overstretched supply lines, the utter exhaustion of their armies, and the arrival, finally, of half a million American troops by that summer. On August 8th, the British, Australians, and Canadians launched a massive counteroffensive, the Battle of Amiens, that reversed the German tide and captured fifty thousand German soldiers in a single day. Ludendorff was to remark famously that August 8th would thus be known forever as the "black day for the German army." A couple of weeks later, the Americans had similar success in the deadliest of all American military engagements in the Battle of Meuse-Argonne, and so the writing was now on the wall for Ludendorff, the kaiser, and the German people. By early autumn, Ludendorff and Hindenburg informed the kaiser that Germany could not win the war. With political upheaval inside Germany stemming from a famished population, with mutinies erupting in the German submarine units, and with a stranglehold blockade by the Royal Navy starving Germany of food and matériel with which to wage war, overtures of an armistice were actively pursued by Chancellor von Hertling and the German generals and grudgingly conceded by Kaiser Wilhelm II.

But here the story disintegrates, for the motives for an armistice were clearly not shared between the Allied and Central power protagonists. From the German perspective, the Armistice was akin to a truce, emphatically not an admission of defeat or formal surrender. For the Allies, the Armistice represented the very defeat the Germans sought to deny and delivered a welcome about-face to the terrifying prospects raised by the almost-successful German Spring Offensive. In short, different perceptions, motives, explanations, and interpretations would immediately emerge about the nature of the cease-fire on November 11th and what outcome it would generate. To most German civilians, the Armistice represented nothing akin to Germany's loss of the war, and since German troops still inhabited occupied foreign soil on that date, the logic of that argument had its merits. Images abound of German troops marching back across the Rhine into the German heartland to the cheers, garlands, and praises of thousands of German civilians welcoming back their glorious troops. This was a moment, in German thinking, for the struggle to persist via diplomacy, a diplomacy merited by savage warfare that the Central powers had inflicted so effectively, or so German sentiment would believe.

To the Allies, this was a time for making sense of the war and determining how to deal with the Central powers, and Versailles would be the setting for this work. The hint of the plan for Versailles had already been shown at the Armistice signing in the Compiegne Forest. The German negotiators who had participated in that process were utterly shocked by what they saw as the unnecessary harshness and vindictiveness of the Armistice, and especially the forced coercion of Allied troops occupying the Rhineland during the Paris peace negotiations as a deterrence against the resumption of conflict. For the Allies, now was the opportunity to strike, no longer militarily, but in terms of nation-building, aggressor restrictions, international governance, and punitive retribution against wayward peoples and nations. At least that was the sentiment which three of the four main Allied nations brought to the table.

The photography from this time at Versailles shows truly that a picture paints a thousand words. One of the most striking, taken in the final week before the signing, shows the four leaders of the Allied powers gathered outside the palace: David Lloyd George, prime minister of Great Britain; George Clemenceau, prime minister of France; Vittorio Orlando, prime minister of Italy; and Woodrow Wilson, president of the United States. Lloyd George, Clemenceau, and Orlando are huddled together, in laughter. Four feet away, outside of the trio, looks on a smiling Wilson, desperate to be included and awkwardly nervous in his body language. The gamble had been played, but it was about to go very wrong. For unlike the French, British, and Italians, Wilson wished to strike a pose reminiscent of Lincoln's insistence of goodwill to the defeated Southern states, which meant his views were diametrically opposed to those of his Allied colleagues. Wilson had, early into the US participation, commissioned a study of international policy that would follow what he believed would be an Allied victory and the defeat of German militarism. Driven by his academic instincts and emerging progressive stance (at least in international relations), Wilson had sought to use the US participation in the First World War as the moment and arena for a grander vision of the world order, a sort of 1815 Vienna revisited for the twentieth century, which would enable the global body politic to forge a new coalition of ideas on the basis of a shared instinct for diplomatic engagement. Wilson had been no naïve outsider to the catastrophe that was the First World War, and for him, this was precisely the rationale that predicated a vital and necessary alternative to how international relations must be hereafter pursued. American engagement in the war was pursued originally only because Wilson believed, valiantly or vainly, that US participation might indeed ensure that this would be the "war to end all wars." American engagement was not about protecting territory, but about protecting principles, and Wilson was resolute in his commitment that those principles must emerge in a postwar world context.

Even while the Germans were preparing their final spring onslaught to gain the necessary territory (Paris and the channel ports) to secure victory and a peace on their terms, Wilson was engaging aggressively at home a different agenda. Founded on a desire for the moral high ground, he set about persuading the American people that a moralistic vision should drive American policy and its leadership in the world, with the goal of the formation of a new international order. On January 8th, 1918, President Wilson outlined to Congress that vision. For him, the First World War, and especially America's participation, was not about nationalistic or territorial ambition, but about a struggle for a new world order, built upon moral principles of respect, reciprocity, and dialogue. Developing his rationale that American entry in April 1917 into the First World War was for the purpose of preserving democracy, Wilson now in early 1918 outlined to Congress his strategy on how that principled new order should be created from the destruction of the war so that the conditions that had created the cauldron of international hatred would be forever removed. And having explained it at home, he boarded his ship to go and make it happen at Paris. In this vision, Woodrow Wilson crafted a to-do list that would piece together what he considered to be the framework for a brave new world, with global security at its core. This was Wilson's eponymously named Fourteen Points plan, which was to become the conceptual and policy strategy where Wilson's fortunes and Versailles' politics were to come to a conflict hiatus. The Fourteen Points strategy was an odd collection of projects, oscillating between somewhat limited and mundane tasks of the age (e.g., Belgium's neutrality restored) to loftier notions of international activity (e.g., freedom of oceanic navigation; no private international treaties). But the pièce de résistance was the last of his Fourteen Points, that of a new League of Nations that would intervene to ensure that war could and would not happen again. Here the idealism of a former academic would reach into global affairs in its most hopeful of ways, charting a course whereby a collective conscience would be shared between nations to head off future disputes and place a secure arm of protection around potential victims of aggression. In short, reminiscent of the model of shared governance that American academia cherishes, Wilson envisaged an organization that could negotiate, referee, and intervene to maintain the peaceful, diplomatic rules of play that would come into effect whenever cases of individual dispute arose between nations or whenever self-aggrandizement appeared to be the intent of any rogue state.

In a sense, at least Wilson was consistent. His rationale for entering the war in April of 1917 was elevated to the noble though imprecise principle of "making the world safe for democracy," and now he was laying out in his Fourteen Points the strategy whereby he could realize that principle. The war won, now was time to win

42

the peace, on the same basis that he had argued to Congress that the United States needed to enter the First World War two years earlier. But whatever strengths may have underpinned this policy, it was in the arena of politics where it was to stumble, both at home and abroad. For in his personal investment in the Versailles process and negotiations, Wilson made the cardinal blunder of giving room for partisan domestic politics to wreak havoc on his plans by failing to invite any congressional Republicans to join him in France. By creating a literal Atlantic gulf between himself and his political opponents at home, he allowed his global agenda to become the target of party-political rancor. If the domestic situation was weakened by his lack of forethought of Republican involvement, his foreign relations were immediately on rocky ground because his Fourteen Points sounded like Wilson, and Wilson alone—and not his allies. His European allies instead coalesced around the idea that Wilson's approach risked "sparing the rod and spoiling the child."

Clemenceau of France viewed the Fourteen Points plan as weak and lenient. He believed a considerably more punitive agenda was needed to rectify Germany's wrongs and to ensure it never again committed similar aggression. The British reaction was sympathetic to the French viewpoint, but slightly different. Prime Minister David Lloyd George was facing an election at home, and his chances of reelection were uncertain. In this context, the appearance of magnanimity might look like weakness, and the British appetite for leniency on Germany was nonexistent. Additionally, Lloyd George was looking further east to the evolution of the nascent Soviet state, and growing suspicions about Communism as a future force. In this scenario he was worried that a "soft" treaty would potentially encourage the more violent elements of the new Soviet state to consider militarism as the first option. These issues aside, Lloyd George personally admired Wilson's Fourteen Points and considered them, in abstract, as compelling. However, that conceptual admiration was insufficient to motivate Lloyd George to rally to Wilson's cause. Fearing defeat in the upcoming election, he threw his lot in with Clemenceau and Orlando, and left Wilson as the odd man out. In this context, Wilson's approach to Versailles was an overreach for his allies. France and Great Britain had suffered longer and worse than the United States had during the war. The scale of their casualties was truly hard to fathom. By war's end, one in three French men between the ages of eighteen and thirty-two were either dead or wounded. Nearly one million men from Britain and its empire were never returning to their homes. French soil had been subject to invasion and occupation, British civilians terrorized by zeppelin raids, and millions of men from Britain and its empire had fought and died on land less than twenty-two miles from the cliffs of Dover. While US participation had been costly, it was modest alongside that of its allies and was remote both geographically and economically from domestic realities. In this scenario, leniency toward Germany was anathema to the European Allies, and generosity would be absurd. While Wilson was likely inspired by the moral perspective of "malice toward none, with charity for all," which Lincoln had asserted toward the defeated South in his second inaugural address, the European Allies would have been horrified by the suggestion that this example from history repeat itself. Wilson may indeed have been honoring Lincoln's legacy, but his call fell on deaf ears at this war's conclusion.

But not entirely. Intriguingly, the nation that took the most notice of Wilson's Fourteen Points as he proposed them to Congress ahead of an armistice was Germany. As Ludendorff and Germany's leaders pondered the military and economic realities that impelled them to seek an armistice, the viability of that option was enlivened by Wilson's call for a palatable exit for all parties out of the war. On the terms seemingly proffered by the most recent of Allied combatants, the United States, Germany reasoned that there was now a chance to move beyond the war in a way that was not a crushing defeat and that left it with prospects for the nation's future and fortune. This was the assumption that the German establishment grabbed onto and that allowed its diplomats to begin fomenting into a plan for the end of the war in the summer and autumn months of

1918, as the inevitable Armistice loomed and a future peace treaty became the focal point of national priorities.

The compromise treaty at Versailles tried to have it all ways for the Allies. The European Allies were willing to concede to Wilson the concept of the league. Of the 440 clauses in the final treaty, the opening twenty-six were devoted to the establishment and the parameters of the League of Nations. In truth, Wilson's vision was attractive to all because it echoed the Vienna hope that friendship and alliances would preserve the order. Wilson was elevating that even further into the notion of a union of all key nations, without individual camps or blocs of alliances, and he and others hoped this would be more effective and critically necessary than the nineteenth-century alliances and ententes had been in preserving the good.

But if the League of Nations was present in the final treaty, and Wilson's magnanimity thus acknowledged, so also were the punitive and harsh ambitions of the European victors, and especially the French. Most of the Versailles clauses, more than four hundred in all, turned to the issue of German punishment, justified by the infamous and misnamed Clause 231, which immediately became known as the "war guilt" clause. As we shall see, this clause was to be the source of considerable historical energy and anguish in the coming years, but in 1919 it provided the moral justification for the many other punitive clauses that the treaty produced. The wording of Clause 231 is interesting, since it does not use the term "guilt"; neither does it read like a confession or admission from the vanquished. Speaking as the subject of the clause, "the Allied and Associated governments affirm, and Germany accepts the responsibility of Germany and her allies for causing all the loss and damage...as a consequence of the war imposed upon [the Allies] by the aggression of Germany." Clearly, it would have been more accurate for this clause to be deemed not the war *guilt* clause, but the war *blame* clause, with the finger of blame being pointed by the victorious Allies. German disgust and disdain at this moralistic stance did nothing to prevent

Clause 231 from gaining immediate notoriety worldwide for establishing German "war guilt" and ensuring that the full range of punishments were warranted because of this language of guilt.

Those punitive clauses fell into three categories: military, territorial, and financial. Some fifty-plus military clauses were designed to prevent the German war machine from being rebuilt. The army, navy, and air force were to be reduced to a fraction of their size, and vast amounts of German war matériel were to be handed over permanently or destroyed, a process already begun at the Armistice. The connection of military to territorial punishment originated with the Rhineland occupation, commenced at the Armistice and now formalized at Versailles with its permanent demilitarization. This had economic consequences for both French security and economy, allowing for the return of the coal fields of Aachen/Alsace-Lorraine to France, lost after the Franco-Prussian War some fifty years earlier. The Rhineland had indeed been the key to the military pressure on the Germans, since from the Armistice it became the location of the Allied army of occupation. That occupation was the reason why many war memorials in the West talk of the Great War's end date as 1919, and not with the 1918 Armistice. Poised in the Rhineland for eight months, the American and British armies waited to see the German response to Versailles, ready to strike the military hammer from within German borders if necessary. Other territorial clauses broke up German lands and reassigned them to emerging nations, none less significant than Czechoslovakia and Poland, with the foresight of Hitler's expansionist agenda less than twenty years later. The final straw that was to break the German camel's back, but that at the time simply got lost in the flurry of Versailles, was the imposition of the financial clauses. Indeed, the infamous Clause 231 was the first to form an entire segment of the treaty, Part 8, entitled "Reparation," which contained itemized financial and economic penalties for Germany to pay as a consequence of the now-established "war guilt."

The main and most noteworthy element of this section was indeed reparations. While the figure was unknown at the time of Versailles (the Germans were thus obliged to sign a treaty without knowledge of the actual financial penalty), the London Schedule of Payments two years later stipulated that Germany was responsible for the staggeringly high figure of thirty-three billion US dollars, with unconditional and nonnegotiable elements accounting for more than one third of that sum. Various reviews in the 1920s sought to refinance the German capacity to meet this Himalayan debt level, but those details did not obscure the reality that the figure was simply astronomical. This was perceived quickly by both Allied and Central powers, and its scale of magnitude, as well as its underlying assumption of guilt, would very soon radically drive the internal German political agenda. To make matters worse for the Germans, the French army reoccupied the Ruhr industrial region of Germany in 1923 in the face of German hesitation to meet the repayment schedule. By this act, the French achieved the result they sought but added insult to injury to Germany that would come back to haunt them in the years ahead. We shall look at the impact of war reparations on German and world history briefly later. For our times, it is worth noting that the enormity, nature, and impact of the Allies placing the cost of the war on Germany is illustrated by the fact that it was only on October 3rd, 2010, that the final payment of its First World War reparations was made by the German Bundesbank to the World Bank. Ninety-two years after the guns fell silent, Germany paid its last bill.

On June 28th, 1914, Gavril Princip shot the Austrian heir to the Hapsburg dynasty, Archduke Franz Ferdinand, and his wife, Sophie, in Sarajevo, and that small act of assassination triggered an apocalypse we know as the First World War. It was the catalyst, or better yet, the spark that ignited a tinder box within a vast arsenal. Five years later to the day, the world leaders signed a treaty at Versailles, thinking they had brought that conflagration to a close. But it was a slow fuse to another tinder box within another and even more deadly arsenal. For the men who fought, however, it was time to go home. To the loved ones waiting, it was time to welcome them back joyously and to rebuild lives and families and jobs and homes. To the widows and the bereaved family members, it was a time to mourn again and to believe that their beloved soldier boys had done their duty and would be remembered and cherished forever for their supreme sacrifice. For the great emerging nations of the twentieth century, it was a time to turn the page and determine how best to be at the forefront of the promise of a new time of peace that would surely hold the assurance of each nation's fortunes and destiny.

For the signatories of the Treaty of Versailles, there was one outstanding issue, or maybe two, that remained to be addressed: firstly, to conclude similar treaties with the other vanquished Central powers now that the main culprit, Germany, had been brought to account for its aggression. Secondly, to ensure that the treaty gain its rightful momentum in both establishing the League of Nations and its hope for a brave new world while holding Germany to account for another one hundred years of reparations for its attack on human decency. The Treaty of Versailles did indeed gain momentum. But history shows us it was not the kind of momentum that the masses of negotiators, diplomats, and politicians and their leadership figures of Woodrow Wilson, George Clemenceau, David Lloyd George, Vittorio Orlando, and even Friedrich Ebert of Germany thought they had set in motion. In gambling parlance, Versailles was akin to a game of global poker. The Allies had raised the stakes and played their hand strongly and had won their hand emphatically. Germany was for a while forced to leave the table. But it would return soon, and the game was about to take on a very different turn for the rest of the century.

5

IF THE WAR GOES ON...

The great twentieth-century German novelist Herman Hesse[1] provided us with a memoir and a mirror on the First World War from
the German civilian perspective. His work, after which this chapter
is titled, was written more than a quarter century after the events he
chronicled, following Germany's defeat in the Second World War
and the collapse of Adolf Hitler's Third Reich. With that hindsight,
Hesse's memoir speaks to us across the past century with pathos and
pained irony, expressing a Germanic elegance and a Christian pacifism that subsequent German history utterly erased. At the First
World War's outbreak in 1914, he invited his compatriots to find a
national consciousness better expressed in the literary giant Goethe
than in the pompously imperial kaiser, though Hesse was worried
that might sound like "ivory-tower intellectualism." Goethe, he argued, "was never wanting as a patriot...but his devotion to humanity
meant more to him than his devotion to the German people." By
1917, and a further two million dead Germans, Hesse had shifted
to an overt political message underscored with religious pacifism,
writing to a cabinet minister in late summer, arguing that the logic
of the war was dooming humanity to the inevitability of an existential void: "Your speech was well constructed; otherwise, it was not
particularly original, significant, or provocative.... Your speech
shows a profound feeling of concern and responsibility for your people, its army, and its honor. But it shows no feeling for mankind.

---

[1] Hermann Hesse, *If the War Goes On: Reflections on War and Politics*,
trans. Ralph Manheim (New York: Farrar, Straus and Giroux, 1970) 16.

And, to put it bluntly, it implies hundreds of thousands more human sacrifices."

By the final year of the First World War, Hesse wrote to a young German soldier, passionately despairing of the choices being made by the powerful and influential which brought about such enormous suffering. A national delusion, Hesse claimed, had overtaken the German people, and in this delusional state the emergent narratives of German thinking had an enduring power that reaped, in effect, what it sowed: "Have you never wondered how it happens that the Germans have been so little loved...and so passionately shunned? Hear me, you were not misunderstood! It was you yourselves who did not understand, who were mistaken. You young Germans have always prided yourselves on the very virtues that you did not possess and blamed your enemies most for the vices they had learned from you."[2]

Hesse's anguished lamentation and condemnation provided a lonely foretaste of the vast collective process known as the *Vergangenheitsbewältigung*, the German people's later mid-century struggle to come to terms with their Nazi legacy. Recently, that same struggle resurfaced mildly in response to Europe's commemorations of the First World War's centennial and the Second World War's seventy-fifth anniversaries. The third and fourth generations have returned, in these anniversary years, to look back with sobriety, sentimentality, righteousness, and bewilderment on a past century riddled with disastrous agency and repetitive structures of violence. For Germany, that memory is still full of angst. Certainly, it was not until the post-1945 period that the process of truth and reconciliation truly began, but what Hesse's writings show is a prior longing in some Germans for an alternative to the military destiny which Germany foisted onto the world and itself during two world wars. In short, we catch a glimpse in Hesse of a long, unfolding fortune of war and hatred that was passed from one generation to another. Hesse posited a hypothetical: if the war goes on. History delivered a

---

[2] Ibid., 111.

reality: it did. How did the war not stop in the carriage at Compiegne Forest or in the grand palace of Versailles, but still go on?

What is made more complex in exploring this question is how we have provided a ready-made answer over the past one hundred years. From the vantage point of the cusp of the second quarter of the twenty-first century, we have two dominating narratives that keep us from properly understanding the first half of the twentieth century. Since childhood, most of us in the West have understood the Second World War as a titanic, binary struggle between good and evil. Between freedom and tyranny. Between democracy and dictatorship. Between decency and demonism. Between truth and error. Between gentility and genocide. Between community and tribe. Between love and hate. And so on. This narrative is derived from experience and the events themselves, which gives us a working template for interpreting the past.

The narrative of the First World War, however, is harder to create or sustain. For we shall see that the British and Germans, for example, have remembered it very differently over the past century and that a binary simplicity is unconvincing. The problem is that as time elapses, we see more clearly the logic coming out of Versailles that connects the first and second world wars. Only with the coming of the second war did we realize that the Great War was not actually the Great War after all or "the war to end all wars" but was, rather, the "first" war. In short, it took the Second World War for us to rename—and reinterpret—the Great War as the First World War. And in the middle of the twentieth century, it was not fully clear how much each war was codependent on the other. How is it possible that the Second World War can assume the historic status of good versus evil when the First World War is rarely described in such binary terms? If the Germans were evil in 1939, did that make them evil in 1914? If the Allies were storming the Normandy beaches in 1944 to restore freedom to Europe, were they doing the same when they stormed the fields of the Somme in 1916?

Answering these questions requires the same analysis of why the First World War simply did not stop after the Versailles treaty.

51

In a sense, the ending of the First World War, or perhaps more accurately its inability to end, provided a greater clue to understanding the last one hundred years than its beginning five years earlier in the assassination in Sarajevo of the Hapsburg heir. In the previous chapter, we saw the Versailles process run its course to a punitive and ambivalent conclusion, with harsh and judgmental measures against Germany coupled with a naïve belief in humankind's ability to resolve future strife through the League of Nations. Here is the clue to the riddle of why the "war to end all wars" did not achieve that aim, nor even take a pause to seek an alternative pathway for the future.

For in answering the question of how and why the war still went on, we need to understand the military and diplomatic agenda that prevailed in the time frame from the Armistice and through the Paris peace process. By November 11th, 1918, it was clear that Germany desired an armistice more than the Allies, and for good reason. The Germans' last gasp spring offensive of the same year had turned to a military rout, and the nation was descending fast by late September into political strife, with a vacillating and weak civilian government, a starving and diseased population, and a mutinous and deserting army. Ludendorff reluctantly informed the kaiser by early October that Germany could not win the war, in large part due to Ludendorff's own stubborn intransigence and increasing psychiatric deterioration. He had known after the August 8th "black day" that the German war machine had broken down beyond the point of return and that an armistice, concluded twelve weeks later, was the only possible outcome. Yet Ludendorff's behavior at this point produced the very worst of outcomes for Germany.

Firstly, Ludendorff believed holding on to foreign land would provide Germany with a stronger negotiating hand in the armistice agreement. The effect, though, was to doom hundreds of thousands more German troops to an unnecessary death or injury by continuing the fight even after he knew the war was lost. And yet Ludendorff showed cunning, in this respect, by brilliantly deflecting blame away from his own disastrous military decisions in the summer and autumn in an increasingly vain and pointless combat option. In truth, Germany committed three major blunders in that short time frame. Firstly, holding on to foreign soil meant pointless death for tens of thousands of more troops. Secondly, by deflecting the reason for the armistice to the civilian government rather than making it the natural consequence of a failed military campaign, it gave credence to the hatred of civilian liberal politics that developed soon after and helped launch the "knife in the back" myth that Hitler later fomented so effectively. If Germany went down, so this playbook would script, it was because of the weak Socialist-leaning politicians in Berlin and not because of the awesome German military machine. And thirdly, Germany thought it could appeal, over the heads of the warring parties, directly to President Woodrow Wilson to gain more temperate and conciliatory terms. This also backfired, since Wilson pushed hard in three sets of correspondence with Germany's diplomats, culminating in a demand for unconditional surrender. In short, the First World War ended very badly and dangerously for Germany and the Central powers.

Meantime, the Allies pounced quickly on the diplomatic option, a choice their generals found alarming. General John Pershing, the American commander and most recent top brass to join the war effort, was anxious that talk of an armistice would prevent the Allies from pursuing total victory, which was now within their grasp. From his perspective, why stop when your enemy is running, but still occupying foreign soil? Better, surely, he surmised, to push on across the Rhine and into the German heartland to destroy totally the enemy's capacity to wage war. Later, the Allied supreme commander, Ferdinand Foch, of France, arrived at a similar conclusion, remarking on the day of the Versailles signing that the Armistice merely suspended hostilities for what he uncannily and accurately predicted would be a twenty-year period. For the French, the Armistice stole the opportunity for a symbolic piece of historic revenge. General Petain had planned to use his French armies to invade German Alsace (Aachen) on November 14 and reclaim its industry and coalfields lost in the Franco-Prussian War of 1870, but that piece of sweet vengeance was stymied by the Armistice just three days before the planned invasion.

The cessation of military action itself on that final day of hostilities prompted not an immediate and exhausted silence on that November morning, but a crescendo of violence and belligerence that was a clue to the unresolved and unresolvable issue at the heart of the Great War, namely territory, power, and resources. The fighting armies and their generals knew that the imminent cessation of fighting at 11:00 A.M. local time, after four years and four months of slaughter, meant that every bargaining chip must be gathered and brought to bear in the months of diplomatic wrangling and peace-making that lay ahead. This cynical awareness that regardless of the cost "we fight on" can be adduced in the death toll of the final six hours of the war. By 11:00 A.M. that morning, another ten thousand men were killed, injured, or simply vanished—three thousand of them Americans—since the signing of the armistice document six hours earlier. Driven relentlessly by the desire to gain key geographic marker points, the fighting was frenzied and savage in the hope that each hand would be strengthened for future negotiations by last-minute territorial gains. In the case of the dead Americans that morning, the objective was the far bank of the River Meuse in the face of numerous German machine-gun nests.

Meantime, chaos was ensuing back in Germany, with the kaiser abdicating two days before the Armistice, revolution on the streets of German cities, and mass panic and violent unrest ahead of the retreating German armies. The chaos of the German homeland was a metaphor for the broader European geopolitical chaos that was unleashed, rather than halted, by the cessation of the formal hostilities of the war. Even while the peace process was underway and headed toward the seminal Versailles treaty outcome, the prevailing reality and mood was one that W. B. Yeats expressed so effectively in his 1919 poem, "The Second Coming":

Things fall apart; the centre cannot hold;
Mere anarchy is loosed upon the world,
The blood-dimmed tide is loosed...

For while we talk about the interwar years of 1918 to 1939, the reality is that European peace only began in 1923, after another four savage years of ethnic and tribal violence along a north-south line running from Arctic Finland to the Mediterranean. The Western Front may have ground to a halt, but along a two-thousand-mile line in Central and Eastern Europe, the violence elevated to new levels.

Firstly, the October revolution of the Bolsheviks in Russia occurred and succeeded only because of Russia's withdrawal from the First World War in March 1918 after the Treaty of Brest-Livotsk with Germany, but this abandonment of the war heralded no outpouring of peace for Russia's people. Within months the revolution had triggered a new internal civil war between the Bolshevik Reds and the Czarist Whites, which was to culminate in another eight million dead and millions more casualties, often civilian, in its savagery. By 1919 the Russian Civil War had ended in Siberia, and by 1920 in Crimea. But the Bolshevik hold on power during those years was tenuous, and the threat of a White counterrevolution ensured peripheral conflict until 1922 and a period of paranoid despotism by the Communist Reds, providing Joseph Stalin, a much underestimated and infinitely cunning politician from rural Georgia, with a model for brutality that characterized his dictatorship from 1929 to 1955. Stalin was a leader in the Russian colony of Caucasus during the civil war who assumed power after Lenin's death, thereby legitimizing a new alignment of proletarian egalitarianism with autocratic despotism. Even the Bolshevik revolutionary Leon Trotsky foresaw that absolute state terror was being reassembled from centuries of Russian hardship into a new Soviet idiom and modus operandi. For his objections, Trotsky was assassinated by Stalin's henchmen with an icepick in his skull while residing halfway around the world in Mexico City.

After its withdrawal from the Fist World War, Russia quickly fell into an ideologically based civil war. By inaugurating a new and pernicious norm of ideological fanaticism for internal government and international relations, extraordinary levels of suffering were the consequence for the Russian people. The Russian Civil War was also disastrous in embroiling former allies into its savagery, thus cementing a hundred years of distrust between East and West. For even while the idea of an armistice was taking shape, the Western Allied leaders were terrified about the possibility of Russia making peace with Germany and the Bolsheviks gaining control of local Soviets (communes) within a future Union of Soviet Socialist Republics. This was the moment when the West determined a stance toward Russia that has continued for a century, aside from a brief period during the Second World War, as evident by the tense relations between Western leaders and President Vladimir Putin's Russia. The cement on that relationship was laid one hundred years ago. For the larger part of that century the relationship has been accurately and broadly understood as a "cold war."

That adversarial foundation started with the Allies agreeing to send expeditionary forces into the Arctic and Finland, ostensibly to protect the Czechoslovak Legion in its retreat to join the Western Allies on the Western front, but realistically to aid the counterrevolutionary efforts of the Whites as they aligned with Finnish forces to defeat the Reds. The American "Polar Bear Expedition" (North Russia Expeditionary Force was its formal military title) may have only sent five thousand forces, but combined with the Japanese intervention in the East of seventy thousand troops, and British and Canadian regiments sent to Finland to join in the efforts, it was clear that the West was committed to assisting the White counterrevolution. This multinational intervention also included Italians, Greeks, Poles, and Serbs. Throughout 1918, while the First World War was moving toward its feverish climax, the Allies had opened new fronts in Finland and northern Russia. Fearing that the new Soviet regime and its Red Army would forever remove the Russian northern water ports of Murmansk and Archangel from Western access, the Allies moved to prop up the counterrevolution in a war that largely has been forgotten in the West. The Allied intervention was doomed once the Red Army scored decisive victories over the Whites in Siberia and the Crimea, and British and American troops promptly withdrew before their losses mounted. But Japan stayed on until 1922, and the Cold War can be dated from the Russian decision to leave the First World War and to chart a new and ideologically separate course for the remainder of the twentieth century. For the West, the die was cast, albeit with a brief period of the thawing of the relationship during the Second World War and the joint struggle against Nazism.

The Treaty of Versailles is considered the primary concluding treaty of the First World War, understandably so given its causal effect on German grievances and global havoc a generation later. Equally significant an agreement as that of Versailles in paving the journey of the twentieth century, however, was the earlier Treaty of Brest-Livotsk between Russia and all the Central powers, including Germany. That earlier treaty in the spring of 1918 effectively froze for this past century the Eurasian landmass into an ideological state of separateness from the remainder of Europe and the Western Hemisphere. Brest-Livotsk gave birth to a new world and a new century, eighteen years after the start of the twentieth century, even while the death throes of the old order were being pursued on the Western Front. What Versailles and Brest-Livotsk shared were not their concluding statements on the past, but rather the new narratives they were to create for the future. Nor were they the only concluding statements of the First World War that sowed the seeds for future strife. Another set of smaller treaties that formalized the end of the First World War set a new course of disequilibrium that was to reshape Central and Eastern Europe and the Middle East. The sixteen treaties in total, seven of which shaped geopolitics during the interwar period, were the catalysts for twentieth-century confusion and instability that continues to reverberate a century later.

This story of how the conclusion of the First World War provided both the death pangs of the old nineteenth-century order and the birth pangs of a new twentieth-century disorder is convoluted, often lost to Western European and American history. But it is a story not lost on the anguished and long-suffering peoples of Central and Eastern Europe. There the knowledge of continued conflict has tinged the collective memory of the past four generations in a way that is different from the collective memory of Western Europeans. The immediate years after the Armistice handed various peoples of Central and Eastern Europe a tumultuous period of revolution and violence. In the treaties that followed the war, the old order was replaced by new territorial arrangements founded with extraordinary disregard for the ethnic and cultural rivalries which had existed prior to the war. For example, the Treaty of Trianon of June 1920 with the former Austria-Hungary effectively exiled three million Hungarians from their home and left them in what is now Romania. The resentment of Hungarians lingered for decades. Similarly, the Treaty of Neville with Bulgaria, five months after Versailles, left a rump Bulgaria with most of its population forced into a newly formed Yugoslavia, Greece, and Romania, and a nation now deprived of a seaport. The irony is that this carving up of the old vanquished empires was, on the surface, an example of the principle of self-determination that Woodrow Wilson had vaunted as his motive for American participation in the war, his Fourteen Points plan, and his goal at Versailles. But instead, these treaties opened a Pandora's box of ethnic hatred that was deeply rooted in Central Europe, with the aim of self-determination for Caucasian peoples who previously had been subjugated under the iron fist of the nineteenth-century imperial powers.

The story of the end of the war with the Ottoman Empire is even more confusing and tragic, resulting in two treaties, not just one, to deal with the so-called "sick man of Europe's" replacement by a new muscular nation, Turkey. Underpinning those treaties was a greater sense of colonialist and imperialist attitudes and goals within the Allies. The dissolution of the Ottoman Empire and its replacement by a nascent and assertive Turkey was, like so much of today's Middle East, intimately connected with the land once known as Palestine and now hallowed as Israel and the Palestinian territory. During the war, in 1915, the British had through their high commissioner, Sir Henry McMahon, sought Arab participation in the conflict against the Ottoman Empire in return for a guarantee of Arab independence and sovereignty, minus the critical coastland of what is today the region from Aleppo to Damascus, as well as much of Iraq. The lure worked, and in 1916 the Ottoman Empire was faced by an armed Arab revolt and insurrection, made famous in the life and story of Colonel T. E. Lawrence, or Lawrence of Arabia. By 1917, however, colonial ambivalence required a shift in strategy, akin to duplicity. The more influential Sykes-Picot Agreement of 1916 was a secret accord between Britain and France that sought to establish greater control of the region than had been communicated to the Arabs in 1915. Sykes-Picot would have given Britain oversight of the Mediterranean coast and France oversight of what is today northern Syria, northern Iraq, and Jordan. The plan would have stayed secret, but the Bolsheviks in Russia blew the Western Allies' cover in late 1917 in order to embarrass the "imperialist states" that were, in Bolshevik estimates, intent on expanding their empires into the Middle East. Even more embarrassing was the emergence, after lobbying for years by Chaim Weizmann, future first president of Israel, of the Balfour Declaration by the British Government in November of 1917. The Balfour Declaration pledged British government support for a Jewish homeland in Palestine, subject to the safeguarding of civil and religious rights of existing non-Jewish peoples there. Balfour was at the time a former prime minister and current foreign secretary under Lloyd George with strong sympathies toward the Zionist cause. What was intended as a humane and visionary declaration, however, threw more fuel onto the fire of Middle Eastern ethnic, religious, and racial tensions. One hundred years later, the intractability of this inertia, instability, and state of permanent conflict is all too evident.

This meddling diversion of the Allies in a region so radically different from London and Paris—and so dangerous an ethnic tinderbox—exemplified a critical failing of the First World War's ending. We see an extraordinary example in the Balfour Declaration of what was evident, too, in Wilson's Fourteen Points and at Versailles, namely high-minded principles and vision predicated on humane values that were catastrophically misaligned with the political realities of the day. The Middle East had already been subjected to the proverbial poking of the hornet's nest during the war, and the self-contradictory and incoherent promises coming from London set the scene perfectly for the "sick man of Europe," the Ottoman Empire, not to die peaceably but in a frantic death gasp. In this context, the peace treaty with Turkey itself fell apart and led to further war. In trying to kill the Ottoman Empire, the Allies forced Turkey to the negotiating table at the Treaty of Sevres in 1920, only to watch the treaty prompt immediate civil war and then genocide. Turkey had signed at Sevres because, like Germany at Versailles, it had no choice. But its signing was the trigger for a military coup in which the great hero of the Ottoman war effort, Mustafa Kemal, was prepared to continue the war against Greece, Armenia, and France. The result was extraordinary violence and what is today known as "ethnic cleansing"—for that is surely what occurred at the Greek city of Smyrna. Spurred on by the Allies, Greece invaded the region in 1919 in what turned into three years of barbaric fighting with the defeated Ottomans. Kemal's success for his Turkish cause culminated in the fall of 1922 with the slaughter and mutilation of the Orthodox Metropolitan of Smyrna and two weeks of carnage that left thirty thousand Greeks and Armenians dead, in revenge for the massacre of Turks in the preceding years. This atrocity at Smyrna was noted by Churchill in his memoirs as having "few parallels in the history of human crime."[3] The outcome, however, was indicative of the whole bloody mess that characterized the period immediately after the official end of the First World War. For Kemal's victory ensured a second treaty with the Allies that ripped up the earlier one

---

[3] Quoted in Robert Gerwarth, *The Vanquished: Why the First World War Failed to End* (New York: Farrar, Straus and Giroux, 2016) 4.

of Sevres from three years prior. Kemal and his new Turkish forces effectively turned the vanquished Ottomans into the victorious Turks, and the spoils of war were an independence for Turkey that was ratified by the Treaty of Lausanne the following summer. This brought the bloody aftermath of the war to its real conclusion, through horrendous violence that was the true epitaph to the First World War. For the Greeks, it meant the forcible removal of more than one million from what is now Turkey, and for the Turks, the removal of half a million from Greece. Lausanne thus became the final treaty to bring down the curtain on a terrible decade for humanity of cataclysmic proportion. Thus, continuing genocide, ethnic cleansing, and total war were the backdrop to the concluding treaties that brought an end to the First World War. Years later, Hitler was to admire the fact that Mustafa Kemal had fought to rip up the first Treaty of Sevres in order to have it replaced by the Treaty of Lausanne and thus gain peace on his and the Turks' terms, and not on those of the Allies.

This Greco-Turkish example was, according to Robert Gerwarth, in his excellent book *The Vanquished*,[4] illustrative of a broader conflict pattern that was immediately produced, energized, and connected to the First World War. Firstly, Gerwarth argues that Mustafa Kemal's success was an example of new kinds of conflict between regular and new armies fought as interstate wars, such as the Polish-Soviet war. What they shared was a vacuum left by the collapse of old empires or systems of governance, such as with the Hapsburg and Ottoman empires, into which nation-state protagonists moved aggressively. Secondly, and consequentially, this capacity to wage war both with official armies and with new militialike forces fueled continuing intrastate violence. We saw this in the Russian Civil War, but smaller examples occurred in Ireland and Hungary, too. And, thirdly, Gerwarth suggests that the underlying current beneath this violence was revolution. This revolutionary

---

[4] Ibid.

impulse was at times ideologically inspired around themes of redistributed power, land, or wealth, such as in Russia, Bulgaria, and Germany, or else ethnically inspired in those collapsed empires such as the Habsburg, Ottoman, and Hohenzollern empires, where repressed minorities sought to establish identity rights under the same lofty principle that Versailles had proclaimed as democratic self-determination. The irony is that these struggles finally brought an end to European hostilities by 1923, but in their wake, the principle of self-determination delivered not Wilson-like democratic administrations but extremes of authoritarianism in the forms of both Fascism and Communism.

One final example of how the First World War directly and immediately triggered further conflict was found not just in Europe and the Middle East but a world away in Asia. Japan and China, traditional rivals and future enemies in a conflict of the worst barbarity, were at Versailles on the winning Allied side. In settling scores at Versailles, the connection of domestic politics to international diplomacy reached high stakes when Japan proposed that language on racial equality be included in the treaty. Japan's economic and military superiority over China, with the kudos earned from assisting Australian troop transportation during the war, bolstered its confidence in now seeking enhanced authority and respect at the table of international affairs. The trouble for Wilson and the Western Allies was their fear of the language of racial equality, which would have jeopardized any hopes Wilson might have had of gaining southern congressional support to ratify the Versailles treaty. Similarly, the British and French had no intention of granting equality to its empire and colony populations. Faced with Japanese withdrawal from the peace process, the Western Allies backed off and gave Japan control of former German territory, including the Chinese province of Shandong. The effect was outrage and protest back in Beijing, with prescience of events seventy years later with the student protests at Tiananmen Square. In 1919, the students formed the May Fourth Movement, which was to give birth to the future Communist Party of China. Once again, Wilson's hope of a world made "safe for democracy" was following a very different pathway. In 2015, a century later, the Chinese government chose to host the global International Committee of Historical Sciences in Shandong's capital city, Jinan, for its quinquennial global convention. It was surely no accident that China chose with heavy irony this location for a gathering of world historians.

Other regions of instability and tension, such as the former German colonies in Africa, would also emerge from Versailles into places of dreadful conflict. Throughout the twentieth and twenty-first centuries, the long struggle to end European colonialism would continue, in the case of Africa through to the eventual establishment of the African Union, consisting of the continent's independent nations, in 2002. Ironically, the wresting away of German control of its colonies at Versailles was justified as an example of granting self-determination to those peoples, but that outcome was to take nearly a century, with the Allies replacing German control of African resources and administrations with their own oversight. True pan-African self-determination was attained only after many decades and through a process of violent postcolonial struggles. The pattern was thus established. The First World War ended both militarily and diplomatically in a way that ensured it indeed did not end at all, despite the vain belief that it would be the "war to end all wars." The numerous treaties in the immediate years after the Armistice were meant to deliver that hopeful promise, but instead they delivered recklessly unfortunate outcomes. All over the globe the First World War ensured both immediate conflict and long-term conditions of hostility. This complex, convoluted, and highly unstable environment emerged because of the war, particularly in relation to the choices that were made on how to end the war.

In replacing the nineteenth-century order with catastrophic failure that upended the rules, governance, systems, hopes, and expectations of humanity in the first decades of the twentieth century, the First World War unleashed a new set of conditions that have shaped our history and our world these past hundred years. With the collapse of the pre-1914 system that had been forged from the spoils of victory at Waterloo a century earlier, a new set of actors and ideas would emerge and struggle for control of the future, without any of the constraints that had generally dictated nineteenth-century norms. As the twentieth century unfolded, the dehumanization of entire peoples, the eradication of the distinction between combatant and civilian, and the legitimation of historic feuds and tribal hatreds came together to empower a dangerous forward thrust from Versailles, in which might would equal right. The example of the Armenian genocide by Turkey, which began in September 1915 and produced 1.5 million dead civilians by the Armistice, illustrates how the war cast its desperate shadow across the century. By the end of the twentieth century, several other genocides—in Bosnia-Herzegovina, Rwanda, Cambodia, Nazi Germany, Nanking China, and the Soviet Union—could all look back to their founding model in the cauldron of the First World War. Such was its legacy. But not completely. For the West would also hold on to other cherished traditions of democracy as a counterbalance to the atavistic and tribal forces that would gain ascendancy. The fact remains, nonetheless, that by the Second World War there were fewer European democracies than there were before the outbreak of the first.

How could that have happened? The clue to the answer lies in the notion of three forces that were created and emboldened from the ashes of the First World War and its violent and elongated ending. Those forces can be broadly defined in political jargon as Communism, Fascism, and democracy, which have for far too long been viewed in their discrete separateness and not in terms of their codependency or coempowerment. Consider a genealogical analogy to explain this. If three siblings are born, they possess their distinctive identities, individual personalities, and lifelong sense of self. They may even detest each other. They may claim they have nothing in common with each other. They may feel superior to the other. And they may go to war with each other. Those options may be real, and yet regardless of this, they share the same biology, hereditary factors, environmental context, and family identity. In short, they have more in common than they may wish. For the past century, we in the

West have talked too much about how distinct, separate, and different we are from those who have behaved badly or who we have sought to denigrate. To our detriment, we have been less willing to examine how much we have in common and how much codependency we share with those others who see, believe, and act differently. There is a very real danger in this overconfidence in our own perspective. As Herman Hesse observed in the young German soldier in 1918, he prided himself "on the very virtues that you did not possess and blamed your enemies most for the vices they had learned from you." Though this may be true, it does not mean that each sibling is devoid of agency, choice, values, or actions. But it does mean that she or he does not enact those in a vacuum. They are part of a broad familial story, and that is precisely how the family of nations has lived for the past one hundred years. The ideological thrust of the past century years has been to pick sides and to believe in the primacy of one's own version and vision, neglecting its interdependency. For us, one hundred years after the First World War, we do not even have the depth of historical perspective—the generational triangulation—that previous generations had to challenge this absolutism. Our parents and grandparents could recall, revisit, and recast the First World War from the perspective of experience and memory. My father today remembers hearing about Versailles as he grew up. We are the first generation that cannot do that. We must dig deeper and peer back further. But it is necessary, because it explains who we are and how we relate to each other.

The German writer Hermann Hesse wondered what would happen if the war went on. It did, and it has continued to be waged in different places and forms for the past century. That is the story of the second part of this book.

PART TWO

CONSEQUENCE

6

FANFARE FOR THE COMMON MAN

Initially, though, the catastrophe of the First World War and the deadly conflicts spawned in its aftermath appeared to settle into a more peaceful stability by 1924, with the fragile promise of a hopeful future for the international community. The wars of old tribalism and convulsions of new nations had by then diminished, and the drumbeat of endless conflict appeared finally to have quieted. Even the fragile Weimar Republic of Germany now began to enjoy some fruits of peace. By 1924, the United States was injecting vast amounts of capital into Europe to stabilize its economies, including Germany's. Indeed, for a short five-year period, it seemed a new world might emerge to replace the nineteenth-century model of aristocratic power and national imperialism. The Roaring Twenties had arrived, and people, en masse and across nations, were now liberated to experience its novelty, frivolity, indulgence, and exuberance. The vast emptiness caused by the inestimable number of war dead may have haunted the bereaved and traumatized the human family as a whole, but the earth kept spinning and its rotation delivered daily a new embrace of life, laughter, and love to replace the grief, at least in the external behavior of the postwar nations.

On the political stage, the mid-1920s produced some powerful examples of new plans for a rebuilt world, new governmental norms, and new electrified economies as evidence that the world after the "war to end all wars" might indeed deliver an era of global peace and prosperity. The emergence of US financing was to play a pivotal role then and ever more, borne from a US financial intervention in 1924 to prevent further economic collapse in Germany and renewed conflict with France and Belgium. This was the Dawes Plan of 1924, which would provide a powerful case study of the assumptions that had underpinned the League of Nations. Angered by the return of the Alsace region to France as part of the Versailles treaty, German coal industrialists successfully lobbied their government for subsidies. This, in turn, produced hyperinflation in Germany, the implementation of trade tariffs on the export of coal to France and Belgium, and the slowdown of German payment of war reparations. The French, who depended heavily on Ruhr coal despite repossessing Alsace, responded by militarily occupying the German Ruhr region, heightening the risk of renewed war unless Germany cooperated on coal exports.

Charles Dawes, distinguished veteran of the First World War, powerful financier, prominent Republican, and future vice president of the United States, was instrumental in designing the plan that then-president Warren Harding's Allied Reparations Commission would enact to head off another European crisis. In return for considerable bond-financed loans, Germany's reparations plan was to be restructured to alleviate its crushing effect on the domestic economy. The key element was a foretaste of the future superpower role of American capitalism in twentieth-century global affairs. The German reparations debt was estimated at 130 billion gold marks, but the bond refinancing would permit Germany to pay only 1 billion in its first year and reduced payments for the following four years, with an influx of $200 million in cash into the German economy. In return, the German Reichsbank granted partial American oversight of its affairs. Furthermore, the French agreed to leave the Ruhr in return for a German commitment to a permanent, albeit reduced, amount of coal exports to France and Belgium. The plan was highly successful in several ways. It defused international tensions, stabilized the German economy, transferred German debt effectively to American investors, avoided a renewed Franco-German war, and ensured Dawes won the Nobel Peace Prize the following year. But it also produced ominous side effects that illustrated the unintended consequences that were to plague future twentieth-century diplomacy.

The two most important of those outcomes were unresolved expectations and unbalanced economic realities. In terms of expectations, the Germans convinced themselves that the Dawes Plan would be the first measure of a longer-term strategy to aid, assist, and strengthen their economy. This expectation received a lukewarm response by the Allies, but nonetheless, in 1929, another plan was developed with Allied approval under the appointed leadership of Owen Young, prominent industrialist and one of the world's first media (radio) moguls, who was tasked with formulating a plan to reduce the burden of reparations on Germany. However, before that plan was developed, a new global economic catastrophe would crash the Young Plan on the rocks and doom Germany to unresolved economic hardship. In October of 1929, the Wall Street crash changed the face of human history and the global economy, dooming the capacity of the Young Plan to assist Europe. Instead, American money immediately reversed course, moving rapidly out of Europe. Credits to Germany were cancelled, thus ending what was in effect a vital stimulus and investment plan for its economy. Rapidly, Germany collapsed into a banking and fiscal crisis that produced unimaginable hyperinflation and a total inability to meet reparations requirements, coupled with its own acute national version of global mass unemployment. By 1932, the Allies acknowledged the unique economic devastation occurring in Germany and agreed to review again its reparations schedule. This time the Allies authorized a reduction in the amount of reparations to $720 million, a quarter of the original Versailles figure, and granted further restructuring of the payment schedule. However, history overtook events again at this point, this time from within Germany. With the ascent of the National Socialist German Workers' Party to power, and Hitler's appointment as chancellor in 1933, the future of reparations was voided and moot, with Hitler rejecting utterly any compliance with war reparations. Some ten-plus years after Ludendorff's creation of the political "knife in the back" myth, German resentment of its economic burdens found another cause that would fuel its future Nazi mythology. The other unintended consequence from the Dawes Plan was similarly an accessory to that demonic mythology: the coal production rules that came out of that plan shifted steel production back into German industry. In the years of relative prosperity and stability after 1924, German steel production rapidly outpaced that of the French, as a direct consequence of the Allied strategy to boost the German economy and thus meet its reparations obligations. Given steel's absolute preeminence in the machinery of war, this concentration of legitimated German steel production augured very well for Hitler's future military ambitions. This patchwork response of the Allies to the vagaries of economic fortune and a push-pull approach to supporting German accountability and capability was consistent with what had emerged earlier at Versailles. A misfortune of Versailles is that it treated the vanquished with both harshness and lenience in precisely the wrong ways.

The Dawes Plan provided a short but critical intervention to address new economic and military threats and thus resolve international tensions peaceably. Similarly, the post-1923 period showed other hopeful signs for future diplomacy and a place for the League of Nations. When the newly appointed prime minister of Italy, Benito Mussolini, brought Italy to the brink of war with Greece in August 1923 over the disputed island of Corfu, the role of international diplomacy faced its greatest challenge since the end of the First World War. Mussolini was seeking to establish the norm of aggressive nationalism, thereby providing a direct and antithetical threat to the diplomatic principles underlying the League of Nations. Dating back to agreements and discussions during the war, Mussolini asserted Italian sovereignty over the Greek controlled island of Corfu. When an Italian general and his entourage were murdered while visiting neighboring areas, Mussolini used the assassinations as the pretext to invade Corfu and incorporate it within a "Venetian empire." The international response was initially to use the league, but the French awkwardly boycotted this convention due to their nervousness of the league scrutinizing French occupation of the Ruhr. The final settlement was negotiated by ambassadorial delegation rather than the league itself, requiring Italy to withdraw from Corfu and Greece to pay a hefty fine to Italy for its purported role in the murder of the general, even though Greek complicity was unproven. At the time, diplomacy won out, but the role of the league was sidelined, and the emotional spoils of victory went to the Fascist aggressor, Mussolini, foreshadowing the next decade in Europe. Tellingly, Mussolini emerged from the crisis both emboldened and vindicated.

These examples, nonetheless indicate that the Roaring Twenties proceeded with the broad conviction that international relations were succeeding in preventing war. That conviction was to last until the seismic collapse of global capital at the end of the decade in the crash of the stock market in 1929. By the 1920s, Europe had established nine new US-style republics, such as Czechoslovakia, each of which were predicated on Wilson's notion of "self-determination," though created with little regard to existing borders, ethnic identities, or economic histories. This increase of emergent democratic nations was, however, a radical departure from the previous dynastic century, whereby aristocracy and monarchies determined the future of peoples and their inhabited borders. Messy it was, but as our times have shown us, Western democracy is indeed messy and in constant flux. What was becoming clear by the post-Versailles period was that while the First World War was not caused by ideological conflict, one of its main outcomes was an overwhelming role for ideology at the center of how nations would pursue their fortunes and futures.

What is also clear is that several conditions for the strengthening of democracy, economy, and diplomacy were available by 1923 and were instrumental in establishing a short period of stability during that decade. Critically, given American finance and influence, the political might of the US could no longer be neglected by Europe even while, from Teddy Roosevelt to Woodrow Wilson, American sentiment moved back and forth between intervention and isolation on the international stage. In 1923, the United States was ready to engage, but by 1929 it was in full speed reversal toward a new isolationism. This was unfortunate since Wilson's Fourteen Points had, in 1919, presented a strategy for engagement and an organization for its realization in the League of Nations. But while Wilson may have partially won the case for the League of Nations on the global stage, he most surely lost it within the arena of American domestic politics. In so doing, the opportunity to make the world safe for democracy would be lost to history. As referenced earlier, by excluding Republicans from Paris, Wilson refueled old partisanship and isolationist instincts. To have his agenda heard by the American people over the heads of the Washington establishment, Wilson crisscrossed the country by railroad after returning from France, particularly the western states, passionately expounding on the virtues of the Versailles treaty and the League of Nations. It was to no avail and proved devastating to his health, rendering him utterly weakened physically and politically. The harsh congressional response to Wilson's plan was also a reflection of others' reactions to the worst aspects of his personality, on display to his fellow negotiators in Paris during the peace process. Clemenceau wryly asked one of his team, concerning Wilson, "How can I talk to a fellow who thinks himself the first man for two thousand years who has known anything about peace on earth?"[1] It was this trait of Wilson's—his self-belief in the power of his own logic, coupled with a lack of empathy and negotiating skills—that finally doomed his vision to inertia both in Paris and back in Washington and left us a noble idea with an unfulfilled legacy: a pleasant dream that disappeared with the waking hours.

The intellectual arrogance and psychological dissonance of the president spelled doom for the Treaty of Versailles at home. For the treaty to be ratified, the Senate would have to approve with a two-

---

[1] Robert Ferrell, "The Perils of Peacemaking in a War-Torn World," in *World War I*, ed. Donald Murphy (New York: Greenhaven Press, 2002) 222.

thirds majority. Leading Republican Henry Cabot Lodge sought to amend the treaty, frustrating Wilson and causing stubborn opposition from the hardline opponents. By November of 1919, some five months after the Versailles signing, fourteen Democrats opposed the treaty, and for the first time in US history, a peace treaty was denied ratification by the US Congress. One month earlier, withered by the opposition, Wilson suffered the first of a series of strokes, which by early 1920 were the subject of public knowledge. His treaty was rejected, his health in terminal decline, and within one year his presidency was over, with the vision and agenda moving to the Republicans for three successive presidents in the Harding, Coolidge, and Hoover administrations. Before he could see any of the peace dividends of a stable and increasingly democratic Europe for the short years of 1924 to 1929, Wilson was dead, and his legacy was seen as one of naivety and failure. In this context, the greater success of US engagement in Europe was evident in the Dawes Plan and the nearly fulfilled Young Plan. The League of Nations, the greatest possible statement of US presidential commitment to global engagement, was doomed to eventual failure, resented by the American establishment and distrusted by Europe's leaders precisely when they needed to implement its standards. Wilson had backed the wrong horse, it seemed, and his Republican successors saw finance as the better way of stabilizing Europe.

This, however, is a harsh judgment. Like many political figures of twentieth-century politics, Wilson's failures were perceived more strongly at home than abroad. For without his advocacy, it is doubtful the league would have prevailed at all. And the league itself certainly did gain worldwide traction for a while. Between 1923 and 1939, a total of sixty-four nations were members of the league, with its highest membership in 1934. Even Germany joined the league in 1926, such was the breadth of conviction that a global diplomatic community could affect a lasting peace, and German membership was sustained until Hitler's ascent to power. Only with the growing Fascist agenda of the 1930s did the inefficacy of the league finally come to light. Until then it held great sway and expressed strong advocacy. The British response to the league contrasts strongly with Wilson's inability to gain American backing. In Britain, its cheerleader was Viscount Robert Cecil, son of the former prime minister Lord Salisbury and later winner of the Nobel Peace Prize in 1937. During the Great War, his vision, like Wilson's, was of a diplomatic organization that could preemptively head off future conflict. In his "Memorandum on Proposals for Diminishing the Occasion of Future Wars,"[2] Cecil outlined in 1916 a Wilson-type vision of democratic frameworks for the resolution of international disputes. By the time of the Armistice, his efforts bore out political dividend, with the Foreign Office establishing a League of Nations Office within its bureaucracy. For the next two decades Cecil's name was inextricably linked to the peace movement, and he was the head of the League of Nations Union from 1923 until its dissolution after the Second World War.

Cecil's contrast with Wilson is obvious. A peculiarly British sort of reaction to the First World War began even before the Armistice was signed, and the league became an accepted part of the formal British establishment's agenda for the interwar years. After the Corfu crisis, it appeared that the British position was vindicated. The final legacy of the league was perhaps a victory of sorts. For while it is true that the League of Nations failed to prevent the rise of the aggressor Fascist nations of the 1930s, and thus permitted the building of the pathway to the Second World War, its necessity as an organization became more, not less, evident. The need for a more effective and more enduring version of the league became apparent precisely because the Second World War so effectively illustrated its shortcomings. On the 18th of April 1946, fewer than twelve months after the end of the Second World War, the United Nations was created. The United States was a charter member of the UN, re-

---

[2] Robert Cecil to the War Cabinet, October 1916, The National Archives, Kew. Memorandum on Proposals for Diminishing the Occasion of Future Wars, CAB 24/10/85.

maining to this day a permanent member of the fifteen-member Security Council, and it hosts the global organization's headquarters in New York City. While in recent decades the UN has been at odds with the United States on some issues, including American foreign policy and intervention in Iraq in 2003, the depth of connectedness and mutual commitment is undeniable. Woodrow Wilson would likely find peace and satisfaction knowing that one century after his death the global political community still has an enduring and active organization of global acceptance, dedicated to the prevention of conflict and the advancement of peace and justice.

This shift in global relations gained broad and deep acceptance over the twentieth century, especially the notion of effective rule by self-determination, with no need for an aristocracy or ruling elite. In short, the fanfare for the common man and woman not only led to emergent democratic states, but a new sense of the social value of human capital and the rights of citizens to determine their way of life. What was more problematic was deciding what this new inclusive approach would look like. A powerful case illustration is the plight of African American veterans returning home from European combat in 1919. In his book *Red Summer*, Cameron McWhirter[3] drew attention to a new awakening of black Americans after the First World War to their possibilities of freedom, an awakening gained while serving abroad with foreign armies from 1917 to 1919. During a horrendous summer period from April to October 1919, a "red summer" occurred, not of a Bolshevik-style uprising but of a violent racist response by white Americans to that emergent African American awareness. During the war, despite Pershing's desire for the separation of American forces from those of the Allies, many black US soldiers experienced new social and racial mobility that had been denied them back home. Pershing's vision of American separatism broke down militarily by 1918 when the Western Front's

---

[3] Cameron Mcwhirter, Red Summer: The Summer of 1919 and the Awakening of Black America (New York: Henry Holt & Co., 2011).

stagnation turned to a war of movement, first in the rout of the Allied armies in the Spring Offensive and then in the reverse thrust in the final months of the war. For many black American soldiers, the horror of the war yielded a silver lining of integration by foreign Allies. Whether in the heat of combat or the heat of the brothel, white and black Allied soldiers from different nations lived, laughed, drank, lusted, fought, and died together in a way that had never been possible previously for the black American soldier.

This unfamiliar exposure to an inclusive and democratic way of being was a dangerous commodity for a black veteran to bring back to America. The forces of reaction and bigotry would not tolerate the notion of a liberated African American, and those forces worked quickly to violently repress any notion that what had occurred in French towns and trenches could be a model for the American way. By October of 1919, there had been fifty-two lynchings and twenty-five race riots around the country, especially in the old Dixie South. Reacting to a black veteran in Georgia wearing his army uniform, and infuriated by the notion that a black man could be a war hero, a group of drunk Ku Klux Klan followers lynched him. This sparked a summer of racial hatred and violence that was a seminal moment in the founding of the twentieth-century civil rights movement.

The deprivation of the African American experience prior to the war was mirrored in different ways in Europe, too. While less racially founded, ethnic, tribal, and religious hatreds had clearly been part of the European landscape for centuries and were now coupled after the industrial revolution to new forces of economic power and abuse. The nineteenth century had industrialized and urbanized Europe to a considerable extent. The effect of the rush for capital, industry, and empire was a massive wealth disparity and a surge in degrading labor conditions for much of Europe's working class. The 1848 revolutions in European cities and the publishing of Karl Marx's *Communist Manifesto* that same year was no random coincidence. Housing and domestic conditions in nineteenth-century capitalist Europe were generally appalling, the likes of which Dickens captured for posterity in his classics. The First World War had taken that industrial model and its use of labor and applied it with enormous and devastating effect in the pursuit of war. But in so doing, the nature of that war produced transformational social forces that did not diminish with troops returning from the front abroad, nor did those forces leave untouched the civilians who had lived and worked to support the war economy at home during the years of conflict.

While the "war to end all wars" failed miserably in preventing future conflict, the optimism of the Roaring Twenties provided the vision to think anew about the norms of social life that had prevailed in the nineteenth century. The war would have to lead to something better, so the mood prevailed, even if militarily that hope was proven one generation later to be in vain. After the war was won, winning the peace was the priority now facing the Allied European democracies. As David Lloyd George, British prime minister, put it a fortnight after the Armistice, the nation and its government owed it to the returning veterans to make it a "country fit for heroes." Programs were established in the former combatant nations based on this sense of responsibility to their returning veterans. Both the American Legion and the Disabled Veterans of the World War (DAV) were founded by the time of the Armistice, and the American Legion had recruited one million members within eighteen months of its founding. The reality facing the combatant nations was not only the absence of vast numbers of war dead from the peacetime economy, especially in the European nations, but an even larger number of wounded, injured, and disabled men who would live the remainder of their lives seeking new civilian roles while bearing old and often dreadful injuries. In the US, a third of a million returning men were eligible for rehabilitation services, such as finding work in the burgeoning ship-building industry. One DAV recruitment notice highlighted the possibility of such jobs for one-armed veterans. Congress responded by passing the Smiths-Sears Veterans Rehabilitation Act within six months of the Armistice and authorized the

spending of the considerable sum of a half a billion dollars in rehabilitation programs for the war-wounded prior to the Wall Street
crash ten years later.

The most enduring and widespread symbol of rehabilitation
was the poppy, still worn today by the British and Commonwealth
nations as part of Remembrance Day, which replaced Armistice Day
after the Second World War. Interestingly, the origins of the poppy
as a symbol reside in literature, in John McRae's "In Flanders Field"
poem from 1915,[4] and championed by a female professor from the
University of Georgia, Molina Michael, who promoted its usage after the Armistice with the American YMCA Overseas War Secre-
taries Organization. Following a period of some dispute, the Veterans of Foreign Wars organization agreed to promote it to assist in
rehabilitation program fundraising prior to the first international
Armistice commemoration in 1922. Today, the Royal British Legion is the primary organization to feature the use of the poppy annually, with great fundraising benefits for injured veterans and extraordinary public relations successes during the centennial years of
2014 to 2018.

It would not be too outlandish to suggest that, for the British
at least, much of this new commitment was borne of guilt pangs
about the suffering of the nation. What is clear is that, both for veteran and civilian populations, their governments conceded the need
to build greater prosperity and inclusion for their peoples. The fanfare for the "common person" may have originated as bugle tones for
the dead, but now its trumpet song was of renewed promise and
hope for the living. Even in the former Central powers a new commitment to the welfare of all prevailed. The largest single residential
building in the world was constructed outside Vienna in the late
1920s as part of the welfare program of the left-wing Social Democratic Party of Austria's agenda. Titled the Karl Marx Hof (Karl
Marx Court), it provided public housing for up to 5,000 individuals

---

[4] John McRae, "In Flanders Field," *Punch Magazine* (1915). See
bibliography for link to archival image.

in nearly 1,400 apartments and was an example of how the slums of the nineteenth century were being replaced across Europe by ambitious housing projects.

Perhaps the most consequential shift in recognizing popular empowerment was the success of female suffrage in many nations in the years after the First World War. During the spring of 1918, after decades of struggle and campaigning, the British Parliament legalized the vote for married women over the age of thirty, and then, just days after the Armistice, women became eligible to be elected as members of Parliament. Within one decade of these Acts, women had won complete equal suffrage rights with men in Britain. In the United States, the campaign for suffrage led finally and successfully to the adoption of the Nineteenth Amendment to the Constitution in August of 1920, one year after Congress had voted to grant suffrage to women weeks before the signing of the Treaty of Versailles. Germany similarly pressed forward with a populist and progressive agenda under its brand-new Council of People's Representatives just days after the abdication and exile of Kaiser Wilhelm and the signing of the Armistice. On November 30th, 1918, the council granted women the right to vote in national elections, dramatically ushering in a new vision of power granted by populist assent rather than dispensed by the ruling elite. While the suffrage movement can be credited with achieving this outcome in Britain and the United States, it is clear that the social changes driven by the war on the home front accounted for the shift in culture that allowed suffrage to rise to the point of successful vindication. In Britain alone, the First World War required nearly a million women to work in munitions factories and chemical and metal industries to support the war effort. Women's attire changed in these factories, with women wearing trousers at work for the first time in history. As with the returning African American veterans, home nations were forced to reconsider historic inequalities, and forces for social change were given the momentum for new levels of egalitarianism for the remainder of the twentieth century. One of the most tangible and

hopeful examples was the breadth of suffrage legislation across nations following the war, and the onward struggle of civil rights for
minorities. Women's suffrage achieved broad, long-awaited success
in the postwar years, but it was not a uniform achievement. While
countries such as New Zealand had already granted suffrage in the
late nineteenth century, the combat nations that had endured the
longest—France and Belgium—ironically were slower in coming to
the table. Eligibility for women to vote in national elections was only
granted after the liberation of France from Nazi occupation in 1944,
and Belgium finally delivered likewise in 1949, even as the idea of
the European Union was being born. Women's suffrage continued
to be a struggle of human rights throughout the remainder of the
twentieth century and continues still today. Only in 2011 did one of
Western democracy's greatest allies, Saudi Arabia, finally grant
women the right to vote, and then in 2018 the right to drive a vehicle.

This dawn of women's emancipation and the century-long road
toward greater gender equality was emblematic of the breadth of
democratic impulses that emanated during and after the war. The
large-scale death of officers from the ruling classes of Europe alongside enlisted men effectively denuded the aristocracy of its next generation and broke the power of landed gentry. It also showed that
the Western Allies were willing to sacrifice nobility for the struggle
at an even greater rate than the proletarian foot soldier. While 12
percent of British enlisted soldiers died in the war, 17 percent of
officers never returned, including eighty British generals. Aristocratic privilege and power were even more absent in the new republics that sprang up in the years following the war, and the vote for
women was an illustration of this new thinking and broadening of
the power base. At its extreme, Bolshevik Russia's response to this
surge in unrefined democratic instincts was increasingly shaped and
dedicated to the concept of world revolution and the smashing of
the bourgeoisie as the necessary steps toward the vision of a classless
society. Thus, the war established a new context and ethos to how

diplomacy, politics, business, economy, and civilian life would operate after its conclusion. What united the Dawes Plan to Mussolini's territorial ambitions and to Woodrow Wilson's train journeys to meet the American people was the emergence of popular assent as critical to political effectiveness, and an awareness of a shift of power after the war from czar and king to the common person. That is not to claim that democracy was fully formed or realized in 1919, but no longer could global relations and internal arrangements operate without the assent of the people being a given a primary place and voice in the machinations of power.

The Roaring Twenties offered different models of how that populist presence might be manifested. None of those models were premised on aristocratic might, but instead on the claim that power would be authorized and wielded by the people. Even Mussolini's Fascist nightmare was predicated on the Socialist vision of Italian power derived from its masses, much as Hitler's demonic agenda sought an absolute devotion to the nation. What would permit these experiments in democracy to flourish until they spectacularly failed or fell with the 1929 Wall Street crash is the availability of that most democratic of commodities of all, the American dollar. For while not all would own the almighty dollar in the same quantities, each dollar would empower its owner with the might of that single unit of currency, regardless of the title or landed history of its owner. American money was reshaping continents, nations, and governments and allowing their peoples to dream of equality, liberty, security, and opportunity in ways that were not possible before the war. With the October 1929 stock market crash, that populist agenda was not abandoned, and neither was there an attempt to return to nineteenth-century power norms, but instead the world pursued clearly divergent pathways to honor the common man and woman. Those pathways would include terrifying totalitarian visions that claimed to speak for the ordinary citizen, even perversely representing absolutism as the purest and most refined version of the will of the people.

Before October 1929 the world enjoyed a few short years of American capital, new systems of representation, organizations of self-expression, mechanisms for global diplomacy, and the hopes of the masses after the most traumatic war in history. It was a short period that was a precursor to what musical composer Aaron Copland later termed in 1942 as his "Fanfare for the Common Man." At that time, Vice President Henry A. Wallace announced that the new century had emerged for the ordinary man and woman and that Copland's symphony was a fitting tribute to that new century. Wallace's claim in 1942 was understandable, given America's recent humiliation at Pearl Harbor and its entrance into the cauldron of the Second World War. The fanfare for the common man and woman had already been sounded one generation earlier, but its tones had been lost in the cacophony of the Wall Street crash, the Great Depression, and the rise of totalitarianism. By 1942, the nations of the world were again pursuing total war, struggling to the death to regain the prosperity, stability, and optimism that had been a short and jubilant storyline during the Roaring Twenties. In the early 1920s, the common man and woman had found their hopes amidst their grief for a few years after the "war to end all wars" was finally over. Vice President Wallace was doing what all politicians do, namely saying that our best days lie ahead of us. Wallace said this during the darkest of times, when fear and death haunted the world once again at an even more horrific level than before. Copland's "Fanfare for the Common Man" offered the hope again for a land fit for heroes once this new titanic struggle against the evils of totalitarianism had been pursued to victory. Earlier versions of that fanfare had been heard after the First World War was resolved, when a new democratic future for the peoples of the world was a possibility. But the First World War yielded other forces, too, that would soon replace the peoples' fanfare with the trumpet of war, and that discordant trumpet would soon drown out all other sounds.

7

MAKE GERMANY GREAT AGAIN

Given what transpired at Versailles, the victorious Allies would have been wisc to follow the aphorism attributed to Machiavelli: "When you see your enemy in water up to his neck, it would do you well to push him under. When you see your enemy in water up to his knees, it would do you well to help him onto the shore." Instead, Germany was neither destroyed nor assisted by the terms of the Versailles peace treaty. While American money stabilized both Europe's ancient nations and its fledgling democracies of the early 1920s, the test of endurance was the baptism of economic fire wrought by the 1929 Wall Street stock market crash. To use the jargon of late capitalism, that truly constituted a paradigm shift.

It is easy with hindsight to claim to trace the path to a renewed Second World War from the conclusion of the first. It is even evident that prominent voices at the time of the Treaty of Versailles dismissed its capacity to endure. Famously, American general John Pershing and French marshal Ferdinand Foch both possessed sufficient military experience and instinct to realize presciently that "this is not peace. It is an armistice for twenty years."[1] But it is an oversimplification to see the journey to the Second World War as simply a continuously paved pathway of what Winston Churchill later described in his memoirs as "another Thirty Years War." This conclusion is too shallow. It is not so much the sheer global scale of fighting

---

[1] P. M. H. Bell, "How World War I Led to World War II," *World War I*, ed. Donald J. Murphy (New York: Greenhaven Press, 2002) 209.

in the first half of the twentieth century that leads us to the conclusion that the first and second wars are intimately connected, but rather the nature of the forces that were unleashed by the first that gives clues as to why the world continued down a path toward another total war. It is doubtful that those forces inevitably caused another global war in the way that an engine or a machine inevitably produces a functioning output. Instead, it is more helpful to see that a complex set of conditions, events, and actions came together—both with recklessness and with misfortune—to produce the outcome of a catastrophic second war in 1939. Dramatic existential choice, far more than inevitable predetermined process, provides the best way of determining how the First World War delivered unto humanity the second. No more powerfully did the first war do that than in giving birth to totalitarianism, specifically to totalitarianism in a binary format. How did that happen?

The causal factors of a second global catastrophe lie in both the underlying forces emanating from the first and the intentional choices and behaviors of the protagonists in the twenty years from 1919 to 1939. This captures the dynamic interplay over a two-decade period, during which a set of actors and actions would combine their reckless agency with the given conditions and misfortunes bequeathed by an ominously misguided Versailles peace. The most dramatic outcome from this toxic symbiosis of agency and structure was a concept of human expression and self-actualization that would embrace totalitarianism as superior to Western liberal democracy, as realized by German Fascism and Soviet Communism. How could these binary opposites both be the offspring of the dead of Flanders and, even more shockingly, how could they offer viable options for the European (and to a lesser extent American) body politic in the twentieth century in the years following the 1914–1918 War? Certainly, for those living in Western Europe or the United States in the second half of the twentieth century there was a confidence of the proven virtue and obvious superiority of Western democracy in all ways over the blatantly oppressive, tyrannical, and inferior systems of governance symbolized by Nazi Germany, Fascist Italy and

Spain, and Soviet Russia. Indeed, any sense of something positive and good emanating from the nation-state of Germany needed the redeeming preface "West" during the latter half of the twentieth century until the collapse of the Berlin Wall in 1989. In short, those living in London or Paris or New York at that time believed their nations had done it better, more humanely, more effectively, and more productively than their historical rivals from a generation before, who had sought to dominate Europe and Eurasia. The West perceived itself as superior and was incredulous that anyone—past or present—could have considered Nazi Germany or Soviet Russia as options. Such was its hubris.

What we see today in peering back across four generations is a very different picture of the interwar years than that of the clearly defined ideological confidence of the Cold War era. Today, with one hundred years of hindsight, we can trace a more complex interdependence and connectivity between the political "siblings" of Western democracy, Central European Fascism, and Eurasian Marxism than we thought after the end of the Second World War and at the birth of the nuclear age. One clue to this is evident in the way Adolf Hitler and German Nazism came to power. Firstly, Hitler and the movement he started did not inevitably have to come to power. The story of the Nazi Party shows this well. The full name of the party reveals a more convoluted sense, and peculiar 1920s context, of ideological and political comingling than those who lived in the second half of the twentieth century realized, when the term "Nazi" had inexorably and permanently become synonymous with evil during the second great war. The *Nationalsozialistische Deutsche Arbeiterpartei*, or NSDAP, was a movement that appropriated various emergent ideologies from the post-First World War years, drawing on concepts of new nationhood and self-determination that Wilson's Fourteen Points proposed and uniting them with a Socialist worldview of proletarian strength, wrapping the Swastika emblem and flag around it, and justifying it with pseudoscientific racialism for good measure. At its birth, this loud and vicious working-class movement had enough elasticity to attract different peoples precisely because it appealed to emotion—fear and anger—rather than to political logic. And it very nearly came to naught.

By the early 1920s, the impact of Versailles was fueling resentment and turmoil and providing fertile ground for the agendas of various German political factions. The "knife in the back" myth that General Ludendorff had initiated in the final months of the first war, to lay the blame for his military mistakes on the table of the Berlin politicians, now presented a golden opportunity to the young veteran, failed architect, and charismatic but insecure egotist Adolf Hitler. Using a simple rhetorical device repeatedly to rally support for the NSDAP, Hitler lambasted all conventional politicians—controlled, he claimed, by their puppet masters in Jewish finance and international Marxism—for betraying the German people and allowing a great Aryan people—*ein Volk*—to be humiliated and ridiculed. But the story of his party's rise to totalitarian might and global threat was not so much linear or predictable as opportunistic. Two hiatus events played into the German response of the 1920s to abandon its commitment to a democratic republic and to deviate toward totalitarianism. Ironically, both of these events relied on the actions of parties outside of Germany. The first was the previously noted Ruhr crisis, which emerged from Germany's repeated inability or lack of will to meets its war reparations schedule. As the tensions rose, Germany withheld timber, steel, and coal exports, so the French army moved into the Ruhr to ensure the exports were maintained. This military intervention, and the economic chaos that ensued, with its massive hyperinflation, famously bequeathed to history the images of German citizens using wheelbarrows to transport their worthless currency.

The effect of the Ruhr crisis was both to galvanize external sympathy for Germany—the American public was shocked that French forces killed more than one hundred German citizens who resisted their occupation—and more critically it raised the sense of desperation and resentment within Germany itself. The resolution to the Ruhr crisis through the Dawes Plan of 1924 presented Germany with an opportunity to return to economic normalcy and political stability within a mainstream political agenda, but tragically the horse had already been let out of the barn. The birth of extremist right-wing movements was a phenomenon that grew immediately after the end of the First World War and was virtually guaranteed by the Treaty of Versailles. The fires were lit at that point, and the flames then fanned by the Ruhr crisis. During the early 1920s, however, those extreme nationalist groups were splintered, even while they shared the same hate-filled manifestos of antisemitism, distrust of internationalism in either capitalist or Socialist forms, and a complete rejection of non-nationalist agendas. Other than that, there was little coherence to the emergent nationalist right until veteran nationalist Anton Drexler formed the *Deutsche Arbeiterpartei,* or German Workers' Party (DAP). Ironically, while still serving in the German Army in 1919, Hitler's superiors ordered him to investigate and infiltrate the DAP on suspicion that it would cause further turmoil. But Hitler quickly became the fox guarding the henhouse, and his oratorical skills were immediately appreciated and endorsed by the very DAP he was tasked with surveilling. Ever the master opportunist, Hitler co-opted the DAP, claiming falsely to be one of its founding fathers and using its platform to launch a grander agenda and a new party with him at its helm, the NSDAP, with none of Drexler's concerns about utilizing the term "socialist" within its title.

At this point, Nazi ascendancy seemed real but only within the closed environment of right-wing extremist movements and not within broader Germany society. Hitler had managed to create a unified political movement that indeed did "unite the right," which, of course, involved not only uniting but also destroying the alternatives. The Ruhr crisis stirred German resentment and presented the NSDAP with its first opportunity to engage in the public arena. Until then, it had been absorbed in developing its internal organization and creating its "brown-shirt" (*Sturmabteilung*) militia. But the Nazis' first foray into the public German arena was a catastrophic failure. Using the tactics of revolution that had emerged from the First World War, Hitler's November 1923 Beer Hall Putsch was a disaster. In his attempt to overthrow the regional Bavarian government, Hitler's calls for revolution from the tabletop of the local beer house ended in disarray, resulting in his imprisonment for eighteen months and the dissolution of the NSDAP by the Bavarian government all in the same November month.

While Hitler brooded in prison and penned his infamous, vile, and incoherent *Mein Kampf,* the fate of the NSDAP and European Fascism could and should have been stymied then. Adolf Hitler might readily have been forgotten to history, with his plans for the mastery of Europe being no more than the idle scribblings of a pathetic, incarcerated nobody with a vicious pathology. Indeed, the advent of the Dawes Plan and the American injection of capital that it delivered took the air out of the Fascist bubble. That capital provided political options that could have drawn Germany and Europe closer to the republican liberalism and economic capitalism that Wilson and his successors desired as the political framework for European stability and peace in the twentieth century. By 1925, the French had withdrawn from the Ruhr, German reparations had eased, and the NSDAP was outlawed; the conditions were surely ripe again for Wilson's vision for Europe. These were the heady years of the 1920s that bode well for capitalism and internationalism, providing a short period when the fragile new democracies of Europe gained some economic stability to buttress their fortunes. But if those conditions presented better fortunes for Germany and the recovering nations of Europe, the rapid and complete collapse of those conditions in 1929 plunged Europe into a heightened state of renewed disequilibrium, danger, and extremism. In this scenario, American capital provided the hope of Europe in 1923, and it also provided the antithesis just six short years later. The Wall Street crash heralded the second great moment of change, the watershed event that allowed a radical departure, a fork in the road of history, which released the totalitarian genie from its bottle and gave a resurgence of energy, rationale, and appeal to both the Fascist and Communist visions. 1929 provided Hitler and the totalitarian world of both left and right with the argument that decrepit crony capitalism was the cancer inside Western democracy and that new political agendas, faces, and voices were needed to espouse the "will of the people." A very different vision was promoted to steel and ready the nation for its destiny after the feeble and failed republican and parliamentary models of governance.

The appeal of that argument was alarmingly broad and deep. It did not require Hitler or the other totalitarian dictators of Europe (Franco of Spain aside) to grab power militarily from an unwilling people or a resistant legislative assembly and then to force those organs to comply with a new totalitarian agenda. All it took was for the people to choose intentionally to find the expression of their will in a strident and absolutist form. In 1996, the American and European public were informed, and many shocked, by the publication of Daniel Goldhagen's seminal and controversial work, *Hitler's Willing Executioners: Ordinary Germans and the Holocaust.*[2] While focusing specifically on the Nazi Holocaust, Goldhagen's work introduced to the public a fierce argument within academic history in the late twentieth century regarding the scale and breadth of complicity of the German public during the Nazi era in the worst atrocities of the state. Goldhagen, whose work won global historical and literary acclaim, coined the phrase from his earlier writings of the "evil of banality," and he argued that Germany uniquely and broadly had exhibited an "eliminationist antisemitism" that stretched back to the Lutheran Reformation. The point Goldhagen was making was that the Holocaust was not an aberration but an extension of popular German culture. This is not the place to evaluate his strong but contentious Holocaust thesis, but his work aptly reminds us of one critical aspect of 1920s and 1930s Fascism, namely that its ascendancy to triumph and power was through popular assent and through democratic processes. The same conclusion was arrived at nearly fifty

---

[2] Daniel Jonah Goldhagen, Hitler's Willing Executioners: Ordinary Germans and the Holocaust (New York: Knopf, 1996).

years earlier by Hannah Arendt, in her definitive exploration of to-talitarianism.[3] In her work, which represents the first major effort after the Second World War to make sense of the rise of totalitari-anism, Arendt concluded that the dictators did not rely on ideolog-ical devotees or committed believers to ensure their grasp on power. Like Goldhagen later, she knew that the ideal population was al-ready available to the dictator's cause in the form of ordinary citi-zens: "For whom the distinction between fact and fiction (i.e. the reality of experience) and the distinction between true and false (i.e. the standards of thought) no longer exist."

An examination of the rise of the NSDAP in electoral terms shows this capacity for popular assent to dictatorship in stark num-bers. In 1928, five years after the failed Beer Hall Putsch and Hitler's imprisonment, the NSDAP was languishing in insignificance while the German economy and political system stabilized and strength-ened. In the Federal elections that year, the Nazis could only muster 2.8 percent of the seats in the Reichstag. Within a decade that trans-formed into 100 percent of the seats in a one-party state, but it took incremental and nonlinear growth following the Wall Street crash for that absolutist outcome to be achieved. Even in 1932, when there were two elections, the Nazi presence shrunk in the Reichstag and still the combined seats of the Communists and the Social Demo-crats were larger than those of the NSDAP. Only with Hitler's ap-pointment in 1933 as chancellor by the decrepit president Hinden-burg, just months before his death, did the Nazis effectively finalize their one-party totalitarian state, rising to a massive 93 percent of the seats in the Reichstag by November of that year. At that point, the oppression and elimination of all other political challengers and the nazification of society became the norm of political and popular culture. But it was a norm that was evident only after the NSDAP successfully climbed its way to power through the process and meth-odology of German democracy.

---

[3] Hannah Arendt, *The Origins of Totalitarianism* (New York: Schocken Books, 2004).

How could the German people have been so naïve and gullible, we asked ourselves from the other side of the Second World War. The point we missed in this angle on Nazism is that it was a product of German popular sentiment and not a force imposed upon that sentiment. In examining it as German outsiders, we had experienced Nazism from 1939 to 1945 through the most destructive war in history and therefore only saw its utter evil. But to the Germans of the 1920s, that perspective was not what they beheld. Instead, they saw a totalitarian vision of the combined appeal of the popular will, an expression of "true" nationhood, and a strength that would deliver on security and economic well-being. That is the picture played up in Nazi propaganda films, with hundreds of young Aryan men and women exercising and smiling as Alpine children clutched flowers for marching soldiers. No need to portray—or even believe in—death squads or extermination camps as the outcome of this dystopian nightmare. To the humiliated and desperate Germans, Nazism offered a redemptive future in which the nightmare itself became the dream of the future—of the Thousand-Year Reich. Strongman Fascism would provide the strength that liberal capitalism and degraded republicanism could never deliver. Moreover, republican democracy intentionally celebrated diversity, whereas Fascism celebrated national identity and unity. "Patriotism is the last refuge of the scoundrel," wrote Samuel Johnson in 1775.[4] Hitler, one of humanity's ultimate scoundrels, knew that a more potent nationalism would be the first refuge of the betrayed, and he intended to utilize that emotive power to its fullest force.

The Fascist agenda of the 1920s and 1930s thus lulled or captivated peoples and organizations and nations into a sense of self and opportunity that precisely addressed the collective urge and need emanating from the agony and shock of the First World War. If the hedonistic 1920s represented the partying Friday night to forget the pain of what had happened in the 1910s, the 1930s represented the Monday morning return to hard and deliberate work for the sake of

---

[4] James Boswell, *Life of Johnson*, 1791.

93

self and one's tribe, with renewed determination, indignation, and invincibility for the future. "Never again," so rightly the self-promise after the horror of the Holocaust, could also equally have been the slogan that the totalitarian dictators promised their peoples after the horrors and ignominy of the First World War. This explains why Fascism was elected in its greatest of manifestations, Germany, and why it even gained some breadth of respect within the liberal democracies throughout the period we call the interwar years.

Other Fascist stories are legend to us, too. Benito Mussolini's style was more boorish and grabbing than Hitler's. His move to power occurred before the rise of the Nazis, when the turmoil of the early 1920s had not been calmed politically or economically with the assistance of American money. Francisco Franco's assumption of power and absolute rule of Spain was the longest lasting Fascist regime in European history. As a teenager who delivered the morning newspaper by bicycle, I can recall the headline of the newspapers on a damp and mild November morning in 1975: "Franco Dead." His tyranny had lasted nearly four decades, founded with direct assistance from Hitler's Nazi regime in providing air support to Franco's Nationalist cause, while the West looked on mutely. Fifteen years after delivering those newspapers, while motorcycling through Spain, I found a well-maintained cemetery in the hills above Madrid honoring the dead Luftwaffe pilots who had been shot down by Republican forces in the desperate and horrendous civil war. Only the Soviet Union provided limited assistance to the Spanish Republic, aided by some of the more colorful figures of Western literary culture such as Ernest Hemingway and George Orwell and the heroic American volunteers who comprised the Abraham Lincoln Brigade. But Western support was lackluster, with influential right-wing thinkers sympathizing with Franco, and no political will for intervention from the Western Allies, something akin to the broader appeasement strategy later used with Hitler. The war matériel from Germany and Italy was substantial, with Mussolini supplying more than seventy-five thousand Italian troops to support the Nationalist cause, as well as vast amounts of equipment. While Spain was too exhausted and depleted of resources to join the Axis powers during the second war, it did supply the concept that a Fascist state could thrive after conflict. It also thrived by accommodating the dominant cultural element of Catholicism, thus reinforcing the notion that right-wing extremism need not be a permanent revolutionary force, but rather an optional system of stable governance. Franco's death on that damp November morning forty years after his rise left Europe with a legacy of appropriated totalitarianism and the troubling feeling that Fascism was quite manageable within the European psyche after the First World War. What is equally impressive, and considerably more hopeful, is that just barely a decade after Franco's death, Spain, as a democratic, constitutional monarchy, was admitted to the European Union and has been one of the most inclusive and collaborative partners within Europe, handling internal tensions such as Basque separatism without recourse to the former oppressive techniques of the Franco decades.

The rise of Fascism thus was mediated by a mix of methodologies, variably including the use of violent and illegitimate struggle and equally the grasping of the levers of power within the constitutional framework of each nation-state. Germany, with Hitler as leader of the NSDAP, did that most effectively and devastatingly. In this way the use of revolution was not necessary for Fascist totalitarianism to win power. But revolution, of course, was intrinsic to that other form of totalitarian government emerging from the First World War, that being built in the Soviet Union. Soviet Russia was a fast learner, and although it wanted out of the First World War, it knew what to utilize from the war culture and methodology to advance its revolutionary and Communist cause. For, in essence, totalitarianism was born and a feature of the war itself. It was the first truly "total war," consuming all aspects of national and international life and requiring of its citizenry a "warfare state" that would reshape all public and much personal life. The Soviet revolutionaries quickly caught on to the magnitude of control and organization that such "totalizing" thinking could achieve, and they had witnessed its effects at firsthand during the war years. The Germans had already coined the term *Kriegssozialismus* ("War Socialism") to describe the total commitment and equality of effort needed from its population during the war, and the Soviets saw in it the confidence and methodology that would consolidate power after the October revolution and through the civil war years. Complete state seizure of utilities, control of communications, and control of all political and judicial processes were thus merely extensions of what the belligerent nations became accustomed to, in varying degrees, during the total war that was the First World War. Now it simply needed reproducing by the Bolsheviks. They began the painstaking task of establishing the one-party Soviet state in the years of peace that lay ahead, prefaced by a Marxist dogma explicitly legitimizing totalitarianism in the concept of the dictatorship of the proletariat, the first step toward Communist utopia. Ironically, as the war years subsided, the Soviets retreated on complete dictatorial control in order to stabilize the population and economy, but the underlying gift of the war to the new Soviet Union was the model they would adopt in style and character in securing their control of the state and in banishing opposition. As Lenin put it one month before the October revolution, "War is inexorable and puts the question with unsparing sharpness; either perish or catch up and overtake the advanced countries."[5] It took the Soviet Union another ten years and a new leader in Joseph Stalin to turn this latent predisposition toward complete autocracy and totalitarian engineering. Only with the advent of Stalin's brutal and breathtaking Five-Year Plan (1928–1932) did the Soviet Union finally complete its totalitarian long march and in five years achieve more industrial change for its citizens than five centuries of czarist autocracy had managed. But it also revealed the evil nature of Soviet totalitarianism, with the Five-Year Plan premised as much on political motives, with trials, executions, and persecutions, as it was on technological prowess and economic theory. In short, Stalin's Five-

---

[5] Jack Roth, "World War I and the Rise of Totalitarian Dictatorships," in *World War I*, ed. Donald J. Murphy (New York: Greenhaven Press, 2002) 228.

Year Plan, in a way predictive of the totalitarian horror of the Nazis' Final Solution, was an absolute vision and program of utter control that permitted no alternatives or perspectives.

This was possible in large part because the populace had been indoctrinated in accepting such conditions by the First World War. The seeds of Stalin's and Hitler's work were sown in the ruined and scorched earth of Flanders and the Eastern Front. Like Russia, the concluding months of the war delivered what was virtually a military dictatorship in Germany, with absolute power no longer vested in the kaiser or the Reichstag but in the army and its increasingly psychotic leader, General Erich Ludendorff. Psychosis aside, or perhaps because of it, Ludendorff was able to position his military junta's failure as the result of febrile democratic politics and was able to mask Germany's failure to win as merely a temporary abandonment of the military option. In short, he kept the treasure of militarism safe and the blame for Germany's predicament on civilian leadership, not the military. This constituted a brilliant move straight from the totalitarian playbook. It preserved for the future the military option and even gave it a rationale that could never be outplayed—vengeance for unjust humiliation. The latter was a double hammer blow for German sentiment, the first strike hitting at Versailles and the second, perhaps as humiliating, delivered by the Ruhr crisis occupation by the French three years later. Yet still Hitler and the NSDAP did not have a path to victory from these legacies of the war. It took the failure of capitalism in the Wall Street crash of 1929, and with that the end of Wilson's liberal republicanism, to hand the Nazis the final building block to assemble their demonic system. We look back at the German choice for totalitarianism via the ballot box as somehow insane and unthinkable. Certainly, its consequences were that, but we only know this with the benefit of hindsight. In the 1920s and 1930s, there were plenty of voices in all strata of society in the West who had also given up on capitalism and its cronies and were willing to seek an alternative extremist solution to ensure security, economy, and national justice.

Hitler knew this in his prison cell in Landsberg in 1924, as *Mein Kampf* testifies. Narcissistically described as his own personal struggle, he echoed in that vile text the same scapegoating and finger-pointing as Ludendorff, lamenting how domestic politics had obstructed the German war machine in the final two years of the war, at the behest of the defeatists and internationalists. For Hitler and the Nazis, only the complete release of military power, without any constitutional limits, guaranteed national success. Intriguingly, sounding like Leon Trotsky's thirst for unfettered and purist Communism, Hitler saw totalitarianism as not only the ideal outcome, but the means to the end itself. Trotsky wanted capitalism to run its course unfettered, so that when the whole edifice came crashing down, the Communist new person and new society would rise from its ashes. For Hitler, the pure path forward meant incrementally using totalitarian methodology to build the new society, the Thousand-Year Reich. The weakness of the civilian government in the last stages of the First World War and in the early years of peace presented Hitler with his supreme opportunity. Those conditions would enable him to convince an exhausted German public of the merits of a renewed and strident militarism and nationalism. Indeed, whereas the Soviet Union intentionally talked the language of internationalism and pluralistic Socialist republics, Nazi rhetoric was monolithic and absolutist in its sense of national identity. This was a brilliant move by the NSDAP. It only needed to ram home the concept of "German-ness," and then everything else would become a threat to that very identity. Hitler also had two levers he could pull that the Soviet Union did not. Germany already had an industrial infrastructure of extraordinary strength. The Soviet Union needed to build one, as Stalin set out to do. Indeed, Germany's economic and industrial infrastructure is what Niall Ferguson[6] argues was at the root of the cause of the First World War, as Germany sought to

---

[6] Niall Ferguson, *The Pity of War: Explaining World War I* (New York: Basic Books, 1998).

build a prototypical European Union of customs and excise agreements, with Germany at the head of the table. Ferguson's argument aside, what Hitler inherited, despite the atrocious cost of the war, was an economic and industrial strength that he could immediately utilize. Wrapping this around the concept of nation, and then supplementing that with the pseudoscience of the biological purity of the German race, gave him an overarching vision and rationale for the Nazi state. And all of that can be found within, and consequential to, Germany's experience of World War I.

By the second half of the twentieth century, the appeal of the totalitarian solution had been replaced by knowledge of its evils and global devastation in the Second World War. The West's experience of that second war permitted a cognitive indulgence about the superiority of democracy, ironically predicated on the same kind of "us versus them" binary thinking that the Fascists and Communists had so effectively availed themselves of in the 1920s. For the Western Allies, this binary logic also worked for the Cold War and the conviction that we had it right, better, and truer than those oppressed and oppressive folk "over the wall." But our failure was assuming that democracy itself was somehow binary and that our version was the only version available after World War I. This was, in a sense, a direct legacy of Wilson's vision at Versailles and remained present even in the twenty-first century in the idea of Western-style nation building in Iraq and Afghanistan. What we struggled to understand during the Cold War was that our ancestors across Europe were faced with choices that all claimed democracy at their core. To the Communists, democracy equated to economic equality. To the Fascists, democracy meant total national unity and self-determination. To the capitalists, democracy meant the export of unregulated capital in the name of liberty. It also accounted for why we look back and wonder how the totalitarian systems could be chosen, why they appealed to so many in the West, and why the policy of the West was appeasement and accommodation until violence, hatred, and war could be contained no more.

At the heart of this unfolding saga lay the issue of identity more than the nature of democracy. Hitler's manipulation of history was essentially a story of German identity and an accompanying narrative of European mastery. Whereas the tenth anniversary of the Armistice showed British angst and guilt about its "lost generation" and confusion as to the purpose of the war, Hitler used the same anniversary to deliver in the National Theatre in Weimar an unambiguous narrative of vengeance and humiliation, built around German identity and a clear sense of national purpose. There was no confusion in the Nazi story about the First World War. Hitler's indignation against Tomas Masaryk's newly created Czechoslovakia was not about the problem of Czech self-determination—Hitler's public statements always alluded to the self-determination rights of peoples and nations, much as Wilson would have argued—but rather that Czech self-determination and its new borders were a direct affront to Germany's nationalist narrative. In that narrative, Czech land meant the denial of German identity and its rightful union of its people, *ein Volk*, so Hitler argued. By supposing that the First World War had effectively created a diaspora of German people, the Fascist agenda represented the "other" as a direct threat to German identity. Since the former Austrian-Hungarian Empire was included under the mythology of "German-hood" (and later used in 1938 to justify the Anschluss and "bringing it back into the fold"), any new state created where German *Volk* had lived was de facto an act of aggression and threat to Germany itself, according to Hitler's warped logic. His modus operandi of the 1930s is wrongly understood as merely the desire for war and empire. That would have made sense with Otto von Bismarck[7] in the nineteenth-century pursuit of power, which lay at the roots of German imperial ambition and the increasing instability of the European power balance that Ferguson argued was insufficient reason for a vast European-based conflict. Hitler's logic, however, was more demonically wrapped into

---

[7] Chancellor of the German Empire and mastermind to German unification in 1871.

a story of German identity, forged with a distorted view of German history, underpinned with false science about racial purity, and fueled by an emotional resentment and loathing of those who did not appropriately honor their sense of self-righteousness. This identity issue provided for Hitler what Hannah Arendt argued in her seminal work of the mid-twentieth century, *The Origins of Totalitarianism*[8], was an answer to the loneliness, estrangement, and fear that underpinned post-Second World War Europe. Totalitarianism, in this sense, was the great Church of Nationhood, assuaging its devotees' fears, insecurities, and loneliness. This intertwining of fake history, emotional pathology, and normative evil permitted only one total and absolute resolution, which was provided by the Nazi state and which required all Germans to be allowed to group together under one identity, one state, and one Fuhrer, wherever they happened to live. To a lesser extent, Mussolini and Franco enacted similar narratives within their own Fascist agendas.

This is not what Stalin was doing. Totalitarianism emerging in the Soviet Union, particularly by the start of the Five-Year Plan, had no interest in the pathology of nationalist identity. Political ideology and control—that of Soviet Socialism—was all that mattered to Stalin and his henchmen, and the apparatus of state was geared to bring whatever peoples and groups existed under that banner, regardless of race or language or identity. But once inside that Soviet space, individual identity and pluralism was utterly subservient to the Russian state and the ideology of Communism. This was a familiar feature of twentieth-century Cold War life, where the Eastern Bloc was first under the control of Moscow and second living under the self-illusion of national self-determination and international fraternity with the USSR. When those qualities of greater pluralism and economic libertarianism did indeed emerge, such as in Hungary in 1956 and Czechoslovakia in 1968, the Soviets rumbled their tanks into Budapest and Prague to remind them of their primary loyalty. This

---

[8] Hannah Arendt, *The Origins of Totalitarianism* (New York: Schocken Books, 2004).

explains why the Soviet Union's form of totalitarianism could evolve and survive. It could reinvent itself into a post-Stalinist version, much like China could reinvent itself into a post-Maoist version, and thus adapt enough to survive. Hence Khrushchev denunciated Stalin in 1956, the same year of the Soviet crushing of the Hungarian Uprising, but tellingly only to a closed and secret session of the Twentieth Congress of the Communist Party. And this reinvention of Soviet society and the capacity for reinvention could only flourish to a point. To allow Soviet society to become truly open, or Glasnost, as Gorbachev famously titled it, would break the mold and put "new wine into old wine skins." The Soviet system was certainly more adaptable and enduring than the Nazi system, and it could reinvent the state and its governance, but never to the point of pluralism, multiparty expression, or economic libertarianism. That would entail crossing the proverbial Rubicon. Only with the Gorbachev era and the fall of the Berlin Wall did the capacity to reinvent finally expire and the USSR disintegrate.

The totalitarian impulse, therefore, was intrinsically connected to both the first and second world wars, but it did not predestine the second war. The Second World War was chosen, not inevitable. The connection was correlational, not causal, as the statisticians would put it. And only with the catastrophe of the second war was Europe finally able to understand how to preserve national identity, economic sovereignty, and pluralistic democracy as an alternative to totalitarianism, and finally put to rest the centuries-old question of the "mastery of Europe." That is surely the story of the 1958 Treaty of Rome and the brilliance of another German, Robert Schuman, in a new, inclusive vision of a postwar democratic European Union. The tragedy of totalitarianism, therefore, lay in both its internal narrative, and the suffering it caused its peoples, and its response from the nontotalitarian democracies, with appeasement or war as the traditional solutions. Some brief discussion of appeasement and accommodation provides a fitting way to introduce how the democracies developed their own narratives to answer the puzzle of the First World War and how to forge their futures after that apocalypse, for appeasement remains woven into the myths of the 1930s and its stories of tortured figures like Chamberlain and heroes like Churchill. Even today those narratives are being retold, with several key historians of the last two decades casting appeasement in a more positive frame of reference, seeing it akin to a policy of "buying time" to prepare for the Second World War.

Recently, Tim Bouverie, in his work *Appeasement*,[9] sought to redress the revisionist theory of those 1930s anguished years of appeasement. Drawing attention to Britain's homogeneous society, he alludes to a conspiratorial understanding between the ruling classes' and organizations' desires to hide from the public the true nature of the Nazi state. Figures who understood the Nazi threat, such as Churchill and Harold MacMillan, were sidelined. For Bouverie, Chamberlain simply did not understand Hitlerian fanaticism. Chamberlain and his government cronies were incapable of developing a meaningful policy to address Hitler's expansive aims of folding into a Greater Germany increasing numbers of purportedly Germanic peoples, for purposes of "living space," or *Lebensraum*. Bouverie argues that far from "buying time" through appeasement, a greater chance of averting war would have emerged from nontolerance of German expansion. In this scenario, the Allies "spared the rod and spoiled the child" in a desperate attempt to avert a catastrophic second war. Strength, armament, and vigilance would have had a greater chance of success, Bouverie suggests, in the same way that NATO curtailed further Soviet expansionism because of its commitment to limit the capacity of Warsaw Pact aggression. What is tragic is that the appeasers simply did not understand the demon they were wrestling with. They assumed their logic, emanating from the horrors of the first war, would persuade world leaders to refrain from entering another total war, even when the totalitarian dictators were pursuing their own logic coming from that first war. Italy's

---

[9] Tim Bouverie, Appeasement: Chamberlain, Hitler, Churchill, and the Road to War (New York: Tim Duggan, 2019).

great interwar poet and politician Gabrielle D'Annunzio said it perfectly in the month before the Armistice: "I smell the stench of peace." To the dictators, right was wrong, left was right, and up was down. Chamberlain had no chance of prevailing in that kind of debating chamber, and the incongruity of his looks and attire at the Berchtesgaten meeting and Munich conference in 1938 matched the incongruity of his policy with the realpolitik of Hitler's playbook. Lucy Hughes-Hallett notes[10] that D'Annunzio's version of patriotic duty represented a totalitarian dream where virility and violence were the very signs of progress. This thinking was not an aberration but a validation of the world that needed to be recreated according to a catechism of an absolutist faith.

The appeasement question brings this terrifying reality to the surface, reminding us across the century that it was the Western democracies themselves that were viewed, to a large extent, with suspicion and derision in the 1920s, and that around Europe, the Fascist and Communist options were viable and attractive. Even the abdicated King Edward VIII was attracted to Hitler, and the startling photographs of him and his wife, Wallis Simpson, cozying up to Hitler and his gang still shock across the decades. But the ex-king merely represented a broader sentiment that enlivened the chattering classes of the Western democracies, namely that Fascism had much to offer and certainly could "make the trains run on time." The evil excesses of emergent antisemitism, violent thuggery, and pernicious oppression were utterly discernible to all by *Kristallnacht* in 1938 but were simply ignored or tolerated as the darker side of a system that did indeed, so the argument went, have merits and economic advantages. Perhaps more than the war question, the question of the moral decrepitude of the appeasement policy and policy makers should feature in the evaluation of Neville Chamberlain and his ilk and their failed strategy for taming the tiger. Chamberlain was a forlorn figure who was out of his depth, and as a veteran of

---

[10] Lucy Hughes-Hallett, *Gabrielle D'Annunzio: Poet, Seducer and Preacher of War* (New York: Knopf Doubleday, 2013.

the First World War, was an example of a very English sort of way of making sense of that war by ensuring it was, at all costs, "the war to end all wars." Sadly, the English would have to make very different sense of their Great War just one generation later, when appeasement was finally seen as the emperor with no clothes. Another generation of "Tommies" would be hurled again into the fray against an even more virulent and fanatical version of Germany than their fathers had fought in Flanders.

In a sense, Neville Chamberlain's anguished and axiomatic role reminds us that in the end it was people, rather than ideologies or policies, who ensured the First World War led to an even more grotesque war just one generation later. As with personal families, people have agency and choice in the public arena, and personalities and histories play into those choices. The second war was not an inevitable event unfolding from the dialectics of history, or the consequences of ideology, or even the inevitable product of totalitarianism. Rather, it was the views and decisions of the people of those times, and especially those in power, that brought renewed global conflict. The socially odd and narcissistically paranoid veteran Adolf Hitler was the key protagonist. Twice he had escaped death in Flanders, once when a shell hit the shelter where he had been sitting with comrades, and once when a British soldier let him run rather than execute him on the battlefield. Providential destiny, combined with rage and resentment, fueled the warped mind of the wounded corporal whose eyes were temporarily blinded by gas and who learned contemptuously of the Armistice from his hospital bed. But the second war was also cojoined by the actions of others, like Stalin, whose coarse rural accent as a young revolutionary from the Republic of Georgia led him to be mocked as a country boy by the Moscow and Petrograd elites, and who determined that sadistic revenge was the most formidable of enabling tools to achieve absolute power; and like Chamberlain, who wrongly believed that preserving the "war to end all wars" principle was the highest aim and that selling one's values to preserve peace at any price was still better than an honorable war—until, of course, it wasn't; and like both Wilson and Roosevelt, who believed capital and liberalism were exportable commodities and that all America needed to do was control the money flow and it would control destiny around the globe. But, of course, these men were flawed individuals who made decisions based on what history had delivered to them in a world of conditions, circumstances, and realities. Fortunes and misfortunes were bequeathed, and now they had to decide and to act. Their ideas and actions were not inevitable or predestined, and neither were their ideologies or political systems. What they chose to do with those conditions, however, is the stuff of history and our past century. In the years of 1919 to 1939, their actions were of global significance and consequence, and would, in less than one generation, bring an even bigger devastation to humanity than had ever been experienced before. In that context their alliances and relationships were, like all peoples, strange and inconsistent. War makes odd bedfellows, and in that Second World War, the Russian ally would return to fight again with the Allies, but this time wearing a totalitarian Red Army uniform. And whereas in the First World War the place of ideology within the motivation for war among the belligerent nations was virtually nonexistent, and instead land and economic power of tantamount importance, by the time the world fell into the abyss of the second war, the ideological clash of democratic and totalitarian worldviews was utterly on the line. Such is the paradox and complexity of the world we inherited from the First World War.

THE WESTERN FRONT

Members of the U.S. Army 132nd Infantry, 33rd Division in
a front line trench taking advantage of camouflage left by the
Germans. The German line is about 1,200 yards from this point
with the Meuse being between. Forges-sur-Meuse, France,
October 3, 1918.

Courtesy Library of Congress

TRENCH LIFE AND DEATH

Machine gun in a front line trench, ca. 1915.

Courtesy Library of Congress

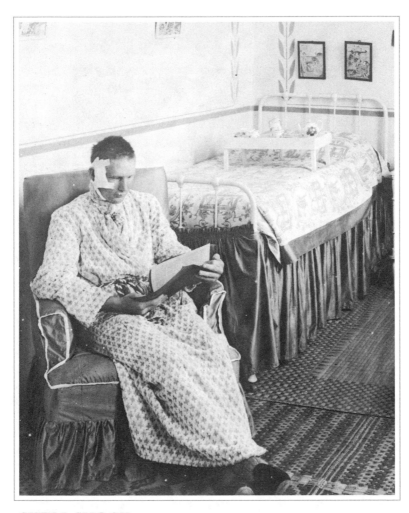

SHELL SHOCK

This soldier was hit in the head by *éclat de shrapnel* which destroyed his ear drum and he was suffering from shell shock. For recovery, he was put in the Sunshine Room installed by the American Red Cross at hospital where there is absolute quiet, harmonious colors, and cheerful surroundings, the necessary medicine in a case of this kind, ca. 1918.

Courtesy Library of Congress

GERMAN WAR BOND POSTER

*Helft uns siegen! Zeichnet die Kriegsanleihe (*Help us triumph!
Subscribe to the War Loan.), ca., 1917.
Courtesy Library of Congress

Mighty Armies Halt Battle One Hour on Xmas; Soldiers Pray

By FRANKLIN P. MERRICK.

Special Cable to The Atlanta Georgian.

PARIS, Dec. 26.—For one hour on Christmas Day, the warriors of the nations locked in deadly conflict in Western Europe ceased to fight. During that brief interval, the clash of arms and the boom of artillery was halted and hundreds of thousands of soldiers knelt in prayer to the Omnipotent.

No armistice was officially declared. It was as if a mightier mind than those of the commanders of the greatest armies on earth had decreed a return of peace, even for so brief a period.

After the short truce had ended, however, the mightiest combat in the history of the world was resumed. Frenchman, Briton, Belgian and German alike put away the visions of home that the day had called forth and took up again the task at hand, the slaughtering of his fellowmen.

CHRISTMAS TRUCE OF 1914

"Mighty Armies Halt Battle One Hour on Xmas; Soldiers Pray." *The Atlanta Georgian*, December 26, 1914.

THE 11TH HOUR OF THE 11TH DAY
OF THE 11TH MONTH

Arrival of Allied leaders in Compiegne Wood where Armistice
was discussed.

Courtesy National Archives and Records Administration

THE ROARING 20s AND A WORLD REMADE

Candid shot of actors Flournoy E. Miller, Josephine Hall, Evelyn Preer, and Aubrey Lyles walking along the Boardwalk in Atlantic City, New Jersey, circa 1920s.

Courtesy New York Public Library

FROM THE ROARING 20s TO THE VANQUISHED 30s

Missouri family of five, seven months from the drought area, on U.S. Highway 99 near Tracy, California. San Joaquin County, ca. 1937.

Courtesy Library of Congress

MUNICH APPEASEMENT AND THE MARCH
TOWARD THE SECOND WORLD WAR

Adolf Hitler greets Neville Chamberlain upon the British Prime
Minister's arrival in Munich, September 1938.

Courtesy National Archives and Records Administration

THE FASCIST SOLUTION

Adolf Hitler and Benito Mussolini in Munich, June 1940.

Courtesy National Archives and Records Administration

SOVIET SUPERPOWER STATUS AND THE RACE FOR SPACE

U.S.S.R., Moscow, temporary Russian exhibit, ca. 1959.

Courtesy Library of Congress

THE CENOTAPH

The Cenotaph, London, England.

Courtesy Wikimedia Commons

VIMY RIDGE

Arras Battlefield, France. Vimy Ridge Canadian Memorial.
Courtesy Wikimedia Commons

DOUAUMONT OSSUARY

Ossuary of Douaumont, Verdun, France.
Courtesy Wikimedia Commons

BLOOD SWEPT LANDS AND SEAS OF RED

888,246 ceramic poppies by artists Paul Cummins and Tom Piper fill the moat around the Tower of London, 2014.

Courtesy Flickr Creative Commons License

GRIEVING PARENTS

Deutscher Soldatenfriedhof Vladslo by Trauernde Eltern.
Courtesy Wikimedia Commons

THIEPVAL

Memorial to the Missing of the Somme, Thiepval, France.

Courtesy Wikimedia Commons

BERLIN WALL COMES DOWN

East German police watch as visitors pass through the newly created opening in the Berlin Wall at Potsdamer Platz, November 1989.

Courtesy National Archives and Records Administration

GORBACHEV AND REAGAN

Reykjavik Summit. Arrival of General Secretary Mikhail
Gorbachev at Hofdi House, October 1986.

Courtesy National Archives and Records Administration

OBAMA AND PUTIN

President Barack Obama talks with Russian President Vladimir
Putin, June 2014.

Courtesy National Archives and Records Administration

TRUMP AND PUTIN

President Trump and President Putin greet during President Trump and the First Lady's trip to Europe, July 2018.

Courtesy National Archives and Records Administration

EUGENE J. BULLARD

Statue of Eugene J. Bullard, First African-
American Fighter Pilot (French Air Corps,
1915), Robins Air Force Base, Georgia, USA.
Courtesy Christopher Blake

A PECULIAR BRITISH STORY

Britain's relationship with its neighboring peoples and the nations of Europe has been an intriguing and peculiar story since the Norman Conquest of 1066 heralded the early modern period. Longer still, for nine thousand years, the British Isles have been geographically separated by the Straits of Dover from continental Europe, the busiest shipping channel on the planet. That geographic separation has been fundamental to the emergence of distinctive cultures and struggles within those British Isles and has also reinforced distinctions from the peoples and cultures of mainland Europe. English, Scottish, Welsh, and Irish history has repeatedly attested to struggles of identity and governance within the British Isles. A thousand years of war and peace with the continental powers has shaped how the United Kingdom of Great Britain, formed in 1707 by the Acts of Union of the English and Scottish parliaments, sees itself literally and figuratively at some distance and different from Europe. During the eighteenth and nineteenth century centuries, British identity, interest, and loyalty lay primarily with its global empire, on which "the sun never set," and not with its European cousins across the short English Channel. Yet that distance from, and proximity to, Europe has been put into stark relief and scrutiny for the past century. At the outbreak of the First World War, Britain was forced into a radical evaluation of its relationships, responsibilities, and connectivity to the peoples who comprise the European nations. Today, Britain has emerged from a vast five-year trauma with the snappy title of "Brexit," and the pattern of history has changed again onto a trajectory of greater independence and separation for the UK.

Britain indeed has an historic push-pull magnetism with mainland Europe, captured by the author Bill Bryson's witty book title *Neither Here nor There*.[1] Napoleon is said to have once dismissed the English as a "nation of shopkeepers," apparently meaning small of thought and insular. Two centuries later, the daughter of a grocer—a shopkeeper—became defined as the Iron Lady, and Prime Minister Margaret Thatcher became the modern-day emblem of Britain's self-confidence and thorny relations with Europe, and especially the European Union. Whether Great Britain will become "Little England" after Brexit is the stuff of crystal ball gazing. For now, we can say that one century earlier from Brexit, Britain's anguish over Europe was to have truly global and historic impact in 1914.

Britain's entry into both the first and second world wars was of surprise to at least the Germans in both cases. In the first war, German sentiment doubted that British resolve and loyalty to Belgium would jeopardize Britain's military might and its empire by what could be considered a nonessential war of choice on the Continent. In the second war, Hitler's perverse view of race led him to a biased expectation that the sharing of Anglo-Saxon blood between the Germanic and English peoples would surely dissuade Britain from choosing unnecessary conflict. In either case, the push-pull relationship between Great Britain and Europe lay at the heart of the dilemma of British engagement. As mentioned earlier, Foreign Secretary Grey cited somewhat confusing motives of British "honour" and imperial ambitions in finally delivering the case for war and lamenting that "the lights have gone out all over Europe." Britain had been pursuing a policy of "splendid isolation" for much of the nineteenth century, preferring individual treaties with single nations on a case-by-case basis, rather than treaties via a bloc of powers or series of multilateral agreements. One of those treaties had been formalized and ratified with Belgium in 1839 as an aftereffect of the Napoleonic Wars, some eighty years prior to the outbreak of World

---

[1] Bill Bryson, *Neither Here nor There: Travels in Europe* (New York: Harper Perennial, 2001).

War I. It was this individual treaty, ironically established as a result of that policy of "splendid isolation," which drew Britain into a conflict of more than four years of dreadful, gridlocked inertia with the armies of Europe. Niall Ferguson[2], formerly of Harvard University and currently of the Hoover Institution in DC, has argued in recent years that Britain's entry into the war constituted one of "the greatest mistakes of the twentieth century," predicated on incoherent policy, contradictory motives, and absent exigencies. Indeed, his stark assessment essentially blamed Britain for turning a continental conflict into a global war, and Ferguson's methodology became a novel and notable one for the discipline of history, essentially positing hypothetical "what ifs" to explore how Britain's options were broader and better than it perceived in 1914. Instead, Ferguson argued, Britain made one of the largest errors of the twentieth century by engaging and elevating the conflict. His most radical and significant "if" centered on a hypothetical German victory quickly over France, which Ferguson argued would have delivered control of the mainland European economy to Germany but would have posed little military or economic threat to Britain and its empire. In the Ferguson thesis, Britain would have suffered little from a short Franco-German war with Germany as victor, an outcome he argued would have produced a prototype version of the European Union some fifty years ahead of its actual birth. Ferguson's controversial thesis is debatable, but his argument, and Britain's decisions in the summer of 1914, do share the fact that Britain had the capacity to elect its investment within, and extension beyond, the exigencies of the European landmass, considering Britain's island geography and border separation. In short, no German army was capable of marching across Britain's fields or across its borders, and so Britain, unlike France, Russia, and Belgium, had options about how to respond.

Britain's entry into the war was thus an example of historical, political, and especially geographic distinction from the mainland

---

[2] Niall Ferguson, *The Pity of War: Explaining World War I*, (New York: Basic Books, 1998).

European nations, affording the island nation of Britain alone the choice of whether to enter the fray or remain neutral on account of it being "neither here nor there." Violation of Belgium neutrality, according to disastrous German prognostication in 1914, was insufficient reason for Britain to jeopardize its sovereignty and empire by joining a continental war of choice, or so the German establishment wrongly gambled. This disastrous assumption of British indifference was mirrored even more powerfully by Britain itself in the way it exercised its political options and fortunes after the end of the war. This is a very British and peculiar story built primarily on two characters. The first is a character of pained romanticism, which in this narrative seeks constantly to grieve the sacrifice and pain of the war, and especially the death of a whole generation of young men. In this narrative, why would Britain ever join a war of choice? This characteristic of British sentiment almost appears to regret the independent decision the country made to enter the conflict. In this storyline Britain has been caught in a perennial memorial of guilty remembrance for one hundred years, conjured up each November in a national fixation with the wearing of red poppies. If this character was from Greek mythology, Sisyphus, the god destined vainly to push the boulder up the hill, would be an apt analogy. The second character is a somewhat more pragmatic and efficient character, resembling the stoic stereotype of the quirky Brit with a "stiff upper lip." This character's role exemplifies the civilian of pragmatic and distinctive independence, who unifies an odd combination of qualities that together form something oddly and distinctly "British." If the Greeks had in their mythology an archetype for this character, it would be their god Sophrosyne, the god of moderation. This left-brain/right-brain story lies at the heart of the British response to the First World War and the international political arena of the interwar years. Let us look at how that story unfolded.

Indeed, it was a story itself—originating as a theatrical play—that gave national expression to the emerging characteristics that would shape national sentiment and give definition to an enduring

110

British perspective. While the National Theatre in Weimar provided the venue for German outrage and resentment, personified in Hitler's dramatic and furious performance, London's Apollo Theatre—fittingly named after another Greek god—provided the context for a radical public reassessment of the war starting at the same time that Hitler was telling a very different story across the channel. This play was *Journey's End*, a 1928 drama created by R. C. Sherriff and acted by a novice young actor, Laurence Olivier, whose name and professional brilliance was to illuminate stage and screen across the twentieth century. The movie version of *Journey's End* was released ninety years later to commemorate the centennial of the war's end.[3] The story permitted a dramatic release of emotion that was to shape British sentiment for the critical interwar years. This period of the late 1920s and early 1930s saw not the same fury and rage as that in Italy and Germany, the brunt of which was clearly directed toward that which concluded the war—the Treaty of Versailles. In this sense, Hitler's and Mussolini's agendas were fueled by an anger focused on 1918 and 1919. For Britain, while the Fascist ascent was underway on the Continent, the key emotions galvanizing the British public were sentimentalism and bewilderment coupled with extraordinary grief. This is the backdrop to *Journey's End*. Ten years after the end of the war, the British were looking back with grief, and to some extent guilt, and asking the question, "Why?" For the Fascists on mainland Europe, that question was irrelevant. If there was a question that summed up their passion and agenda, it would be "When?" Moreover, since the Allies had been the victors in 1918, British anguish focused not on the conclusion of the war, but on its beginning. For Britain, the key date for the First World War was 1914, not 1918. To large extent that has remained the key date for the British collective consciousness of the war for the past one hundred years.

---

[3] "'Journey's End' and The First World War," *Imperial War Museums*, December 2018.

This consciousness has resonated and endured across decades and informed much of the recent centennial commemorations in the UK. But the Fascist response of the interwar years, being so distinct from that of the British, shaped the continental European collective memory of the war in a radically different way. Political and military agendas, not grief and sentimentality, were the initial motivations and outcomes post-1919 for the mainland European nations, and in the case of the Fascists, memory of the war was only valuable or necessary to inspire vengeance. Thus, political strategy was the driving impulse on mainland Europe after 1919. The British response, however, was more mixed and moderated during those interwar years. By the early 1920s, Britain began to develop not so much a *strategy* regarding the First World War than a *story* about it. Indeed, the enduring "message" of the First World War was one that finally became expressed via literature, film, and art in order to relay a broad cultural sentimentalism, pathos, and agony for a lost generation of young and implicitly innocent men from Britain and its empire. Especially powerful in creating this mythology were the writings of the First World War poets and the later emergence of widespread access to television just at the time of the fiftieth anniversary commemorations of the war in the mid-1960s. This British moderation had two faces: firstly, a naïve regret and acknowledgment of the futility of the war, and secondly, from that conviction of its painful futility, a strategy for the 1920s and 1930s that sought to prevent another occurrence—a strategy meant to ensure that, above all else, the war was indeed the conflict "to end all wars." These emotional and political reckonings were cojoined and informed each other. Together they provided a very powerful and intoxicating cocktail for the British psyche. How did they unfold?

Firstly, the artistic and cultural expressions of the "futility" argument were unleashed publicly by the play *Journey's End* to stunned response and extraordinary acclaims from enormous audiences, and in a sense the emotions released by *Journey's End* have not stopped since then. This was a moment when a British story of the war—ironically, concerning its senselessness—was finally taking place, providing cathartic expression after a ten-year period of incubation and silent grief following the Armistice. At the same time, the First World War poets became a mid-twentieth-century staple for the curriculum of every school student and perpetuated this Sisyphean mythology of endurance and suffering. Whether a "corner of a foreign field" or poppies blowing "between the crosses row on row," these idioms and images saturated the literary consciousness of the nation. Still reproduced every autumn in anticipation of Remembrance Day (November 11th), the wearing of poppy pins by politicians, citizens, television personalities, and professional sports players is a cultural norm, akin to the US predisposition to fly the national flag on front porches across the country. This resonance of the war via a literary medium has shaped an entire and enduring perspective and even exported that perspective across the globe. By way of illustration, in my home town of Macon, Georgia, the voice of the World War I poets is manifested on the war memorial on Coleman Hill, where under the names of the seventy-nine deceased of the 151st Machine Gun Battalion of the Rainbow Division, the epitaph reads: *"Dulce et Decorum est Pro Patria Mori."* This phrase, originally from the Roman poet Horace, was the inspiration and title of Wilfred Owen's last poem, written just a few weeks before the Armistice and before his own untimely death just days prior to the cease-fire. But poetry is not history and even poetry can be misleading. Horace's phrase, which Owen adopted as his poem's title, translates: *"How sweet and fitting it is to die for one's country."* That might on the surface appear a fittingly patriotic sentiment for a war memorial. Unfortunately, though, Owen's poem concluded by calling the phrase "the old lie." It was a deception and a lie that Owen called attention to and which he asserted would never be told to future generations if the reader witnessed the indescribable gas deaths of the suffocating victims in their trenches. So, even poetry was misread and misapplied for ulterior purposes, not dissimilar to how Bruce Springsteen's song *"Born in the USA"* was misquoted by President Ronald Reagan as an illustration of American greatness, a theme which Springsteen was critiquing.

113

Secondly, when it came to reviewing the First World War, the malleability of the medium enabled the artistic universe in British life to create products of ongoing resonance over the past century to serve each generation's interpretation of the war. One of the most powerful examples of that was the BBC series in 1964 *The Great War*[4], which commemorated the fiftieth anniversary of the outbreak of the war in 1914. Narrated by two other giant performers of the twentieth century, Ralph Richardson and Marius Goring, this enormous twenty-six-part weekly production by the BBC gave the British public a contemporary version of the same story of the war, this time coupled with graphic imagery, moving pictures, and the full horror that until then words, paintings, and stories had conveyed. With individual episodes imaged with titles such as "For Such a Stupid Reason Too," "Hell Cannot Be So Terrible," and "And We Were Young," the effect was stunning and tragic. *The Great War* had more audiences and greater responses than any previous BBC production and was sold around the world, especially among what became known as the Commonwealth nations. For the British, the series was a huge expression of a national mea culpa. Ironically, given the role of propaganda in the First World War, the BBC even manipulated the imagery in its title sequence to ram home the horror story it was seeking to bring into the homes of the mesmerized British public for twenty-six consecutive weeks in 1964. An opening sequence image that came to define the production featured a familiar image of an infantryman in the Irish Rifles, staring vividly into the camera. But the original documented photo taken during the war showed this anonymous solider in a trench with his compatriots, readying themselves to go "over the top." By the time *The Great War* was broadcast, the image had been edited with the same soldier relocated into a waterlogged shell hole, next to a skeleton corpse in tattered uniform. The BBC had thus "photoshopped" its image in keeping with the established message about the war that resonated with the 1960s perspective. This malleability can be found also in

---

[4] *The Great War*, Documentary, London: BBC, 1964.

the readings of the First World War poets, whose work is repackaged according to the sentiment of the day. A great example is another Wilfred Owen poem, "Exposure,"[5] written in the spring of 1918, which describes the suffering of the soldiers in the trenches. For decades, however, it was understood as signaling esteem for the sacrifice of the troops for a national cause, thereby ascribing a noble purpose to the war. This certainly jibed with Owen's decisions to keep returning to the front during a four-year period. By the 1960s, however, that interpretation of "Exposure" was redundant, and in the climate of that period, the poem was broadly recast as an antiwar statement. The reality is that Wilfred Owen was likely not writing an either-or poem, as both the sentimentalists and the cynics would like to think. Instead, it makes sense to read Owen's work as embracing the nonbinary "both-and" paradox that is the core of the British story of the war from its time forward.

In this context, the 1964 BBC production of *The Great War* was similarly using contemporary technology to convey, not create, a broad and paradoxical perspective that had emerged over the fifty years since the war. The BBC production did a masterful job of retelling a story, which reinforced a concept of "Britishness" at the heart of the identity of a people and nation, and which still resonates today. Shared across various art forms, this symphony of voices has told a unified story across generations of a peculiar British sense of self and loss, with its attendant emotions of sacrifice and guilt. In this narrative, the First World War delivered a dreadful, experiential manifestation of a deeply rooted British connection to land and environment, which reinforced British identity as being about both a people and a place. Fifty years after the start of the war, former prime minister Winston Churchill published his final work, which drew attention to this very point about British land and identity.[6] And place—or earth—was a very powerful reality on the Western Front

---

[5] Wilfred Owen, "Exposure," 1918, *Poetry Foundation*, 2020.

[6] Winston Churchill, *This Island Race* (London Cassell & Co., 1964).

for the millions who endured it. This concept of place speaks to the island experience of Britain as a core identity, in a way that is different for the United States. Britain stands upon, and is created from, a sea-encircled landmass, sublimating the experience of trenches and mud and weather and fields from the hellish place of death to the supreme expression of British noble sacrifice. This is visible, for example, in the art of Paul Nash, a defining war artist and soldier whose work even received an official military commission to convey to the public the images of the war. Nash today still haunts us with his portrayal of the chaos of soil, light, air, land, physical presence, and void. His work enlivens the physical earth with the metaphysical nature of the war, providing a hideous spirituality that draws the soul toward oblivion:

> No pen or drawing can convey this country—the normal setting of the battles taking place day and night, month after month. Evil and the incarnate fiend alone can be master of this war, and no glimmer of God's hand is seen anywhere. Sunset and sunrise are blasphemous, they are mockeries to man, only the black rain out of the bruised and swollen clouds all though the bitter black night is fit atmosphere in such a land. The rain drives on, the stinking mud becomes more evilly yellow, the shell holes fill up with green-white water, the roads and tracks are covered in inches of slime, the black dying trees ooze and sweat, and the shells never cease. They alone plunge overhead, tearing away the rotting tree stumps, breaking the plank roads, striking down horses and mules, annihilating, maiming, maddening, they plunge into the grave, and cast up on it the poor dead. It is unspeakable, godless, hopeless.[7]

This is the exact inverse of the pastoral motif of British sensibility and essence that William Blake had captured a century earlier

---

[7] Paul Nash, *Outline: An Autobiography and Other Writings* (London: Faber and Faber, 1949): 1–271, 211.

for posterity in his poem "And Did Those Feet in Ancient Time."[8] For Blake, the soul of England resided in its pastoral roots, grounded in the land itself. Bookending his poem, England's land is the gateway to the divine:

> And did those feet in ancient time
> walk upon England's mountain's green:
> .... Nor shall my sword sleep in my hand:
> till we have built Jerusalem,
> in England's green and pleasant land.

In Blake's vision, the land is where the divine and the temporal meet. Rather than us ascending to heaven, Blake saw the divine coming to earth, to sanctify its soil, to build the eternal Jerusalem in the temporal sphere, and England would be the place for that visionary home. For Nash, the soil was the place also where hell could rise and occupy the home of man, and that hell was captured in his nightmarish, dystopian portrayal of the Western Front. Blake's heaven was near; very near, and indeed, we can live in it when we walk on England's green and pleasant land. And, conversely, Nash's hell was near, very near, and indeed, we can die in it when we walk in Flanders's tortured fields. The classic sixteenth-century Dutch artist Hieronymus Bosch expressed visions of the Last Judgment[9] and its consequential ghastliness of hell with grotesque, twisted figures and tortured souls. Nash brought that same ghastliness to life, but in a Last Judgement vision that was, in fact, an apocalyptic total war in which hell came up to earth, and earth did not need to go down to hell. And the place where hell had revealed itself on earth was in Flanders in the years 1914 to 1918. This is the fashion, or zeitgeist, of the meaning Britain ascribed to the war and one that

---

[8] William Blake, "Jerusalem ["And did those feet in ancient times"], 1810, *Poetry Foundation*, 2020.

[9] Hieronymus Bosch, *Last Judgement*, 1482, Academy of Fine Arts, Vienna.

gains enormous expression in literature, in aesthetics, and in the emerging technology of television throughout the twentieth century. The British character has been shaped by its island identity that has subliminal meaning and sacred potential. A place, a people, and a hope rooted in island soil with eyes turned heavenward. But now many were uprooted from their island and sacrificed in the wastelands of Europe. Worse still, the British claimed this was for honor and pure nobility, but in retrospect it appeared their young men were sent pointlessly to that place of hell. In this tragic pathos, one finds the existential pain to support Niall Ferguson's claim that the First World War was the greatest mistake of the twentieth century.

This overarching narrative has endured across our century and works on a dialectical tension of honor and error in the British meaning found in the war. In one sense, Ferguson's claim gained traction because it was not that shocking. He simply represented one end of the continuum, though mostly the public sentiment has not been able to come to terms with quite as radical a conclusion. No discussion of the British sensibility and its impact on the world of culture, the arts, and literature would be complete without reference to a seminal work of the late twentieth century that attempted to describe a peculiar British perspective. Paul Fussell, an American veteran of the US Army landings in Normandy in 1944, was an academic whose field of British literature enabled him to develop a powerful and radical statement about the war and its impact on literature. His work was titled *The Great War and Modern Memory*,[10] and it defined a whole new debate about the war. Today, it still stands as a brilliant and original piece of literary analysis. Fussell argued that the experience of the war shaped all future artists and writers not only with a tragic harshness, but also with a redefined understanding, or "memory," of the world prior to the war. Fussell saw the war as not only changing history going forward, but in changing our memory of the past. He argued this phenomenon was present in

---

[10] Paul Fussell, *The Great War and Modern Memory* (Oxford UK: Oxford University Press, 1975).

the various literary creations of the twentieth century, and particularly in the British experience. His work gained global attention and broad literary acclaim with numerous awards. In more recent decades, he has been accused of using a filter to interpret writings and creations in a way that the evidence suggests otherwise. In short, Fussell has been critiqued as seeing everything through a prism of grief-tinted spectacles. At the start of the centennial commemorations in Britain in 2014, Daniel Swift published in the magazine *History Today* a summary of the problems with Fussell's analysis, arguing that he was strong in understanding the writings and analogies used to explain the war, but much weaker in his theoretical understanding that these writings were also a reevaluation of the times both before and after the war. As Swift summarized, "It is great literary criticism and lousy history."[11] In that summation Swift reflected much of the argument over the decades directed at Fussell, namely that he was blind to the diversity of literary and artistic responses to the war. His critics argued furthermore that there were many reassuring, positive appreciations of the war within cultural history, with affirming messages about its value and meaning derived from British life both before and after the war. What this debate misses is that maybe Fussell and his critics were both right. For we now have a full one hundred years of experience to draw on, and it is clear, and has been argued here, that it is not an either-or situation. The British instead have a bilateral and internally tensioned view that works well together.

This tension runs as follows. The war was hell and pointless and a tragic waste of young life. Equally, the war was noble and honorable and an agonizing sacrifice to guarantee a future where decency prevailed. These concepts are not antithetical but rather symbiotic. Indeed, one argument makes sense only if the other argument pre-

---

[11] Daniel Swift, "The Classic Book," *History Today* 64/8 (August 2014): 61.

vails. In early 2020, a dramatic movie about World War I was released titled *1917*.[12] The obvious cinematic merits aside, it was this bilateral reality that tensioned the movie so effectively for its audiences. In the film, two featured young enlisted soldiers, alongside thousands of their comrades, are thrown into oblivion for a noble cause in extraordinarily horrendous circumstances. The movie *1917* represented a deeply ensconced and profoundly intriguing way in which the First World War has found a niche in the soul of the British psyche.

But Britain is also a political nation-state as well as a living people, and its distinctive response to the war did not only inhabit the cultural consciousness of its artists and writers and the grieving dining rooms of its bereaved families. It also became a vital and peculiar facet of Britain's public life and determined to large extent how Whitehall and Parliament would chart British destiny. This is the second major character in the British story of the First World War. The British not only have mourned their war dead for one hundred years, they also have used that experience to shape their political vision and strategy over the decades. Indeed, the bilateral tension of "noble guilt" described above went on to shape how Britain was to make sense of the war politically going forward and shaped the distinctive qualities and peculiarities that were Britain's priorities in the public and global arena. The interwar years thus became the time when Britain's emerging sense and perspective of the war was visible in the political and strategic direction that the country embraced. As David Reynolds notes in his masterful work *The Long Shadow* (2013), the focal point of the meaning of the war, emanating from 1914 for the British—as opposed to the German focus on 1918—fueled the British passion for the themes of the "war to end all wars" and "never again" to be prioritized in the politics of the state. Reynolds argued that while Adolf Hitler was urging the German public to a renewed contest to avenge Versailles, the British response was

---

[12] Sam Mendes, director, *1917*, Universal Pictures, 2019.

to ensure that 1914 was never repeated, and the politics of the interwar years were absolutely dedicated to that testimony and aim. The League of Nations galvanized public interest and sentiment in that respect like nothing else, for in the league lay the possibility of an organization that would redeem the former sacrifice and sustain a rational process to prevent a future recurrence of the worst nightmare of renewed conflict and attendant global agony.

Whereas the league came to be vilified as inept by both the Allies and Axis nations in the 1930s, and subsequently replaced by the United Nations after World War II, its reputation was still strong in Great Britain. Largely through the efforts of Lord Robert Cecil and his office, it gained traction in the political landscape and public mindset of the British and their leaders just at the time when other nations were turning away. While the 1930s saw the collapse of the global economic order and the resurgence of rearmament and the drumbeat of war, in Britain there continued a broad and robust confidence that the late Woodrow Wilson would have admired. By the early 1930s, more than four hundred thousand individuals, mainly Britons, were members of the League of Nations Union, which was headquartered in London and was led at various times by the former foreign secretary Sir Edward Grey and Lord Robert Cecil. Importantly, the league resonated with the mood of the British public and its emerging bilateral interpretation of the war. Reynolds traces this to an interesting event in a quiet northeast suburb of London, Ilford, in the 1930s.

There the local newspaper, *The Ilford Recorder*, which is still published today, ran a survey on attitudes toward war and disarmament in tandem with the local League of Nations Union branch. The effect was electrifying, with extensive and overwhelming interest in the success of the league from residents and a desire to see policies at the national level that would promote its objectives. The Ilford survey spurred the national League of Nations Union to issue, in the autumn of 1934, a "Peace Ballot" to the voting public of Britain. This ballot focused on five questions about the value of the league, the desirability of disarmament, the curtailment of the arms industry and trade, the efficacy of sanctions and/or military intervention on rogue nations, and, oddly, the abolition of air forces via international agreement. Nearly twelve million Britons answered the Peace Ballot, with staggering levels of assent in the affirmative to each question. Most responses were at the 90-plus percent level, with the lowest level of 70-plus percent in response to the option of necessary military intervention. The response constituted one-third of the entire voting public and gave a resounding "thumbs up" to the work of the league when the results were published in the spring of 1935. As Reynolds notes, this was in every sense a peculiar British occurrence and utterance. The British wanted peace, wanted the First World War to end all wars, wanted organizations that would promote and protect peace, and, in the final analysis, would be prepared reluctantly to pursue military struggle if necessary.

This was occurring precisely at the time when Adolf Hitler was purging any potential opposition in Germany, in the infamous "Night of the Long Knives." That event was a signal of Hitler's real intent and interest. Goering and Himmler persuaded Hitler to focus national efforts less on ideological National Socialist revolution, the goal of Ernst Röhm and his *Sturmabteilung* (SA), and more on stability, economy, and rearmament. In short, a coming war. In those preparations, Hitler's absolutist instincts were sufficiently pragmatic to eradicate any potential ideological rival, which motivated his purge of the distracting and distrustful SA. These concurrent events revealed the underlying priorities of the British and German outlook and leadership. Britain was faithfully committing to wage peace. Germany was faithfully preparing to wage war. This British peace priority, personified in the leadership of Neville Chamberlain and reflective of public support of the League of Nations Union, was at best noble and naïve, and at worst blind and wishful thinking. Even after the Spanish Civil War and Hitler's clear use of that as a rehearsal for a major European war, the appeasement policy played out long after Chamberlain's hand possessed worthless cards, or pieces of paper inscribed with Herr Hitler's signature. This momentum of opposites is what ultimately came to its fateful clash in 1939, when Hitler's hawk of war set the agenda for global affairs over Wilson's and Chamberlain's dove of peace.

It is also this momentum that left the 1914–1918 War as a difficult narrative for the British, and maybe for the British alone. Every other protagonist of the First World War had an easier answer to the question of why they participated in its national memory. For the Germans, it was easily labeled as a wicked national humiliation that required retribution. For the Russians, it was a pre-Soviet czarist folly of imperialism. For the Americans, it was a new moment to make the world safe for American democracy and American capital. For the Middle East, it was a new opportunity to struggle for Jewish self-determination and Muslim self-expression. For the young republics of Central Europe, it was a time to forge new nations and identities from the wreckage of old dynasties. Even for the Irish, it was a moment of binary polarity from either side of the sectarian divide to see that the wounded stories of ancient Reformation battles be retold and refashioned in a new struggle for Irish independence or union. But for the British, there was no easy answer. There was pain, guilt, and beautiful, evocative literature and art that drew the audience into the pathos of the war without delivering the body-blow punch of political explanation for a nation transfixed by tragedy.

National angst is still somewhat unresolved despite the outcome of the second war, which gave the British a wonderful, self-promoting script of Churchillian resilience, bulldog independence, and a David-and-Goliath-style, lonely struggle against tyranny until a standoffish New World was finally forced into the fray. For while the British have united their narratives and connected their themes about the first war, they have not been as successful in reconciling or harmonizing the national narratives regarding how each of these two world wars relate to each other. While the passing of time has made it easier to see the links between these two conflicts, the British have a way to go to tie their own loose ends. The first war's narrative, to the British, is shocking, empty of easy words, and gruelingly painful. The second war's narrative, on the other hand, is heroic, gritty, purposeful, and prideful. The former is about losing an island identity. The latter is about defending an island identity.

123

This binary sense of history, and the enduring problem of the British narrative about the First World War, resurfaced again in the decades after the Second World War. Reinforced by the BBC's *The Great War* series, cultural messaging distilled these two separate narratives into two views: firstly, that the First World War was unnecessary and tragic, and that nobody wanted to go to war in the first place; and secondly, and conversely, that the Second World War was a global struggle of civilizations between forces of good and evil, and its engagement was necessary for the triumph of democracy.

By the 1960s, those narratives ran deep in British consciousness. Following the BBC series *The Great War* five years later, Sir Richard Attenborough brought to the big screen in 1969 the hugely successful comedic play and musical *Oh! What a Lovely War*,[13] featuring the same theatrical giants who had voice parts in the earlier BBC series. This new cinematic film was based on the theater play created by Joan Littlewood[14] on the eve of the fiftieth anniversary of the outbreak of the First World War, which itself was synchronous with a thoughtful book by the maverick politician and future minister of defense under Margaret Thatcher, Alan Clark. His book *The Donkeys* (1961),[15] was based on the phrase "lions led by donkeys" and the argument that the heroes of the First World War were the ordinary enlisted British men—the true lions—but that their misfortune was to be led by imbecilic "donkeys," namely the generals. The phrase itself has long been used, ascribed originally to the Ancient Greek philosopher Plutarch, and utilized commonly in the nineteenth and twentieth centuries. The so-called "Desert Fox" of the German Army, *Generalfeldmarschall* Erwin Rommel, is said to have applied the same phrase to the captured British troops at Tobruk

---

[13] Sir Richard Attenborough, director, *Oh! What a Lovely War*, Paramount Pictures, 1969.

[14] Joan Littlewood, director, *Oh! What a Lovely War*, Theatre Workshop, 1963, Theatre Royal, Stratford East.

[15] Alan Clark, *The Donkeys*, (New York: Random House, 1961).

during the Second World War, contrasting their valor with the ineptness of their leader, British field marshal Bernard "Monty" Montgomery. Half a century later, the brilliantly witty *Blackadder Goes Forth*[16] television comedy popularized this caricature. Again, produced by the BBC and using the same fictional characters over four periods of British history, the final *Blackadder Goes Forth* series was set on the Western Front of the 1914–1918 War. The quality of humor and wit was superb, but in the fashion of the Shakespearean stage, it was its tragicomic nature that bewitched its audience. Additionally, the serendipitous timing of the final season was intriguing, for the final series was released in November 1989, the same month that the Berlin Wall came down and the Cold War changed forever. In the heart-wrenching final episode, the cast of characters we had come to know over four seasons stepped out of their trench and went "over the top" into a hail of machine-gun fire. Meanwhile, the aristocratic and foolish General Melchett was cast drinking Burgundy wine some miles behind the lines in a French chateau. With a haunting piano soundtrack, these familiar and beloved characters stumbled and died in a war-torn no-man's-land, which then visually transformed into a bucolic meadow of poppies. The dead Englishmen thus returned to their spiritual "Albion" home via a pointless slaughter, in some small part of a foreign field.

Blackadder Goes Forth was a superb piece of comic drama that maintained the British narrative of the agonized sacrifice of its ancestors for a public living seventy-five years after the events. And the series also created for its audience a commentary on the current geopolitical context of the late 1980s, at a time when the Cold War was to undergo a radical transformation. The serendipity of its coincidental release with the fall of the Berlin Wall was dramatic and powerful. In the final episode of the series, the connection between the "futility" narrative of the First World War and the bewildering nature of the Cold War was emphatically and explicitly enunciated.

---

[16] Richard Boden, director, *Blackadder Goes Forth* (London: BBC, 1989).

The concept of "Mutually Assured Destruction" (M.A.D.), the basic rationale for the Cold War nuclear arms race between NATO and the Warsaw Pact, was scripted back into the plot of *Blackadder*. The characters in the final episode ask themselves, as they step out of their trench and into no-man's-land, "What is the point of the war?" With Monty Python-like creativity, one of the final exchanges between the characters harmonized this British disbelief about Flanders and the Nuclear Age:

> Private Baldrick: (Baldrick has been granted permission to ask a question.) "The thing is: The way I see it, these days there's a war on, right? And, ages ago, there wasn't a war on, right? So, there must have been a moment when there not being a war on went away, right? And there being a war on came along. So, what I want to know is: How did we get from the one case of affairs to the other case of affairs?"
>
> Captain Blackadder: "Do you mean 'How did the war start?'"
>
> Private Baldrick: "Yeah."
>
> Corporal George: "The war started because of the vile Hun and his villainous empire-building."
>
> Captain Blackadder: "George, the British Empire at present covers a quarter of the globe, while the German Empire consists of a small sausage factory in Tanganyika. I hardly think that we can be entirely absolved of blame on the imperialistic front...the real reason for the whole thing was that it was too much effort *not* to have a war."

At this point, the Blackadder production script pivots from the enduring British narrative of a pointless, confusing, and messy rationale for the First World War. Captain Blackadder answers the private's question by directly connecting the 1989 climate of the Cold War and its M.A.D. methodology, which had defined global politics since the end of the Second World War and which was about to go, at that time, through massive episodic change in a few days at the Berlin Wall.

Captain Blackadder: "You see, Baldrick, in order to prevent war in Europe, two Super blocs developed; us, the French and the Russians on one side, and the Germans and Austro-Hungary on the other. The idea was to have two vast opposing armies, each acting as the other's deterrent. That way there could never be a war."

Private Baldrick: "But this is a sort of a war, isn't it, sir?"

Captain Blackadder: "Yes, that's right. You see, there was a tiny flaw in the plan."

Private Baldrick: "What was that, sir?"

Captain Blackadder: "It was bollocks."

This brief examination of one immensely popular British TV comedy from the 1980s shows how malleable the theme of the First World War has been to the British across various decades. The war rapidly became a flexible motif that worked to illuminate British life and provide a uniquely British insight to make sense of different situations. The First World War has thus lingered in British consciousness for more than one hundred years as an ominous vacuity as the nation tried to make sense of its suffering, its identity, and its place among the nations of the world. This loss endured as a wound that would be reopened with other challenges for the nation throughout the twentieth century. Another example from the 1980s illustrates this point. During that decade, an infamous mining strike occurred as a result of the Thatcher government's determination to close uneconomic coal pits. The ensuing strike lasted twelve months, brought great industrial dispute, mass poverty in many mining communities, industrial violence, and sporadic power outages across the country. Margaret Thatcher refused to back down, and the strike became one of the great threats against her premiership and her government. Although she finally prevailed, the nation was transfixed by one of her Tory patriarchs, former prime minister Harold MacMillan (dubbed "Supermac" at the time), who, at the age of ninety years, delivered his maiden speech in the House of Lords. In that speech, he lambasted his own Conservative government for its behavior and attitude toward the miners, even while he supported the policy of closing uneconomic mines. MacMillan reminded the government: "Although at my age I cannot interfere or do anything about it, it breaks my heart to see what is happening in our country today. A terrible strike is being carried on by the best men in the world. They beat the Kaiser's army and they beat Hitler's army. They never gave in."[17]

Other nations have found ample material in their own narratives to make sense of the ignominy of the First World War. The British have elevated that to a new level and have saturated their national identity with its events and impact over the past century, and still do so today. That is why the Tower of London's display of one million ceramic poppies, "Blood Swept Lands and Seas of Red," was so poignant and resonant. When Queen Elizabeth II placed the final poppy in the moat, the British narrative of the Great War across the century was honored and presented for the world to behold. The poppies' location in the moat around the Tower of London is intriguing because the tower was built as an island fortress and prison, surrounded by water and armed to resist internal and external threats to its island stronghold. A better metaphor for how Britain has struggled to explain the First World War could not be expressed. For the war took "our boys" from their heavenly island home and slaughtered them in the watery hellhole of Europe. Whereas the Tower of London had been a prison for centuries, for this past century it has been the foreign field of Flanders, the prison to British sensibility and meaning about the war, and a prison tomb to its dead. Those million dead of Britain's empire never returned across the water to their island home, but at least they made it halfway back to the moat. In that evocative centennial place in 2014 a

---

[17] Houses of Parliament, Hansard: HL Deb (13 November 1984) vol. 457, cc219-306.

red poppy signified they were halfway home, no longer languishing across the water in a foreign field, but now returned in spirit and symbol to the soil of their island home once more.

9

AND THE WALLS CAME TUMBLING DOWN

On November 9th, 1989, after a tumultuous period of disruption within the Soviet Union and its aligned Eastern Bloc allies, another breathtaking historical pivot occurred in Central Europe with the breaching and demolition of the Berlin Wall. The Berlin Wall had been the single greatest symbol of the ideological chasm that had inhabited Europe from 1945 and the end of the Second World War. Churchill's much-quoted and haunting term the Iron Curtain, first delivered at a speech on March 5th, 1946, at Westminster College, Missouri, referred to that impenetrable border which ran from the Baltic to the Adriatic seas, with capitalist and Communist nations facing each other broodingly across barbed wire, mined fields, cement walls, and machine-gun posts. This Iron Curtain, which stretched across hundreds of miles and numerous nations, was the legacy quickly erected in the wake of the defeat of Nazi Germany at the conclusion of the second war. Yet the landlocked capital German city of Berlin—with its western district administered by the democratic FDR and its eastern district administered by the Socialist GDR—singly provided the greatest tangible symbol for the vast, binary political identity that was to become Central Europe for the remainder of the twentieth century. For more than forty years, Berlin and its wall fixated interest around the globe and became a symbol of identity that allowed everyone to claim, in concert with President John F. Kennedy, that "Ich bin ein Berliner."

But the collapse of the wall was part of a broader crescendo of change behind the Iron Curtain that belonged to numerous individuals and leaders in many places, not just the politicians and people in Berlin. Certainly the "Polish pope" John Paul II and his compatriot Lech Walesa, leader of the Gdańsk shipyard trade union Solidarity (*Solidarnosc*), deserve credit for fanning the flames of democracy behind the Iron Curtain in the 1980s. Those flames had flickered briefly in earlier times in Hungary in 1956 and Czechoslovakia in 1968. But the Soviet Union had on those occasions used "hard" and "soft" military interventions, especially after failed overtures of friendship to the West following the death of Stalin, to stamp out any sparks or embers of democratic heat in its republics and Eastern Bloc satellites. The opportunity for change was lost, and authoritarianism reestablished for another generation. That situation radically and unalterably changed with the emergence of the somewhat tragic and mesmerizing figure of Michael Gorbachev, the eighth and last general secretary of the Communist Party and president of the Soviet Union. Gorbachev assumed overall leadership of the Central Committee and the USSR in 1985 after the death of the hardline Konstantin Chernenko in March of that year. And Gorbachev's transition appeared more generational and welcome, since Chernenko had succeeded two previous traditionalists in just two prior years, namely Yuri Andropov and Leonid Brezhnev. The time was right for a young and exciting leader, not a repetition of a dying old Marxist veteran of the "Great Patriotic War," the Soviet name for the Second World War.

Having risen through the ranks of the Communist Party, Michael Gorbachev could have reasonably been expected to maintain Communist orthodoxy and solidify its control for a new generation. The USSR might have anticipated in him a younger, vibrant, and more engaged type of Marxist-Leninist who had the communicative instinct of a modern politician and populist attraction to ordinary people and workers. But Gorbachev's human face was just the tip of an iceberg that would sink the Soviet old order once and for all, for Gorbachev immediately set about a cultural change in the Soviet Union that would ensure most Western observers became familiar with at least two Russian words: perestroika and glasnost. These two words contained the ideas that would upturn an entire ideological worldview and an historical superpower. Loosely translated to "restructuring" and "openness" respectively, the seeds of the end of the Soviet Union were sown in these ideas as well as by decades of a stagnant economy preceding Gorbachev's enlivening vision. If Kennedy's Camelot had breathed fresh air into the halls of Washington in 1960 and warned the world of Soviet expansionism, Gorbachev's perestroika wreaked a hurricane through the Kremlin twenty-five years after Kennedy's warnings. But the collapse of the USSR was never Gorbachev's intent, and today he is a figure of extraordinary varied reputation, despised by many now in Russia, while hailed as a hero in the West. Pivotal events marked his tenure and can be partitioned by two eras, one before the nuclear accident at the Chernobyl Nuclear Plant in the Ukraine in April of 1986, and the other after that catastrophe. During both eras he, along with his Western counterpart US president Ronald Reagan, was able to move nuclear disarmament forward in huge material and perceptual ways, despite the obstinacies of hawkish figures in the West such as Margaret Thatcher, and an old military guard back home in the USSR that did not trust him. Those military men and politburo conservatives would eventually attempt a failed coup in the summer of 1991, leading quickly to the breakup of the USSR, the voluntary formation of the Russian Federation, and independence for most of the former Eastern Bloc countries. In truth, Gorbachev's reform agenda had earlier seeds in the three years after Stalin's death in 1953. At that time, Premier Nikita Khrushchev had flirted with the idea of a loose Russian federation and greater association with the NATO countries. But due both to internal politics and external disinterest from the United States, Khrushchev reversed course on a thawing of relations and a new détente with the West. The opportunity for a new dawn would have to wait for another premier, Mikhail Gorbachev, who arrived on the Soviet scene thirty years later.

The tumbling of the Berlin Wall remains the primary testimony to the new way that Gorbachev wanted the question of the "mastery of Europe" to be settled, though he would never have put it that way. Indeed, he proposed the replacement of NATO and the Warsaw

Pact alliances, the binary sets of international treaties established after the Second World War to defend the West and the East against each other. Gorbachev instead sought a unified set of agreements across the Cold War lines to develop a new "Common Home for Europe" strategy, which envisaged a pan-European and Russian framework of cooperation, the polar opposite of the Cold War methodology. In this scenario, the fall of the wall would yield an even greater potential for union than that offered by the existing European Union. As events showed, the incorporation of former Eastern Bloc satellites into the EU during the 1990s was testimony to a new European common home that Gorbachev had helped envision and promote. The first step toward that expanded European unity commenced, ironically, in the very same nations that had plunged Europe, in the summer of 1914, into disunity and self-destruction. Seventy-five years after Austria-Hungary led Europe to war in 1914, the modern nations of Austria and Hungary cut down the barbed wire on their small border area of the Iron Curtain in the summer of 1989, and the heat of democracy truly commenced the melting of the old Cold War.

The USSR did not intervene then, nor did it when the Berlin Wall fell that November. And in the wall's falling, the final fulfillment of the concept of German unification, won violently previously through Bismarck's "blood and iron" policy in the 1871 war with France, was again realized, but this time through peaceful protest and popular assent. In this dramatic moment, indeed, the bookend to the First World War was now fixed, at least in terms of resolving the question of the "mastery of Europe." For by reuniting Germany once more, and now in a way that the West and East would manage diplomatically and democratically, Europe could finally argue that its most basic, volatile, and unresolved division was healed. In this sense, what Versailles could not achieve in the wrangling of the elite and powerful in 1919 was resolved successfully three generations later when the citizens of Berlin took matters upon themselves, without recourse to their powerful elites, and finally designed a modern working map of European democracy and stability. The story could end here with optimism and resolution, but as in most matters of human affairs, one person's fish is another person's poison. For in the three decades that have evolved since the Berlin Wall fell, considerable toxicity has seeped into the cultural and political environment of those Western and Eastern European nations, which all claim the mantle of twenty-first-century democracy. What was desired and partially gained in November 1989 by the removal of Communism from the map of Eurasia has since been risked by an uncertain commitment to the institutions necessary for democracy to thrive in those places where dictatorship and authoritarianism have deep roots. The actors of Versailles failed to grasp this same issue in 1919 when they hoped their treaty would "correct" the errors of the past and ensure a future for Europe where order, security, and democracy would be the norms. One hundred years later, our generation has witnessed a repetition of a similar misguided logic of presumptive triumph once again. How is this so?

Perhaps most obviously, when the Berlin Wall fell, as did the Soviet Union and its apparatus of state two years later, many Western governments assumed that its version of history and democracy had somehow "won" the Cold War. The West did not give sufficient expression to the notion that the end of the Cold War was somehow a winner for both "sides," or for even humanity, but instead viewed it as a particular Western victory. It was seen as a vindication of the Western democratic worldview. In this self-talk, history had proven the West's case, and the struggle was thus concluded. The greatest academic expression of this was in the 1992 publication *The End of History and the Last Man*[1] by Francis Fukuyama, now senior fellow and political scientist at Stanford University. Developing on his earlier article at the time of the collapse of the wall—that at least asked the question rather than provided the answer ("The End of History?")—Fukuyama's core argument went beyond the plausible and sufficient argument that 1989 was the bookend of the First World

---

[1] Francis Fukuyama, "The National Interest," in *The End of History and the Last Man* (The Free Press. 1992) 3–18.

War and its legacy. Instead, Fukuyama could not resist expanding on 1989 as a kind of cosmic event, a teleological vision of the final victory of capitalist democracy and liberal republicanism. It was, in his words, "the endpoint of mankind's ideological evolution and the universalization of Western liberal democracy as the final form of human government."[2] Woodrow Wilson would have been jubilant if he had been around to read Fukuyama. In the intervening years, Fukuyama has stuck to his guns, essentially arguing that the "end point" for humanity is democracy and self-governance, though recently he has begun discussing how advances in science and technology are critical to that story and outcome.

In Fukuyama's highly influential and esteemed work, therefore, the case was set out that the West had been right all along and had crossed the finish line with all ideological alternatives coming in behind. In this linear view of the ascendancy of democracy, the West was both beholden and right to resist the kaiser in 1914, the Fuhrer in 1939, and the commissar comrade in 1945. The symbol of a fallen Berlin Wall thus lay not in its immediate impact for the people of Germany and Berlin, but rather in its expression of a grander vindication of the Western worldview. The rapid succession of events of that era was indeed breathtaking. Timothy Garton-Ash, professor of history at Oxford,[3] characterized it well in claiming that during that time, what was unthinkable on a Monday had already occurred by that Friday, and this rapid change may have played into this irrevocable sense of the supremacy of the West.[4] Moreover, with the demise of the USSR two years later and its replacement by systems of government that claimed a new version of democracy at their core, it was too tempting for a heady rush to judgment that the West

---

[2] Ibid., 16.

[3] Timothy Garton-Ash, *The Magic Lantern: The Revolution of '89* (New York: Random House, 1990).

[4] Brian Klaas, moderator, "The Survival of Democracy in Eastern Europe, with Ivan Krastev, Timothy Garton Ash and Brian Klaas," podcast, *Intelligence Squared* (12 November 2019).

could now shape, inform, and develop the East, paving a sort of one-way ideological road in which Western products—both economic and epistemological—would be transported and accumulated by eager Eastern consumers in their rush to democratic self-actualization. Aside from its naivety and hubris, Garton-Ash points out that it was mistaken to use one of the most nonlinear events of all recent human history—the fall of the Berlin Wall—to develop a linear narrative about the triumph of Western democracy over a course of decades. The "end of history" argument proposed by Fukuyama was doing just that, seeing 1989 as the final resolution of the old struggles of capitalism, Fascism, and Communism in the sunset of the latter and the sunrise of the former; in that sense, he thought history was "finished." Before Fukuyama, the mid-century scholar Daniel Bell had proposed in his book *The End of Ideology*[5] that a technologically advancing Western culture would be eclectic about its narrative and that overarching ideologies had been exhausted. We would, he proposed, choose from a buffet of convictions and principles that could cohere piecemeal with technology. As we shall see, Bell was indeed prescient. But Fukuyama went further still, arguing that one ideology had replaced all others, and that was liberal capitalism.

This sense of a terminal end to the old order echoes the environment of 1919, when the Allies believed that a brave new world without war was within humanity's grasp if a new equilibrium, with American capital as its fulcrum, could address the question of how to ensure European stability. That question had now been settled through a tragic global war, so the treaty designers surmised, and that Western capitalism could now be exported to the new democracies and vanquished nations of the First World War to provide the alternative to war. The designers of the Treaty of Versailles monumentally and tragically miscalculated that it would restore European stability and that capitalism would provide the pathway forward to sustain that stability. With that in mind, it was believed that the

---

[5] Daniel Bell, The End of Ideology: On the Exhaustion of Political Ideals in the Fifties, (New York: The Free Press. 1960).

ancient historic struggles for identity and mastery of Europe could finally be put to bed—the "end" of their nineteenth-century history—so that they could now begin to live as we would have them live, made in the image and likeness of Allied systems and economies. Fast forward from 1919 to 1989 and the irony is very apparent. Even if the West's economic system could be picked off the shelf and exported to our vanquished foes, Western democracy and economy after 1989 quickly lost the very fluidity, pluralism, and variety that had made it so effective, and it morphed into another monolithic entity or formula. In short, it lacked an understanding of humanity. The clue to this was visible in the many images of the Berlin Wall. Before the wall fell, chaotic and colorful graffiti was always on its Western face but not on the side facing eastward. The expressions of agency, color, voice, and emotion were varied and plural precisely because they were democratic, and not simply a commodity to be exported to the former Eastern bloc peoples, who were assumed to be aspiring capitalists in their escape from political authoritarianism. This was an arrogant blunder and a repetition of 1919 all over again, with an odd twist. For the Europe of the 1920s was so devastated economically, and then contrived politically after Versailles on such new and arbitrary borders, that economic stability was probably the one commodity that could work, and indeed did so effectively until the Wall Street crash of 1929. Only when capitalism's economic virtues dried up did "identity" become the driving question of the 1930s, much to the opportunistic delight of Hitler in Germany and the other dictators. But by 1989, the identities of those peoples had evolved for decades in the former USSR and Eastern Bloc. Indeed, lip service had been paid to national identity and expression in the Eastern Bloc, even as the economic test that had been the original Bolshevik raison d'etre obviously and repeatedly failed. So, in 1989, the West assumed that all it needed to do was replay the economic strategy once more in order for the newly emancipated and post-Communist nations to become mirror images of Western Europe and the United States.

President Bill Clinton had successfully utilized the mantra "It's about the economy, stupid" in his election campaigns, and its success suggested to some not only the value of its application to US elections but as a general principle of the late twentieth century in peoples' aspirations for self-expression and security. That assumption proved wrong, and the only lesson evident from the past three decades is that when it comes to post-Communist Eastern Europe, the Baltic States, and the Russian Federation, "It's not about the economy, stupid." For while the American model of economy was thrust forward as the orthodox catechism for humankind after "the end of history," it became clear by the end of the twentieth century that the former Communist and egalitarian societies had inadequate mechanisms in place to ensure that this promised new wealth would be distributed across social strata in any meritocratic way. Instead, it rapidly came to reside only in the hands of the oligarchic few, many of whom were self-serving kleptocrats. In short, the story of democracy since the fall of the wall has had more in common with the post-1929 story of failed promises than in its pre-1929 years of Wilson's liberal democracy. And after 1929, capitalism and democracy had very tarnished reputations indeed.

The year 1989 marks a moment of lost opportunity for the West, in which it came with some hubris to believe too much of its own self-talk. For the nations behind the eastern face of the wall, this lost moment represented a double hammer blow. Whereas formerly under their Marxist-Leninist commissars they experienced a modicum of equality, but with economic and political austerity, now they were subject to what Garton-Ash described as an inequality of respect from the Western capitalists. In 1989, the liberal democracies of the West had been given a brief moment not to claim victory, but to offer human respect and a helping hand, rather than an economic formula, for the people whose identities, aspirations, and inclinations, many Westerners assumed, simply needed economic emancipation to be realized. Instead of dialogue, these Eastern Bloc nations received a heavy dose of supply-side economic theory. Ironically, too, in most cases the transitions they underwent toward that

Western economic "solution" in the Eastern Bloc were not delivered via hardline and violent revolution (Romania aside) but relatively peacefully. The "old guard" Communist leaders generally stood aside and disappeared without a struggle once the wall and the other symbolic "walls" of each Eastern Bloc nation fell. The people claimed back their lives and fortunes only to see them, over the next decade, defined by realities of cold hard cash from the West that slipped through their collective fingers.

German reunification achieved the most elegant and promising outcome of this capitalist-Communist dialectic, since at the heart of that unifying enterprise lay the historic cultural belief of more than 150 years in a shared Germanic identity and togetherness. While in the past this had triggered the most vile and violent reactions of racial aggression and militarism, in 1989 the country finally established and fulfilled its greater Germanic unity in a new Germany which sought to respect both the identities as well as the economic needs of its former GDR Eastern citizens. It is tempting to wonder if this recent German success story was achievable precisely because of the former disasters they had delivered to the world. For previous experiments in German unity and enlarged Lebensraum had inflicted tyranny and misery on first Europe and then the world. This 1989 version was, in comparison, a story of human political triumph, not one of shame and oppression. And while Germany remains an ongoing success story in large part, albeit with ominous recent internal tensions, the other Eastern Bloc countries have spent thirty years struggling more than Germany. They are aware that the West views them as "losers" of the Cold War and that the West expects them to simply embrace its capitalist program. This failure to recognize satisfactorily the complex identities and cultural aspirations of the peoples behind the former Iron Curtain has been a contributing factor in the resurgence of the far right in Eastern Europe. The new brand of populism which has taken root in various nations is not simply a by-product of economic disparity and the lack of meritocratic distribution of new wealth; it is also related to their perceptions of themselves as second-class citizens and the desire to find national pride. Thus, in the Eastern Bloc the return of religion, family, and nation are major public themes that have emerged to compensate for the failure of broad economic well-being and a sense of Western disdain for national identities. Whether in Victor Orban's Hungary or in the new patriotic constitutionalism emerging in Poland, the desire for a post-Communist existence has not been an immediate rush to embrace a Western identity and model, but rather to model a self-expressed sense of identity and national hope.

This may, in a way that is different but parallel to the story of Germany's reunification, represent a similar concluding phase in the plot of Central and Eastern Europe's story that began at Versailles. The Treaty of Versailles created a framework, both geographically and politically, of extraordinary instability that merely suspended the issue of the "mastery" of Europe. That issue remained unresolved even after a second global war and the subsequent division of Europe into NATO and Warsaw Pact blocs. Versailles offered Europe the vain hope that nation-building would work via the cojoining of Wilson's principles of democratic capitalism and arbitrary national identities built upon ancient ethnic fault lines. But instead of a stable European home that forever put war to bed, Versailles created an unstable environment waiting to collapse. When Western money dried up in 1929, that environment did indeed collapse and unleashed passions of unstable tribalism which spiraled Europe toward military dictatorship to reassemble the pack. Only now, four generations from Versailles, can we see how the course of the twentieth century required continued conflict and realignments before an enduring framework for Europe could finally establish stability and democracy.

Two important steps toward sustainable peace and political stability were required in the second half of the twentieth century. Both of these steps were seismic changes derived directly from the First World War and its ending. The first and most enduring of evolutions was the establishment of what is now known as the European Union, originally in the Benelux trade treaties of the 1940s. The second, more contemporary and more unpredictable, was the collapse of the Soviet Union and Eastern Bloc and the emergent geopolitics there today. Western Europe's move toward union and Eastern Europe's move toward disunion each represent dialectically opposing trajectories toward a final resolution to the disequilibrium thrown up by the First World War of 1914 to 1918. In terms of Western Europe, the emergence of the EU represents an extraordinary about-face to centuries of rivalry and decades of incalculable violence that characterized the first half of the twentieth century. Responding to the fact that the search for economic dominance had plunged Europe and the world into crisis in 1914, the Europe that emerged from the ashes of the later second war effectively decided that union and cooperation were infinitely preferable to division and rivalry. This represented something very different from the treaties and alliances of nineteenth-century Europe. Starting with the European Coal and Steel Community treaty of 1950, the original combatants of Belgium, France, the Netherlands, Luxembourg, Italy, and Germany formed a trade union that grew over the coming decades into the vast experiment in balance between sovereignty and union of member states known as the European Union. Less than one hundred years since the outbreak of the First World War, the EU was in 2012 awarded the peace prize by the Nobel Committee "for [having] over six decades contributed to the advancement of peace and reconciliation, democracy and human rights in Europe."[6]

This accolade came after complex decades of discerning the process and structure for European cooperation, expanding membership of individual member states, and the critical task of balancing pan-European integration while safeguarding member states' sovereignties. No other nation, and no other national leader, was vexed by this issue more than the United Kingdom and Prime Minister Margaret Thatcher. By the end of her ten-year premiership,

---

[6] Nobel peace prize to the European Union: https://ec.europa.eu/home-affairs/what-is-new/news/news/2012/20121012_en.

Thatcher's political strength had evaporated at home, and the question of Europe had riven her Conservative Party. At the heart of this perennial British angst over the Continent was a policy decision that was to change Europe again for decades. This was the Maastricht Treaty of 1992, with its philosophical and semantic conundrum of the "principle of subsidiarity," which sought to find a way of describing the relationship of the particular to the whole, the member state to the broader union. The Maastricht Treaty was as significant a step for the EU as was the creation of the earlier economic treaties and the former European Economic Community. The Maastricht Treaty, which the UK eventually ratified alongside all other member states, essentially propelled Europe toward a model of a "United States" of Europe and enhanced European identity. Its radical achievements were the concept of European citizenship, thus ensuring the free movement of people as well as trade across member state borders for purposes of residency and work. Additionally, and specifically to ease this movement, a new exchange rate mechanism was established between the different currencies of the EU as a preliminary step toward the creation of the euro as a global currency, with a euro currency zone that incorporated twelve of the member states at its outset. Today, that number has risen to nineteen eurozone member nations, including smaller principalities outside the EU such as Vatican City, Andorra, and San Marino.

Today, as the European Union approaches an age of seventy-five years, it remains one of the most complex, inspiring, and ambitious projects in geopolitical development and international unity in centuries, and its longevity appears intact and resolute. Its core operations, the European Commission and European Parliament, ensure both an administrative system and political establishment that guide the processes of engagement and integration across twenty-seven nations. Headquartered respectively in Brussels, Belgium, and Strasbourg, France, the historic irony of these locations could not be greater or more optimistic. For just one century earlier, these were the same places where the First World War originated and pitched Europeans and then global citizens into the most appalling strife and loss in human history to date. Yet the EU remains a bold work in progress and a resolution to history's miseries that has not yet endured the full test of time, as Brexit highlights, and the United Kingdom resumes once again a separation of identity from the Continent. Similar branded movements have swirled around other member states (e.g., "Swexit" and "Frexit") without the popular strength yet to trigger further exits.

Paradoxically, the second great step that provided the EU with the opportunity to alter the pattern of centuries of historic strife was the collapse of the Berlin Wall and the demise of the Soviet Union. The tumbling of the wall saw a cluster of former Eastern Bloc nations look westward toward the EU for their national destiny, rather than eastward for continued association with the emerging Russian Federation. This made sense, given the economic messaging that came from the West after the fall of the wall. Today, eleven former Communist nations are members of the EU, comprising more than one-third of total EU membership. Five of them are members of the eurozone, and twelve former Eastern Bloc nations are now members of NATO.

The EU is testing these new associations as the second generation of former Eastern Europeans questions in greater numbers the merits of Western economics. The EU has, however, managed a more successful middle way of balancing for its newer Eastern members the economic realities of market-based democracy with their aspirations for national expression. Further East still, those non-EU nations, and especially Russia, have lurched more quickly toward authoritarianism as post-1989 disillusionment with capitalist democracy gained traction amongst the former Communist peoples. Today, Vladimir Putin of Russia stands as the epitome of Eastern leadership in Eurasia, and in Putin we see the clear trend toward the piecemeal picking of ideology, economic diversity, and whimsical political systems built around the concept of a strong figure or single party. How, for example, Polish constitutional nationalism within the EU will compare with Belarussian authoritarianism outside the EU is too early to tell. What we can say is that radical ideology, launched by the Bolsheviks in 1917 and advanced by the Fascists in the 1920s and 1930s, led to an age of entrenched rivalries that dominated the second half of the twentieth century, until the wall fell in 1989. Now the political style of Europe appears postmodern, with greater arbitrariness and fluidity in the public arena and its ideas. This is the 1920s once again, with an explosion of hopes, ideas, and power struggles that were harnessed by democrats and dictators in shaping the future. Their emergence after Versailles saw the birth of ideology and a century of conflict. The extraordinary paradox is thus stated. A nonideological world war gave birth in its conclusion to an ideological world until that world began to crumble in 1989. We thought it was crumbling only in the Soviet Bloc. But, in truth, it is starting to show fault lines in the West today.

Of course, ideology did not lead inexorably or solely to totalitarianism alone in the post-Versailles world. While large swaths of mainland Europe fell under the spell of Fascism, Britain's peculiarity manifested itself yet again in its avoidance of extremes and preference for compromise and the centerground of politics. Drawing on traditional institutions of governance, the British were ready to appropriate emerging notions of Socialism that the trade union movement promoted, after the Second World War. Britain found itself in the unusual situation of being able to look westward toward American capitalism and its free markets as the preferred economic model and also look toward the Continent for labor movement and social democratic principles of organization. In short, politically, this was yet another example of a very peculiar British story. This is not to minimize the presence of nationalism within the UK or the absence of ideological impulses both prior to and after the First World War. The search for Irish independence, for example, had nearly erupted prior to the war, and certainly in 1916 the Easter Uprising showed a determination of Irish nationalist fervor that would resurface four years later in the establishment of the Irish Free State and the start of the Irish Civil War. Only in 1998, with the Good Friday Agreement, did the long and sad history of the "Troubles" become resolved, but even that has been thrown into question by Brexit and the question of the Irish "backstop." If Irish nationalism was a reality in the UK, so, too, did Scotland exhibit similar nationalist fervor in 1913 with the disestablishment of the Church of England and the call for Scottish sovereignty from Westminster. Today, the same calls are loud again, with most Scots broadly desiring continued membership in the EU and fearing a post-Brexit independent United Kingdom.

But British nationalism has always appeared inclusive and paternalistic, not menacing or dominating, and this is what emerged in 1914. For the British sense of the "rights of small nations" was what propelled Britain not into an ideological clash with Germany, but into a moral one, in terms of popular perception. One generation later, with Nazism at Germany's helm, this evolved into both an ideological and moral conflict. It was, though, this 1914 moral persuasion that enabled Britain to create a coalition of commitment from across its union of nations and its empire abroad, erecting, in effect, a tent where many voices, languages, colors, and religions would gather to the British cause in 1914. While the British Empire was not truly democratic, a sense of Britishness united those who fought from across its empire and across its union. This capacity to put aside individual national grievances to come together under the expectation of "For King and Country" was a remarkable achievement. Even in the Easter Uprising of 1916, some Irish nationalist sympathizers saw the Irish purchase of German weapons as treacherous. This explains why, until the Good Friday Agreement, both the Ulster unionists and the Irish nationalists have cherished annually their respective community traditions of commemorating the First Day of the Battle of the Somme on July 1st. On that occasion in 1916, both the 36th Ulster Division unionists and the Irish Rifles from the nationalist counties marched together into the massacre that saw the most casualties in history for the British Army. The First World War thus provided an overarching cause that eclipsed all others. The power of the war to bring together disparate groups under the British flag was indeed extraordinary. In 2020, more than a hundred years after the Somme, an Irish athlete playing on the

British soccer team from the northern city of Huddersfield was verbally abused by the fan crowd for refusing to wear a red poppy on his jersey during Remembrance week in the UK. Such was the legacy that endured across the century and across the partisan Irish divide. Thus Britain, in the First World War, was able to rally not an internally nationalist fervor, but rather a united sentiment against German imperialism and a moral imperative to go to the aid of "five-foot nations" against the German giant.

Later, the sectarian hatred of Ireland was such that each community—loyalist and nationalist—could appropriate the history of the First World War into their own mythologies, such as the Battle of the Boyne of 1690, with the Protestant triumph of William III (Orange) over the deposed Catholic James II. The war was able to put a stop to such nationalist instincts within Britain, but after its conclusion and the Versailles twin principles of self-determination and nationalist rights, the lid was taken off across Europe, and the forces of chaos were unleashed in its wake. Yet Britain's persistence in connecting diverse impulses continued across the twentieth century, even as its empire sought independence and Britain granted its colonies independence in incremental ways that largely avoided the excesses of violence characteristic of the empires of other European nations. The stories of Dutch, Portuguese, and French postimperialism make Britain's postimperial history appear relatively benign and elegant. This capacity to do "both-and" for Britain persisted internally after the second war, with the Labour Party landslide of 1945 and the establishment of the welfare state. This accommodation of capitalism and Socialism was an extraordinary choice, and perhaps feat, for the British people. As Britain celebrates the seventy-fifth anniversary of its National Health Service in 2022, the American public still stands today paralyzed at the prospect of what is oddly deemed "socialized medicine," even as US soaring health care costs and limited public accessibility illustrate a fundamental ideological and pragmatic dilemma. Yet this British "peculiarity" is not without tension. The story of Labour and Conservative, Margaret Thatcher and Tony Blair, and the EU and Brexit are all part of an internal dialectic between capitalism and Socialism that the British tend to sustain as a fluid form of social democracy. These and other British stories also speak to the push-pull of British identity, sovereignty, and unity with peoples across the channel and across the globe. The old claim that the sun never sets on the British Empire no longer applies. Britain's global footprint is smaller today. But the afterglow of that sun continues to shape a British comfort with day and night, with self and other, with capitalism and Socialism, and with Europe and America. This duality led Britain into a war in August 1914 which then triggered a global conflict that has shaped us ever since. Britain also held out as initially the solitary resistor to tyranny in a second war in 1939 that would have delivered the legacy that "might is right" if it had not assumed that role; European stability would have likely been achieved but at the shocking price of absolute tyranny. Ironically, one hundred years later, Germany and Britain alike have been vindicated. Europe needed a core central power of economic strength that would galvanize the Continent, and today that nation is Germany. Bismarck would be pleased with that outcome. And the world needed a corrective force in the struggle for the right kind of European stability, which required a nation that could utilize both levers of engagement and separation throughout the twentieth century to help maintain that equilibrium. Today, that nation still is Britain. The Duke of Wellington, Napoleon's victor, would also be pleased.

One final and essential case of the axiomatic role of ideology in global affairs from 1919 to 1989 is that of the People's Republic of China, perhaps the least understood and most significant of players in our current geopolitics as we approach the second quarter of the twenty-first century. China is likely to emerge shortly as the world's premier superpower, replacing the United States. The US is not yet ready for a silver-medal role, and it is pertinent to wonder how the US will adapt psychologically to its coming relegation of status. The twentieth-century history of China is outside the scope of this book, but three events shed light on how the Chinese story is resonant with broader trends that emerged from the Great War. Firstly,

China's victimization and suffering at the hands of Japan in the 1930s was inextricably connected to Japanese indignation of Western arrogance toward its former World War I ally. Japan's sense of hurt, and its subsequent economic vulnerability resulting from US trade policy in the Pacific, prompted its U-turn away from the democracies and toward the Axis nations of World War II. In short, the First World War dealt Japan a bad deal, and China was punished as a result. Secondly, this in turn set the scene for conditions that led to Mao Tse Tung's Long March to power in 1949 and the absolutism of Marxist-Maoist ideology in shaping one quarter of the world's population, imposing totalitarian oppression in its wake. The Maoist Cultural Revolution had all the hallmarks of Communist totalitarianism, refined in Stalin and replicated in Mao. Ironically, because they had so much in common, China and the Soviet Union detested and feared each other over the decades. Brothers may hate each other, after all. Finally, we now can observe how China has sustained astonishing economic growth and put down populist student protests, most notably in 1989 in Tiananmen Square. This is yet another illustration of the capacity of contemporary governments to be comfortable with "both-and" and not "either-or" strategies. China is, as an example, embracing contrarian notions of economy, government, mores, and strategies that no longer require one dominant or overarching philosophy. In short, China is beginning to behave in the context of its own history as eclectically as Britain has done for a long time, or as Putin's Russia has been doing since the end of the Soviet Union. Now, President Xi Jinping's China appears to be doing something similar, in his one-party, free-enterprise, Communist-oriented, high-tech, culturally collectivist society. Universities in the West often offer "interdisciplinary" studies to students who are not certain of their intellectual passions or what major to study. Developed nations are increasingly practicing interdisciplinary thinking as they seek a way forward in the twenty-first century. And in doing so, they are replicating a contemporary version of the Roaring Twenties from one hundred years ago, when capital was available, albeit in the form of the dollar, where new ideas and nations were springing up, and where dominant advantages were not readily available until the dictators grasped them in the 1930s. We are living now in a new Roaring Twenties. It is exciting. It is unclear. And it is volatile.

In this sense, when Woodrow Wilson embraced the First World War as the opportunity and responsibility of the United States to "make the world safe for democracy," he let the genie out the bottle that has yielded a century illustrating the very reversal of that principle. In 1945, just after the end of the Second World War, the leading British Labour Party minister, Aneurin Bevan, quipped, on considering Wilson's phrase, that it would have been better if "democracy had been made safe for the world."[7] This is the reality of the story of democracy as experienced and retold in the modern era. We see it in the populism that has become such a buzzword to describe the turn of events in the West in shaping both democracies and nondemocracies in ways that traditional institutions struggle to understand or contain. The Trump phenomenon in the United States and the Brexit result in the UK are examples of how traditional ways of doing things in democracies, and the institutions that those traditions have built, have little sense now of how to manage or even comprehend populist sentiment. If democracy implies systems of tested inclusive thought, populism implies an explosion of untested exclusive emotion. Populism, in this sense, is one side of the coin of democracy, oppositional to the side that is about order and governance. It is no accident that the populist movement most current in the United States started as the "Tea Party," appropriating patriotic notions from American history, and uniting them to revolution and independence. But the Tea Party patriots of 1773 were also insurrectionist rebels and terrorists, and democracy continues to struggle with that paradox. How we reconcile these recurrent tensions is the stuff of historic power-making. For centuries, people

---

[7] *Tribune*, 13 July 1945, quoted in John Campbell, *Nye Bevan and the Mirage of British Socialism* (New York: Norton, 1987): 142.

have argued over the French Revolution's call of *liberté, égalité, fraternité* and whether or not they are internally contradictory. The same tension confronts us today in the EU, in Eurasia, in China, and in the US. In 2001, Dani Rodrik, an economics professor at Harvard, developed the "impossibility theorem"[8] to explain our current iteration of the French Revolutionary problem, namely that nation-state, democracy, and global economic integration are mutually exclusive, and that only two of the three can ever coexist. Rodrik may be correct, but no one seems to be listening. Today, we are samplers, ready to appropriate ideas and strategies from around the globe in a fashion akin to dining out at a smorgasbord. Take as much and as many as you will.

Aneurin Bevan's mid-twentieth-century observation about making democracy safe was testament to a different reality, sharpened by the calamity of two world wars that were ostensibly fought in the defense of democracy itself. Yet, Bevan noticed, while democracy has been the great hope of humanity for centuries, it is also a very volatile vision and mission, a sort of tinderbox substance, not simply offering wonderful ideals that speak to all peoples, but carrying more inflammatory impulses too, no matter how much President Woodrow Wilson believed in its efficacy and universalism on April 6th, 1917. Eighty-five years later, another US president, George W. Bush, once again took up Wilson's torch of the hope of democracy, making it the moral rationale behind his "nation building" policy in the 2003 Iraq War. The Fallujah insurgency the next year in response to Bush's intervention illustrated the exact same critique that Wilson's strategy had encountered in the decades of the 1920s and 1930s. The same challenges to democracy are apparent even as we assume that democracy will provide the answers to the questions that had led originally to strife and unrest. We find the same problem, for example, in the much-vaunted Arab Spring of 2011 and the

---

[8] Sam Knight, "What Will Brexit Britain Be Like?" *The New Yorker*, 31 January 2020.

consequent horrendous Syrian Civil War that followed. Less violently, but similarly surprising, we find democracy stirring up dissent, not quelling it, in the present-day United States's radical Trump phenomenon, the United Kingdom's Brexit development, and in Eastern European democracies as they struggle with nationalistic xenophobia. In these and other examples we see something that is messy and distasteful and does not work out how we thought it might or should. We see, in short, the unintended consequences of democracy, or its side effects. If the Greek *demos* is the etymological root of the word "democracy," and *demos* means "crowd," what does it mean when the crowd behaves like a mob? The First World War showed us that it did not lead to an ordered Europe drawn equitably by Allied leaders on a map on the floor of the Versailles Palace, but rather a destabilized Europe arranged tyrannically by panzer divisions crossing international boundaries and crushing human and national aspirations at the behest of a demagogue. And all this was pursued through untold suffering and led once more to global catastrophe in the name of democracy. The task of our century is to find a way both to cherish democracy and yet to recognize and manage its volatility. For a short time, when the Berlin Wall came tumbling down, we who had grown up in the West in the second half of the twentieth century believed that democracy had finally won. Our vision, our ideas, our thoughts, and our worldview had triumphed, so it seemed. In truth, we were pleased with ourselves and forgot the scriptural warning that "pride goeth before a fall." Little did we think that our gift of democracy would become something unfamiliar, suspicious, and uncomfortable in the hands of those to whom it was gifted.

10

A BRAVE NEW WORLD

In 1932, Aldous Huxley published his legendary novel, *Brave New World.*[1] Taking its title from Shakespeare's *The Tempest*, Huxley drew on the play's character Miranda and her ironic observation about human nature:

> How many godly creatures are there here!
> How beauteous mankind is! O brave new world,
> That has such people in't.
> —*The Tempest*, act 5, scene 1[2]

Huxley wrote from his French home during the Great Depression when clouds of conflict were again gathering. Countering the optimism of writers such as H. G. Wells, Huxley feared for humanity's future. He saw stability as the ultimate aspiration of civilization, while the world order of the 1930s threatened chaos. Huxley also believed that core human needs and virtues were being replaced by a growing obsession with technology. In so doing, we risked embracing a naïve view of inevitable progress through ever-increasing and powerful forms of technical knowledge that would, so Huxley considered, leave behind the human individual. Huxley feared people would voluntarily hand over control of humankind's destiny. It was Huxley, not George Orwell, whom Neil Postman viewed as the

---

[1] Aldus Huxley, *Brave New World* (New York: Doubleday, 1932).

[2] William Shakespeare, *The Tempest* (New York: Simon & Schuster, 2009): 203–206.

prophet of our age in his book *Amusing Ourselves to Death*.[3] Interestingly, the late Postman's son, Andrew, wrote in the February 2nd, 2017, edition of *The Guardian*[4] that America's election of President Trump was testimony to a brave new world that his father had written about in his 1985 publication.

In what sense can the emergence of new sciences, technologies, and forms of progress in the twentieth century be positive or negative? For Neil Postman, the epistemological framework that flowed from these changes failed us by promising utopia and delivering dystopia. If, in the first half of the twentieth century, humankind engaged in mass destruction and killing, in the second half, Postman claimed, we were "amusing" ourselves to death through our hedonistic inclinations. This chapter explores the major new developments in the public world that came directly out of the First World War and how they have been available for our disposal, for good or for bad. We have previously seen how the political framework of the twentieth century was refashioned around ideology after Versailles concluded the war. With that change, the axiom of the "rule of the people" became the great quest for meaning in the 1920s and 1930s. While representative politics was shifted seismically by the war, so, too, were extraordinary changes in science and technology that have been absorbed into our contemporary world. In 2020, the United States held a general election which incorporated voting constituencies that only dreamed of emancipation prior to 1918. Those parties and groups heatedly focused debate on numerous cultural issues, including public policies for health and medical access that were only made accessible through the misfortunes of those who fought and were treated in the war. The revolutionary impact of the war on

---

[3] Neil Postman, Amusing Ourselves to Death: Public Discourse in the Age of Show Business (New York: Viking, 1985).

[4] Andrew Postman, "My dad predicted Trump in 1985—it's not Orwell, he warned, it's Brave New World," *The Guardian*, (2 February 2017).

medicine was as rapid as the speed at which war technology evolved in the four years of fighting. For example, Ellen Hampton[5] has noted that in those years, the nature of medical transportation moved from horse and wagon to ambulance, and surgery evolved from the kind reminiscent of the American Civil War to the use of X-rays and anesthesia. The major medical advancements achieved during the war years are evoked by the mnemonic of the "three A's": ambulance, anesthesia, and antiseptic.

In the early weeks of the war, in late summer of 1914, all combatants were shocked by the scale of amputations carried out in field hospitals around the battlefield. By the time the six-day Battle of the Marne concluded in mid-September of that year, just six weeks after initial hostilities had commenced, the French had incurred three hundred thousand casualties. Of that astronomic number, 10 percent underwent amputation. Ironically, 70 percent of these amputations were not the result of direct combat, such as bullet or shrapnel, but were the consequence of the infection of Clostridium perfringens, the bacteria that is commonly known as gangrene. The prevalence of these risks and associated amputations inspired both French field doctors and American medical researchers to explore the emerging science of antiseptic treatment. French doctor Alexis Carrel and British biochemist Henry Dakin, working in conjunction with the Rockefeller Institute for Medical Research in New York, had secured the first use of X-ray technology to assist in treatment for the wounded. In this small example, burgeoning American armaments exports were also shadowed by American medical exports as a result of the First World War. The relationship between the medics at the front and the Rockefeller Institute spurred further research into combat treatments and the identification of what was to become the Carrel-Dakin method of sterilization. This entailed the use of sodium hypochlorite in irrigating open wounds, preventing the growth of the Clostridium bacteria. The speed and scale of these

---

[5] Ellen Hampton, "How World War One Revolutionized Medicine," *The Atlantic* (24 February 2017).

medical enhancements illustrated a general principle of innovation throughout the four years of the war. Namely, that the experiences, resources, and operations relevant to the summer of 1914 were radically different by the time of the Armistice in 1918. The war required radical and immediate improvement for the combatant nations simply to maintain the stalemate, and the logic of the war pushed for immediate inventions to outwit enemy and to sustain comrade.

The massive expansion and advancement of battlefield medical services was thus an immediate response to the start of hostilities, and the need for those services grew exponentially throughout the war's duration. In addition to the battlefield medical units, the role of volunteer organizations was critical in supplying care to the vast numbers of casualties. One of the leading volunteer organizations in the Allied cause was the American Ambulance Hospital, which arrived at the battlefield just one week after war began in August 1914, reviving a role in Europe from forty years earlier in the Franco-Prussian War. In addition to vast care, these medical facilities provided the living laboratories for medical research and experimentation. For example, George Washington Crile, a veteran surgeon of the Spanish-American War and future officer of the US Army, pioneered the first use of nitrous oxide as an anesthetic for battlefield surgery. Additionally, Crile is credited with developing battlefield blood transfusions and the emerging use of sterilization to control the spread of disease. He and his colleagues also developed a vaccine for typhoid just as living conditions in the trench warfare of 1915 became appalling. This ingenuity from both French and American medical services entailed the use of concurrent research and the cojoining of new technologies in medical and nursing care, creating an environment for mass medical innovation at a time when the need grew at an exponential rate because of the conflict. Crile's work is remembered in posterity for him being honored with the naming of both a US Navy ship and a lunar crater from the Apollo expeditions of the 1960s. The paradox in this situation was the diametrical tension between the deterioration of the human condition as the bedrock for the improvement of medical and technical knowledge. As Mary Merritt Crawford, the only female doctor at the American Ambulance Hospital, later noted in her memoirs, "A war benefits medicine more than it does anybody else. In a way the advances in technical and medical knowledge were balanced by human retreat backward into cruelty."[6]

If emergency battlefield medicine advanced in leaps during the four years of the war, so did recuperative care for the returning injured veterans. Indeed, for those who did return, the scars of war were such that lifelong treatment was a reality for millions. The physical scars of war were, of course, visible for the remainder of the victims' lives and were often indescribably shocking reminders of battlefield injuries. Again, the American Ambulance Hospital was instrumental in developing new procedures in the case of maxillofacial surgery for facial reconstruction. These victims, and the returning amputees, were the most visible reminders to the home public for decades to come of the nature and cost of the war. In the 1920s, as Armistice Day parades became annual events to remember the dead, the images overwhelmingly recorded wounded veterans with awful scars and missing limbs being wheeled or walking with crutches along the routes. The scale of this can be deduced from the example of Australia, part of the British Empire at the time. One hundred and sixty thousand physically wounded veterans returned to Australia after the war. Of these, thirty-seven thousand underwent maxillofacial surgery to repair or hide head wounds. These numbers are staggering, especially when considered in the context of the overall Australian commitment to the war. Three hundred and fifty thousand Australians had served overseas, and sixty-five thousand had been killed. In short, nearly three times the number of dead returned as veterans with major physical injuries, about one in two of the total overseas Australian commitment. Such was the scale of injury that the need for medical and surgical innovation was ever-present.

---

[6] Ibid.

And then there were the insidious injuries sustained psychologically and emotionally that were not visible to the public yet haunted the lives of the veterans and their families privately. The term "shell shock" had been popularized during the war after first being used by a British doctor, Charles Myers, in 1917. Shell shock, or "war neurosis,"[7] as the psychiatric establishment began to term the condition, referred to the utter nervous collapse, physical dysfunction, behavioral incapacity, and terrifying fear that descended on hundreds of thousands of trench fighters who experienced the trauma of artillery barrage. This was a natural response to a fatal threat. Of the ten million dead, the Smithsonian Museum estimates that 60 percent of fatalities were the result of artillery actions. Yet, paradoxically, it was observed over time that victims were not limited solely to those under barrage but evident as a much broader condition affecting soldiers across the battlefields and in various combat roles. Indeed, by 1916 it is estimated that more than 40 percent of men in the fighting zones were experiencing some kind of "war neurosis." Certainly, by the time of the Armistice, more than eighty thousand British Army servicemen had passed through medical facilities for treatment of the condition, and it was becoming evident that the condition was not simply a physical consequence of extreme stress under barrage.

Psychiatric institutions across Britain expanded in response to the onset of this phenomenon, twenty of which were established by the end of the war. Yet while the medical establishment slowly began to consider how to support these victims, within broader society, they were often ignored or treated with disdain. The confusing and distressing nature of the condition prompted as much avoidance as compassion in the public mindset and even accusations of cowardice from some in both military and civilian circles. The agony of the condition and an emerging perspective on the pointlessness of the war inspired the war poet and decorated officer Siegfried Sassoon to

---

[7] "Shell Shock," *BBC History Magazine* (3 March 2004).

pen his poem "Survivors,"[8] which powerfully laments the terror of the victims. Sassoon himself was removed from the front and convalesced for shell shock, first at Oxford and then at Craiglockhart War Hospital in Scotland. His case well reflects the political dimension to the escalation of the condition and the public response. By 1917, Sassoon's perspective on the war was evolving into an ambiguous one, including opposition to the scale of its death and suffering. This ambivalence, combined with his stature as a poet and mental health patient, meant that military authorities began to doubt the commitment to the war of many shell shock victims. In his poem "Survivors," Sassoon's ambiguity and cynicism are evident:

No doubt they'll soon get well; the shock and strain
Have caused their stammering, disconnected talk....
They'll soon forget their haunted nights; their cowed
Subjection to the ghosts of friends who died,
Their dreams that drip with murder.

Sassoon's experience provides an example of the phenomenon in which officers suffered from the effects of shell shock more than ordinary soldiers, perhaps a reflection on the British cultural expectation that officers would "show the stiff upper lip" to their men, meaning repress their emotions. Such repression, in turn, would lead to a vicious cycle of increasing the damage and duration of the condition. The same cultural norm also had an effect on the treatment techniques of most psychiatric establishments, which replicated techniques of behavioral modification more commonly associated with prisons rather than hospitals. Consequently, solitary confinement, disciplinary measures, and emotional deprivation were as common therapeutic methodologies as more humane treatments of rest, improved diet, and physical recreation. The most famous exception, noted for its revolutionary methods based on compassion

---

[8] Siegfried Sassoon, "Survivors," *Counter-Attack and Other Poems*, 1918, The First World War Poetry Digital Archive.

and therapy, was at the Abbott's Seale psychiatric institution in Devon, where former army major Arthur Hurst pioneered humane methods that produced very successful outcomes in a short time. He even reconstructed the Flanders battlefields on the Devonshire moors to enable his patients to relive war experiences but with different outcomes. Unfortunately, Hurst's more humanistic approach to the treatment of shell shock victims was the exception to the rule, rather than the norm of the medical establishment.

Sassoon's own experience of the war and his psychiatric treatment at Craiglockhart, which modeled the traditional disciplinary approach, were superbly retold in a trilogy[9] written by novelist Pat Barker in the 1990s. Of course, Barker was writing at a time when we had another term for "shell shock" that the American Psychiatric Association approved in 1980: post-traumatic stress disorder, or PTSD. Reviewing the case files of Vietnam veterans from the 1960s and 1970s, the APA had concluded that the soldiers' symptoms were consequential to their war experience and revealed as many as seventeen symptoms, each consistent with the behaviors evident three generations earlier in the First World War. Alarmingly, the APA also concluded that up to 10 percent of the civilian population experience PTSD from nonmilitary trauma causes, including assault and abuse. The phenomenon of PTSD has, of course, occurred throughout human history, but its mass appearance was in the First World War, and it has been universally acknowledged ever since. On a personal note, my maternal grandfather undoubtedly exhibited undiagnosed PTSD symptoms, like millions of other war veterans, which, in his case, manifested as lifelong traumatic nightmares of battlefield death after his experience as a veteran infantryman of the London Rifles. He regularly experienced, as Sassoon put it, "dreams that drip with murder." Today, the US Department of Veterans Affairs estimates that up to 20 percent of US combat forces return with symptoms of PTSD, and such a number, if accurate, suggests that

---

[9] Pat Barker, Regeneration; The Eye in the Door; The Ghost Road.

the scale of the problem in the First World War was infinitely greater than the official numbers of registered patients.

For those who did not suffer PTSD or physical injury, the war still left its mark on the lives of the returning veterans. Economists estimate that 80 percent of the unemployed in the 1920s were veterans from the combatant nations, including the German former corporal Adolf Hitler. The economic vulnerability and loss were to some extent compensated for by the emergence of new networks and organizations to provide a framework for rehabilitation into civilian life. France particularly took the lead in forming as early as 1921 "The Union of Disfigured Men," which evolved over the next seven years into a veterans' association with places of refuge, recuperation, and socialization in wealthy chateaux throughout the country. This awareness of the scale of injury and need for radical structures illustrated just how much World War I was the arena where suffering and loss was truly democratized. As noted earlier, the officer classes were as susceptible to death, injury, and trauma as the working-class recruits, and, indeed, many of the poorer British were rejected from service as being unfit while their aristocratic countrymen were expected to take the lead. Up to 35 percent of British volunteers, primarily from working neighborhoods, never entered military service because of poor health. The same war, however, threw aristocracy and monarchy into the fray. The late Queen Mother, mother of the current monarch Elizabeth II, lost her own uncle at the Battle of Loos in 1915, a loss that grieved her apparently for life.

The war's atrocities brought on technological advances alongside new medical achievements. The technology that defined the First World War and the scale of destruction it could inflict reveal that the pace of change and knowledge was exponential during the four years of conflict. Aviation provided one the best examples of this principle of acceleration. Aircraft flight was born with the Wright brothers in 1903 at Kitty Hawk in North Carolina. Yet in the next decade, the progress of flight beyond that seminal event had been minimal. The type of available aircraft in 1914 illustrates the slow development and basic nature of flight warfare. In 1914, the need for military aircraft was new, and its primary use was for reconnaissance. Combat between airmen was occasional and crude in 1914, with pilots using grenades and revolvers in their sparring. By 1918, however, more than 220 sophisticated types of aircraft were in use, with synchronized machine guns and bombs incorporated into aircraft and zeppelins capable of long-distance bombing raids. This development was unthinkable in the spring of 1914. As well as flight itself, the accompanying engineering developments were revolutionary. The invention by the Dutch engineer Antony Fokker of the interrupter gear mechanism in 1916 meant that machine guns and propellers could be synchronized. This heralded a whole new lease of deadly air power in the Fokker series of German aircraft, which aided powerfully the German war effort in the skies. Prior to that invention, pilots often shot their own propellers to pieces in combat duels. As engineering developed, so did speed. In 1914, the maximum speed of the German fighters the Rumpler Taube and the Albatross B.II were both under sixty-five miles per hour. By the end of the war, the British Sopwith Dragon could achieve a speed of 150 miles per hour. Today's Joint Surveillance and Target Attack Radar System (JSTARS) in the US Air Force and the capabilities of orbiting satellites for ground-based military strategy find their roots in the game-changing role of crude and simple reconnaissance aircraft created four generations ago for the same military ends.

Air technology also advanced in other ways than simply fighter combat. Today's air traffic control originated during the war with the development of two-way radios in the US that were then utilized for military purposes after the United States entered the conflict. By 1917, air-to-ground communication had been established, effectively permitting live data for reconnaissance purposes and the coordination of air-ground strategy. Similarly, the use of UAVs (unmanned aerial vehicles), a staple of today's military strategy, originated with the development of a drone by the US Navy in 1916, which was improved upon sufficiently enough to be used as an early "flying bomb" toward the end of the war in 1918. Hitler's continuation of this aerial strategy achieved its most famous history in the

V-1 and V-2 "flying bombs" of World War II, used in the London Blitz. And, finally, in the canon of aviation innovation, the British Navy's development of the aircraft carrier is essential: in 1917, the navy initiated the takeoff and landing of aircraft onto the deck of the *HMS Furious* once the ship's enormous eighteen-inch (caliber) guns were removed.

This combination of technological advancement and the integration of military tools was evident in the extraordinary development of naval and sea-based warfare. Although submarines find their most basic origins in the American Civil War, the 1914–1918 War prompted massive advancements in naval and submarine technology. The irony is that essentially the naval element of the First World War was mainly limited to a British blockade of German ports to starve the German war effort of matériel and the German people of food. That irony is even larger given that the origins of the First World War find tangible roots in Britain's fear of the growing might of the Germany Navy. Yet actual naval battles in the war were rare, with their names memorable solely because there were so few: Heligoland Bight, Jutland, Dardanelles, and Dogger Bank are part of British cultural memory due to their uncommonness. The German U-Boat development was of greater impact, and certainly of greater potential, given the extraordinary role and effectiveness of German submarine warfare in the early part of the Second World War. In the first war, the U-Boat was a lethal new element of warfare, and its introduction prompted similar technologies in the invention of both depth charges and hydrophones to counter their effectiveness. By early 1916, they effectively countered the German submarine threat to military and merchant shipping, and U-68 achieved unfortunate fame as the first submarine sunk by depth charges that spring.

In this sense, the First World War introduced new technologies on a limited scale that later were developed and utilized on a massive scale for the remainder of the century, and they still shape conventional warfare strategy today. For example, the greatest tank battle

162

in human history—the month-long Battle of Kursk between German and Soviet forces in World War II—involved the use of more than ten thousand tanks. This occurred less than thirty years after the first introduction of the tank as a weapon at the Battle of Somme in 1916 (which was largely symbolic rather than effective) and then its first-ever use strategically at Cambrai a year later. The British Mark I and II tanks and the French Renault FT tank were not ultimately game-changers in the First World War. In the case of the British tanks, more crew died of carbon monoxide poisoning from inadequate ventilation in the tanks than from actual combat. But by the end of the war, the potential of this instrument, like that of the U-boat, was immediately recognized to the extent that the French led their victory parade in Paris after the Armistice with their FT tanks. This was in recognition that the three thousand FT tanks produced in total for the war effort had been acclaimed as the "victory" tanks by American soldiers, who, in 1918, saw their potential to alter dramatically the course of battle.

The rapid advance of technology and weaponry that characterized the twentieth century was to a considerable extent initiated in the First World War. Its combatants were completely unprepared for the military technologies that utilized their deadly experience as a laboratory for refining advances in technical and medical knowledge. The indiscriminate use of poison gas, inaugurated on April 22nd, 1915, at Ypres, Belgium, was an example of a new mindset of cruelty and a new knowledge of delivery that still resonates today after a century of mass annihilation. The memorial today at the site near Ypres where the Germans released 150 tons of chlorine gas from more than six hundred canisters poignantly identifies all the ensuing uses of chemical warfare across the century, up to and including the recent Syrian civil war. Whether in the form of flamethrowers or tracer bullets or shrapnel bombs or chemical bombs, the "war to end all wars" was, in fact, the war to define all warfare henceforth, certainly in the spirit of total war that the new technologies permitted. The costliest battle of the war, the Battle of Verdun, was predicated by the German general Falkenhayn on the premise that he could "bleed France white," according to his memoirs. The three quarters of a million casualties in the battle are testimony to the effects of combining an ancient human attitude of hatred to a contemporary technological creativity; the resulting obliteration was total in a war that started without clear reason or ideological contest.

The scale of the war provided equally the context for economic and technological advancement that today accounts for the United States' superpower status, even as China appears poised to share that position. In his final speech as president, Dwight D. Eisenhower warned, in January 1961, of the dangers to democracy of the "military-industrial complex." For Eisenhower, the connection between the instincts of the military apparatus and the logic of capitalism was a deeply troubling relationship. As a veteran of the First World War and the supreme allied commander of the second one, the warning was both ironic and noteworthy. What Eisenhower alerted the world to has largely fallen on deaf ears over the decades. The military-industrial complex continues to fuel vast sums of profits procured in the developments of huge arsenals of military equipment, with the US far outspending any international rivals. Estimates place the current level of global annual spending on the military and its armaments at about $1.75 trillion, with the United States accounting for 37 percent of that figure. The origins of this vast economic model can be found in World War I. By late 1910, leading industrialists in the US had convened in secret on Jekyll Island off the Georgia coast to discuss terms for establishing a federal reserve that could guide and sustain the banking and finance system. By the spring of 1918, the United States Federal Reserve was successfully fundraising ten billion dollars (or approximately $175 billion in today's value) in war bonds from the public to fund US involvement and to continue to export matériel to Europe. By enabling the public to purchase thousand-dollar bonds at heavily discounted interest rates from banks, the money circle from funding to fighting was ensured. Coupled with the earlier "neutrality dividend" that the war had delivered the US by manufacturing, exporting, and loan-financing huge arsenals to the fighting nations, the military-industrial complex was truly unleashed and American capital guaranteed as the primary funding source in international armaments for the next one hundred years.

The United States' emergence as the world's dominant economic and military superpower was thus no accident of the twentieth century. It was, rather, a direct consequence of its engagement in the First World War: firstly, as supplier and secondly, as participant. At a cost of vast human loss and suffering, a brave new world of economic dominance, military advancement, medical progression, and technological innovation was created. These advances were, of course, not siloed from other massive social changes noted earlier that the war yielded for future generations. Whether in the emancipation of women through the suffragette movement or the slow and tortured journey to civil rights or the rise of the trade union movement, new realities for public life and governance were created by the massive changes experienced both at home and in the battlefronts in the years 1914 to 1918. In this respect, the war dividend was the "rule of the people" in both the democracies and the dictatorships, though that principle was only capable of flourishing where democracy was sustained. This new sense of popular participation had precedence in earlier centuries. The industrial revolution had already reshaped the way people lived, and the earth on which they lived, for more than two hundred years. But in the democracies, the radical realignment of governments around participatory principles received unparalleled energy as a result of the First World War. The old hierarchical world order could not be put back together, and new forces emerged that would indeed shape our century and subsequent generations. America's first black president, the exploration of space, female political leadership in Europe, the birth of the digital revolution, the emergence of social democracy, the European Union, health care provision for most of humankind, and the nuclear age— these and countless other examples remind us how indebted we are, both for good and bad, to the generation of our great-grandparents, whose expectations and experiences were radically reframed after their world became undone in the summer of 1914.

The First World War thus presents us with the paradox that WWI physician Mary Merritt Crawford astutely observed: the more human behavior retreated backward into cruelty and destruction, the more human knowledge advanced. In medicine, science, technology, and the military-industrial complex, the Great War could be measured as "great" not only in terms of the scale of human strife, but also in terms of the scale of human knowledge. This links us and our lives very powerfully to our fourth-generation ancestors. The century that divides us from them is on the one hand both a vast gulf and at the same time a thin veneer. In his extraordinary documentary film *They Shall Not Grow Old*[10], the filmmaker Peter Jackson digitized, colorized, and inserted voices into original black-and-white moving images from the war. Overlaid onto the visual images, he also included the accounts of British veterans who were interviewed in the 1960s. The finished documentary is superlative and a testimony to how much the motion picture industry owes its origins to the war years. Intriguingly, one of Jackson's veteran voiceovers remarks on how much the war changed during its four-year course. He recalls in the film how the war became unrecognizable from its beginning to its end, and that if a soldier somehow escaped participation during much of its course but reappeared at the end, he would think he had returned to a different conflict. This principle applies to us as well when we examine the scale of change of the past century, and yet connectivity and continuity unite us across the generations.

In this sense, our fourth-generation ancestors bequeathed to the future a legacy that recklessly continued along a pathway of conflict and global division. But this inheritance included a silver lining to that dark cloud in the form of huge advances in knowledge, science, and technology, available equally for good or evil—the best of times

---

[10] Peter Jackson, director. *They Shall Not Grow Old*, Warner Brothers, 2018.

and the worst of times, as Dickens remarked. The First World War was the crucible that molded a future for humanity that has emerged over four generations, and the nature and scale of the war allowed for both our better angels and our worst demons to cohabit our century. The scale of suffering caused its survivors universally to believe it would be "the war to end all wars," delivering a brave new world for humankind, even as it pushed history onto a trajectory of new conflicts at varying levels. This binary dynamic of the war shows that its forces reaped extraordinary misfortune upon successive generations and yet also produced advances in human knowledge that would change forever the lives of those future generations. This is the paradox of the war. Certainly, the dark side of the human condition is a manifestation of the First World War that left it hard to explain and mesmerizing to observe. That, to some extent, explains the wild confusion and then ideological fanaticism that characterized the decades after its conclusion. But it is surely also paradoxical that the First World War gave us our familiar world today, the one that we embrace as valuable and beneficial. In this sense, our fourth-generation ancestors experienced a war that required them to be brave—even reckless—and then delivered to them a brave new world. The century we inherited continues to deliver those binary forces, those human conditions of both opportunity and destruction that we still observe and reframe in our world today. And for those millions who did not survive that apocalyptic moment of history in the years 1914 to 1918? How they speak to us across the century, and what messages we tell ourselves about their passing, is another enormous clue to our generation's understanding of the significance of the First World War.

PART THREE

CONSCIENCE

CHAPTER 11

KNOWN UNTO GOD

After the Battle of Waterloo in 1815, British dentists visited the battlefield to exhume the dead and remove their teeth in order to supply dentures to their living patients back in London. While the Great War one hundred years after Waterloo may have treated its combatants often with scant regard, it did, thankfully, reserve a much grander posterity for its dead in the extraordinary monuments erected throughout Europe and the world to memorialize that vast loss of life. Since that time, the inanimate stone and marble memorials across the world have stood as symbolic statements for future generations. They have prompted reflection on the meaning of the war across the decades, providing successive generations the opportunity to see in them their own perspectives, emotions, and narratives. In this respect, these elegant memorials are akin to mirrors for the living as well as testimonies to the dead, prompting as much reflection on the present as insight into the past. The First World War has lived on for one hundred years in much of what we take for granted in our lives, and in much of how we make sense of the story of our lives. This is David Reynolds's "long shadow"[1] of the war across the century. But the metaphor of light and dark also works in another way, for the memorials of the First World War have also illuminated how each generation has perceived the nature and meaning of the war. The First World War indeed cast a shadow, but its grand and numerous memorials have also cast light on the war's significance to each subsequent generation, even unto today's

---

[1] See also chapters 1 and 8.

fourth generation. What clues do we find to how we perceive our lives and times in these vast edifices?

Perhaps most importantly, the monuments to the war dead have served multiple purposes across the decades and have enabled successive generations and nations to project onto them their own stories. This was partly their intent, powerfully captured in perhaps the most famous of all Allied war memorials, the Cenotaph in London's Whitehall, which then inspired those in other Commonwealth countries. The Cenotaph is dramatized still every Remembrance Sunday in November with a service of commemoration, military parade, and royal wreath laying, in the same fashion as that inaugurated on November 11th, 1920, by King George V. Sir Edward Lutyens, designer of many memorials, constructed the Cenotaph with simplicity, elegance, and invitation. Its brief inscribed words pay homage to "The Glorious Dead." Otherwise, its dimensions suggest a large, stone, vertical oblong—like a coffin—onto which the observer can project any thought or idea. In short, the Cenotaph was designed to allow the observer to inscribe mentally any thought and emotion onto its structure.

In this sense, each generation could write anew its understanding of the meaning of the memorial and the war that it memorialized. Sometimes, such a process was alarming. A discomforting and jarring example of the capacity to contemporize edifices according to the observer occurred infamously with the awe-inspiring Canadian memorial at Vimy Ridge in France, built to honor Canada's dead. The Canadians chose the design of the Vimy Ridge memorial through a competition, in the autumn of 1920, to honor the sixty-six thousand fallen Canadians of the war, some one in ten of its fighting soldiers. One hundred and sixty architects competed, and the winning design was awarded to Walter Seymour Allward. The vast and splendid memorial is located on a prominent ridge in the Somme region, site of the successful Canadian assault on Easter Monday of 1917. The massive construction, with twin pillars soaring hundreds of feet and surrounded by twenty statues, is visible from thirty miles away on the plain. A huge statue of a bereft Lady

Canada stands alongside the towers, and at the base of the memorial a brief inscription dedicates the memorial on behalf of all Canadians "to the valour of their countrymen in the Great War." It was finally completed in 1936 and immediately became a global emblem of the stature and magnificence of the memorials that were trying to give appropriate homage and respect to the scale of loss of the war.

Yet just four years later, after the fall of France in June 1940, an eager Adolf Hitler brought a Nazi-state entourage to view the Vimy Ridge memorial, perversely hijacking it for his own National Socialist cause. His visit to a memorial dedicated to a former adversary was not out of respect or defiance. Instead, Hitler saw in it a message for the Third Reich, standing as a magnificent example of grandeur that the Thousand-Year Reich should emulate in Berlin and across its conquered nations. It was, for Hitler and the Nazis, an inspiration of transcendence, permanence, and might and would be a fitting example of the stature of the Reich for the next millennium. Hitler was so enamored by the Vimy Ridge memorial that he instructed Nazi architects to study it and commanded that no desecration would be permitted. Other, smaller memorials around the Ypres salient did not enjoy such respect, with German troops regularly machine-gunning them as they passed by in armored vehicles in the Second World War.

The example of Hitler's appropriation of the Vimy edifice for purposes of his fanatical European strategy is idiosyncratic but instructive of the broader permeable meaning of an impermeable object such as a stone memorial. This phenomenon is enhanced when the experience being memorialized is of such vast scale, breadth, and depth of pain. That vastness needs to incorporated into the purposes of the memorials in their original context. Our ancestors from four generations earlier faced an extraordinary challenge in the years following the war—the challenge of making sense of the past and giving expression to the future. In so doing, their primary need was to provide justification for the war. Whatever Woodrow Wilson's claims about making the world safe for democracy, the lingering experience of the outcome was not one of heroism, but one of an uneasy doubt and shame. The evidence is strong that the war left the world with a redemptive hope of it being "the war to end all wars." Only in so doing could it be justified. Part of that justification inspired the desire to honor the dead in permanent grand memorials as atonement for the loss inflicted upon the millions of casualties and their loved ones.

This recognition of the need to honor the dead had already emerged during the war. An officer of the British Red Cross, Major General Fabian Ware, was a key figure as early as 1915 in recording the locations and identities of fallen British and empire soldiers. This was the genesis of what is today the Commonwealth Graves Commission, then the Imperial War Graves Commission, responsible for maintaining the cemeteries of British and Commonwealth soldiers around the world. Major decisions were made that provided the literal groundwork for the future memorials and cemeteries of the First World War and subsequent conflicts. Firstly, and most controversially for the families at home, the decision was made that repatriation of the dead was not possible and that the fallen would rest close to the site of their death. This, in turn, led to the evolution of military cemeteries, where crude battlefield graves would be replaced in the years after the war by serene and elegant cemeteries across Europe. These cemeteries held the remains of the dead from various nearby sectors to restrict the range and number of individual cemeteries. Nonetheless, throughout Flanders one still finds numerous roadside cemeteries that might host fewer than one hundred graves, such as that for the 153 men of the Devonshires who fell together on the first day of the Battle of the Somme and are buried together in their own small cemetery. The largest British cemetery in the world is Tyne Cot Cemetery, in the Ypres salient, which holds more than twelve thousand graves and has a recently renovated museum that reads aloud on a looped recording the individual names of every soldier lying there.

The nature of the war and its duration had ensured that vast numbers of combatants were simply MIA (missing in action) or had simply disappeared. A tiny element of those were deserters, who were summarily court-martialed and executed, but the real MIA from the First World War were the hundreds of thousands of vanished men, transformed either into dust or body parts from artillery barrage, or absent through sinking into the vast fields of mud. Where corpses were still relatively intact, identification in many cases was nonetheless impossible since items such as dog tags or personal effects were often obliterated in battle. Thus, for many soldiers, their lives ended violently, anonymously, and without location, and for their bereaved families, their loved one disappeared without a trace. The scale of this absence phenomenon was shocking. Of the thirty-eight million casualties of World War I, approximately 20 percent were missing in action, a staggering 7.75 million. Of that terrifying number, there were millions who were buried in a grave, but without identification. Demographers use the term "lost generation" for those who came to adulthood during or after the First World War, referring to a generation of disillusioned and hedonistic skeptics who were born in the two decades prior to the twentieth century, characterized forever in such figures as Ernest Hemingway and F. Scott Fitzgerald. But the title of "lost generation" is befitting not only for the survivors of the war who had to make peace with the future, but also for the millions of men who literally disappeared in the horrors of the battlefields. The British Empire alone lost 212,000 men without trace. Reckoning with the scale and uniqueness of this phenomenon represented a new ontological reality within human experience and forced those who were struggling to find a strategy for honoring the dead to come to terms with not only the war's pain and agony, but also its nihilism and oblivion.

The solution was found in new language and customs that instead of ignoring this huge vacuum, elevated it to cosmic scale and prized it within deep national symbols. The Imperial War Graves Commission had already determined that the graves and their tombstones would not distinguish between officers and enlisted men. This leveling of the status of the dead provided a means for giving an identity to every unidentified corpse or missing person, which was the genius product of author and poet Rudyard Kipling. Kipling drew on his own existential anguish to offer an enduring poeticism and poignancy that captivated the bereaved. Having lost his own son, John, without trace at the Battle of Loos in September 1915, Kipling spent the next five years in desperate denial of his demise and continued searching for his son in the vain hope that he was a prisoner of war. Kipling had shifted his position on the war from jingoism to cynicism as a result of this loss. In 1917, while working for the Imperial War Graves Commission, Kipling chose the sentence that was to become engraved on 212,000 tombstones and forever replace the nihilism of loss with the hope of heaven:

A SOLDIER OF THE GREAT WAR
KNOWN UNTO GOD

The engraving put the first part of the sentence at the top of the stone, usually above a cross. Below the cross the concluding phrase "Known Unto God" was inscribed. As a poet, the potency of this decision was not lost on Kipling. Firstly, it captured well the pathos and hope of the bereaved, and secondly, it allowed for the loss and absence to be sublimated into an eternal spiritual presence and home. This was intended to comfort the bereaved who lived with the terrible sense of a truly "lost" loved one, providing them with a tangible reference point and marked space. The individual solace afforded by the "Known Unto God" motif also provided the framework for national stories and traditions that emerged quickly in the years after the war. In seeking a reassuring replacement for the nihilistic vacuum of the vanished millions, nations were able to orchestrate symbols of permanent honor in the shrines and tombs of the unknown soldier each created in the 1920s, employing elaborate procedures to ensure that a truly unidentifiable corpse was laid to rest in stately splendor as the physical embodiment of national loss. So, in the early 1920s, at the Arc de Triomphe, at Westminster Abbey, and at Arlington National Cemetery, the Allies enshrined their anonymous losses and translated those into a perpetual focal point in the emblem of a national tomb encasing an unidentifiable corpse from the First World War. The Tomb of the Unknown Soldier (or Unknown Warrior in Britain) captured the essence of national identity and provided a mirror across the generations for reflection on the tragic grandeur experienced by each nation. In terms of the selection of the corpse, two issues were of fundamental importance before the Tomb of the Unknown Soldier could be ceremonially unveiled to the world. Firstly, it was essential that the corpse unambiguously was a soldier of that specific nation, confirmed either by fragments from its uniform or through some other national identifying artifact. Secondly, the final selection of the corpse as the entombed "unknown" involved various elaborate methodologies, ensuring the soldier could never be individually identified. The concept of the Tomb of the Unknown Soldier was fitting and moving for its times, but impossible for consideration in today's world of DNA testing.

Several vast monuments from the First World War are uniquely powerful in expressing this polarity of anonymity and identity, especially when physical remains could not be found for those listed on military-service rosters. In this vacuum, the Allies built pantheon-like mausoleums to give transcendent meaning to the enormity of earthly loss. The battlefields of the Western Front were the primary killing fields of the war, and both the British and French erected these empty mausoleums directly on the fields where their hundreds of thousands had vanished. For the British, the five great battles around Ypres, from 1914 to 1918, and the Battle of the Somme, in 1916, were the chosen settings. The ancient Flemish city of Ypres, for centuries the heart of the wealthy Flemish wool trade, was reduced to rubble as it exchanged hands repeatedly between British and German armies during the war. Located in a salient, a promontory of land surrounded on three sides, it was the perfect target for artillery batteries that were placed in low lying ridges on each side, just a few miles from the city center. Yet after the war, without waiting for any official authorization, the citizens of Ypres rebuilt and restored the city to its former splendor, using the original bricks and stones that lay around as rubble. By the late 1920s, Ypres was again a medieval gem thanks to its people, a splendor that thankfully survived the Second World War.

As the city of Ypres was being restored, the British built a massive neoclassical arched memorial on the ramparts of the medieval wall by the canal. Straddling the main road out of the city center to the town of Menin, the Menin Gate Memorial of red brick and stone opened in July 1927, with monarchy and dignitaries of the Allied cause in attendance. Most powerfully and significantly, the Menin Gate's walls and ceilings are covered with the names of fifty-four thousand missing British soldiers, the inscription by Kipling on the top of the arch reading: "To the Armies of the British Empire Who Stood Here from 1914 to 1918 and to Those of Their Dead Who Have No Known Grave."

Here is the clue to the Menin Gate's power: it reassembled the motif of "Known Unto God" that had been used for individual, unidentifiable corpses into a vast army of the lost on a grandiose, almost cosmic, scale. "Known Unto God" referred to an enormous, transcendent collective as well as lost unnamed individuals. Additionally, in placing the Triumphal Arch of the monument over the road (like Marble Arch in London or the Arc de Triomphe in Paris), the architect Sir Reginald Blomfield achieved the effect that all living travelers along that Menin road thereafter had to pass literally within the midst of the lost collective, surrounded by the names of an army of missing people whose identities shrouded the traveler on their way. This theme was so powerful that one hundred years later it was resurrected in an extraordinary war centennial commemoration in which silhouettes of individual soldiers, both in small transparent plastic models and in full-scale six-foot black metal outlines, were placed all around the British countryside in all sorts of public places, with the commemoration title "There But Not There." In commemorating the centennial, the British charity dedicated to veterans' rehabilitation, "Walking with the Wounded," had, in 2014 to 2018, used these "ghost soldiers" as mementos and fundraisers. On my work desk stands one of these twelve-inch plastic silhouettes. Its smallness works evocatively in the same way as does, conversely, the vastness of the Menin Gate Memorial. These memorials allow the contemporary observer to perceive the lost person, but it is his absence, not his presence, that is standing beside you. He is a "ghost soldier" whose absence haunts the ongoing generations as they seek to make sense of his loss and that of millions of other "unknowns" earlier in time.

The Menin Gate concept was replicated on the Somme battlefield five years later in 1932, but there the massive Thiepval Memorial did not straddle a road, but the murderous fields themselves. Built as a series of interconnecting arches increasing in proportionate size, and finally reaching a single tower at the summit, this enormous construction stands over 150 feet above the ground and is visible from miles around the Somme region. The Thiepval Memorial was an Anglo-French project, but its Portland stone tablets only record the names of the missing soldiers from the British Empire. It has none of the poetics of a Kipling poem in its epitaph, but instead has large chiseled capital letters engraved on the two supporting towers beneath the apex tower. High on the left tower, the observer reads: "THE MISSING." On the right tower, the phrase concludes, "OF THE SOMME." Underneath that startling and blunt heading, the names of more than seventy-two thousand missing of the British Empire were engraved on the inside and outside of the arches, including that of Major Cedric Charles Dickens, grandson of the classical author. Thiepval was, like the Cenotaph in London, an architectural product of Sir Edward Lutyens. The earlier Cenotaph, dedicated just two years after Armistice to "The Glorious Dead," had offered the living an empty tomb or blank slate, a tabula rasa, onto which the bereaved could symbolically project their memory and emotion onto an empty space. The Thiepval Memorial, dedicated twelve years after that of the Cenotaph and sixteen years and one month exactly after the infamous first day of the 1916 Battle of the Somme, sought a different purpose and role for the observer and mourner. For at Thiepval, the bereaved placed themselves directly into the hollow of a vast empty space, almost a cathedral-like nave, with tens of thousands of named dead surrounding the mourner-observer on all sides, as if calling from heaven or pleading from hell. The scale of Thiepval is figuratively and literally cosmic, and as such, the loss, shame, and guilt of those beholding it is overwhelming. The construction of such a monument was possible only after the horrors of the war had sunk deep into global consciousness and wonderment. The modest Cenotaph in 1920 quietly whispered to the mourners, beckoning their silent projections of pained memories. The towering Thiepval Memorial in 1932 brought heaven down to earth and shouted accusingly the names of tens of thousands of individuals to the guilty living. The Lost Generation of the 1920s was thus held to account on the Somme battlefield at the Thiepval Memorial by the lost army that had disappeared under their feet into the soil without trace.

The battles of the Somme and Verdun were linked militarily in 1916. The Somme was a desperate Allied attempt to relieve pressure on the French at Verdun. The enormity of the human loss in both battles produced, both for the British (the Somme) and the French (Verdun), an unknown scale of loss and with that enduring symbols in their remembrance. The symbolic constructions at Thiepval and Verdun were designed to express a national message and catharsis for the living and pull subsequent generations back into some reflection on the meaning of the events for the future. The British chose Thiepval to bring the observer inside a vast chasm of the names of the missing, its architecture resembling clasped hands and yearning gazes reaching and looking heavenward. Sublimation of history was the goal of Thiepval, so that the missing persons were only lost names to us here on earth but were known souls unto God. For the French, a different intent motivated the unparalleled and terrifying Douaumont Ossuary that was the monument to the Battle of Verdun and its one quarter of a million dead and three quarter of a million casualties. The German general Erich von Falkenhayn intended his army's siege of Verdun as a humiliating repetition of France's decisive defeat at nearby Sedan in 1870 in the Franco-Prussian War. To avoid a repeat of history, Falkenhayn calculated the French would defend Verdun to the last man, knowing the Germans had the opportunity "to bleed France white," as his memoirs recounted.

The siege of Verdun ran almost the entire year of 1916, with the Germans failing to capture the fortress town, but with one million souls on all sides forever removed from the battlefield. As Thiepval was opened in 1932, so was the Douaumont Ossuary. Unlike Thiepval, its lure was not upward but downward, almost into a cosmic-scale coffin, where individual and national identity disappeared in a vast hellish underground chasm. The Douaumont Ossuary contains the visible mixed skeletal remains of more than 250,000 French and German soldiers. The random bones of former adversaries are today jumbled together as skeletal reminders of the anonymity of death in the First World War. The tower above resembles a vast bullet or shell, aimed heavenward, not like clasped hands in prayer, as Thiepval suggests. The comingling of hundreds of thousands of French and German dead was surely a different message to the world other than simple nationalistic pride, though the French did build their largest cemetery, with more than sixteen thousand graves, on the grounds of the ossuary. Today, the horror and anonymity of the Douaumont speak less to the identity of lost soldiers being known unto God and more to the bewilderment and incredulity of such anonymous loss being unanswerable and a mystery that surely only God could possibly explain.

Memorials of the First World War thus took on life and meaning for future generations, speaking not only for the dead for whom they were created. In so doing, no greater example of the malleability and enduring nature of the war's memorials can be found than in the Tannenberg Memorial, in what is now Hohenstein, Poland. Tannenberg has been a place deeply fixated in Central European consciousness for centuries, being the site of the first Battle of Tannenberg and the defeat and slaughter of ancient Prussian Teutonic knights by Slavic forces in 1410. Ignominy from long ago was avenged for Germany in late August 1914, however, when vastly stronger Russian forces were stunningly and quickly defeated by German armies under Ludendorff, Hindenburg, and Hoffman, sealing their military reputations for the remainder of the war. The Battle of Tannenberg was even more shocking because the war had not even completed its first month. Tannenberg provided a sense of relief for Germany just as the news from the West was becoming more anxious, with the Schlieffen Plan's essential requirement of a rapid defeat of France faltering badly in the actual execution of the war. Tannenberg effectively secured German control of East Prussia for the remainder of the war, but the failure of the Schlieffen Plan, and Russian rethinking following Tannenberg, effectively ensured that for the next four and a half years Germany was facing its biggest fear: a circle of iron and war on two fronts.

At this point, Tannenberg took on new dimensions for the future. Once the First World War had been lost, Germany was determined to salvage pride and prestige from the battle at the start of its failed war. Construction of the great Tannenberg Memorial commenced on the tenth anniversary of the battle and finished three years later. This occurred during the time of the German Weimar Republic, and the finished monument resembled a medieval fortress in the shape of a six-sided fort with massive towers. The symbolism of the 1410 battle could not be more obvious. Moreover, Tannenberg would be the place where it would honor its current dead and become a national crypt. Despite his personal misgiving, Hindenburg's mausoleum was built alongside twenty tombs of the German Unknowns, symbolizing the collective death of the earlier medieval nation. Into this context, Nazi propaganda and fanaticism took deep root. By 1933, the Tannenberg Memorial was the scene of Nazi rallies and ceremonies at the time of the anniversary of the battle, and when Hindenburg died the following year, Hitler was able to consolidate his dictatorship and pay lip-service homage to the president by conducting an elaborate funeral and internment at Tannenberg. At this point, the original monument had already taken on multiple purposes for subsequent generations, but it was not to stop there. By 1945, the approaching Soviet Red Army turned history again on its head. Hitler ordered the exhumation of Hindenburg and his wife and the partial demolition of the exterior of the memorial where the mausoleum had been located. Only in 1949 did the Communist Polish government order the destruction of the Tannenberg Memorial to signify the defeat of Fascism. Yet as with many of the war's legacies, the Tannenberg Memorial continued to haunt subsequent decades. In the 1950s and the 1980s, Tannenberg was incrementally demolished but in slow, piecemeal fashion, as if no one could totally exorcise its ghosts. Today, it lies unrecognizable among fields of overgrown brush, like many of the fields of the First World War.

This continuing feedback loop between each generation and the war has allowed peoples to interpret that traumatic past event and then reapply its messages to their own contemporary circumstances. By "remembering" the First World War this way, it continues to live up to its original designation of the "Great War." Intriguingly, that process has started again outside of Europe recently. The British and French began the process of remembering—and creating their unique stories of remembrance—very quickly after Versailles, when their national wounds were still fully exposed and raw. The two other great Allied combatants of the First World War, Russia and the United States, have trod a very different path of remembrance for one hundred years, and only now have decided to create new national narratives about the war. With the advent of the centennial, both nations began to rediscover a place for the First World War in their current identities.

For the Russians, the war's centennial coincided with its painfully reestablished status once more as a non-Soviet nation. During the Soviet years, the First World War had occupied an awkward place in the dominant Communist narrative. Officially, it was dismissed as the "War of the Imperialists," tainted by czarist and pre-Communist agendas. Indeed, the Germans had transported Lenin back to Petrograd to foment revolution, and the implications of German-Soviet cooperation in 1917 sat awkwardly with the later rivalry and war between Nazi Germany and the Soviet Union. Today, Russian president Vladimir Putin's sense of opportunity is unparalleled in world affairs, and his newfound interest in both the First and Second World Wars are examples of his ability to position

Russian interests today with current geopolitical strategy. This was evident recently in 2020 regarding an odd spat Putin had with the government of Poland regarding its role in the cause of the Second World War. In this public and heated argument, Putin was not seeking a post-presidential career in academia or engaging in historical debate. Instead, he was engaging in current affairs and power plays that further Russia's expansionist agenda and its efforts to shape international geopolitics. The same is true, in a less opportunistic manner, with regard to Putin's earlier interest in the First World War. In 2012, Putin announced that August 1st, the date of Russia's entry into the First World War, would be a national holiday from that point on. Two years later, he cut the ribbon on a grand new memorial in Moscow, "The Monument to the Heroes of the First World War." Two other national historic sites dedicated to the war were unveiled in the same centennial year of the outbreak of the war in the Russian Federation.

In this context, the First World War today unites cherished Russian themes that were awkward within a Soviet context but that fit nicely into a top-down, historically grandiose, and post-Soviet Russian worldview. By uniting the Orthodox Church with patriarchal motifs of Russian greatness, Putin has deftly reframed pre- and post-Soviet themes with impunity, thereby rekindling hopes of Russian superpower status by appropriating events and stories that conveniently inspire such dream-making. Russian greatness and dominance today can be upheld and vindicated by Russian sacrifices of old, in the Putin strategy. While the Second World War—named the "Great Patriotic War" in Russia—wonderfully fueled the Soviet agenda of the struggle of Communism against Fascism, that second war alone provided what the Soviets needed. It was clean, ideological, and successful. The First World War had none of those advantages to the Soviets. But to Putin and a Russia that speaks democracy but practices authoritarianism, showcasing a cuddly bear Olympic mascot while its troops invaded Crimea, the First World War has no awkward connotations. It is a gem waiting to be rediscovered. So, it has been. Today, the First World War is rehabilitated with the Russian narrative and its interpretation of Mother Russia's grand role in history. That is the purpose of its new memorials and its national holiday. The dead millions of Russians from 1914 to 1917 are finally resting in peace within the renewed national Russian psyche.

The Americans, too, have sought and struggled to make current sense of the First World War. The centennial of World War I has aligned closely with the seventy-fifth anniversary of D-Day, an event which many Americans see as critical in the destruction of Nazism in Europe, but which the aforementioned Russians dismiss as a small act compared to the vast struggles of the Eastern Front in World War II. In 2015, one year after Putin unveiled his First World War monuments, President Barack Obama signed into legislation the creation of the United States World War One Centennial Commission to prepare and conduct the national remembrance of the war. Each state duly followed, creating its own state commission. What is interesting is the somewhat unclear pathway by which the US reached this late moment of recognizing the centennial and the event it commemorated. Indeed, the US almost stumbled into an understanding of the First World War and a contemporary memorialization that can inform the current generation.

It was only in that same year—2015—at the time of the creation of the national commission, when legislation was finally passed for the building of a National World War I Memorial in Washington, DC. That construction project, fittingly located in Pershing Park, was finally completed in 2021, long after the original goal of having it open on the exact centennial date in November 2018 of the original Armistice. The national memorial's slow progress reflects previous uneven efforts at memorialization. The Liberty Memorial Tower in Kansas City, Missouri, was constructed in 1926 as the nation's first tower of remembrance, but by 1994 it had to be closed due to dilapidation and little public interest. Ten years later, the tower was restored through the efforts of a few legislators, and in 2004 President George W. Bush signed the legislation that created the national museum adjacent to Liberty Memorial Tower.

However, the plan for a memorial in the nation's capital (other than one that the District of Columbia had commissioned decades earlier) only gained attention and some support with the increasing national interest in the Second World War. As that second war receded into history, and its veterans began to pass away at faster rates, some individuals championed the cause of also honoring the earlier First World War. One key proponent in that endeavor was the last living American veteran of the First World War, Frank Buckles, who had attended the unveiling of the Liberty Memorial Tower in 1926. He assumed the honorary chair role of the Memorial Foundation, a role he maintained until his death at the age of 110 in February of 2010. In short, individual groups and persons struggled on, in the 1990s, to fund the National WWI Museum in Kansas City, Missouri, and to galvanize public demand for a national memorial. The National World War II Memorial was opened in 2004, yet on the current construction timetable, it will be nearly two decades later before the country unveils its national First World War memorial.

The forgotten nature of the war in American consciousness has already been examined. What is new about this belated desire to bring about greater public awareness is what has also galvanized Russia recently: namely, that today's memorializing is less about memory and more about serving current issues and aspirations. Russia has found a contemporary rationale and agenda for memorializing the war a century after its conclusion, and now so does the United States. In these past two decades, American interest in the creation of a war narrative has been triggered by the emerging sense of the distancing of the Second World War and loss of its veterans, and, more ominously, by the injury to the United States' twentieth-century superpower confidence by the attacks of September 11th, 2001. The dramatic and traumatic birth of the War on Terror, and the twenty-first-century struggle with terrorism, and particularly Islamist fanaticism, has provided America with a nostalgia about its earlier struggles and victories. Through that nostalgia a working narrative has found its roots in today's generation of Americans as it discerns a meaning for the US in the 1914–1918 War. In so doing, memory serves not to explain the earlier event and the national role at that time, but rather provides a context and illustration for a story that addresses today's national identity and needs. In our age of the War on Terror, the doughboys of 1917 are revisited as heroes who inspire us now by their example of courage and sacrifice across the ocean.

Even at the local level this is evident. The centennial of the war enabled states and communities to find the heritage of the past in the opportunities of today. The Museum of Aviation in Georgia, for example, unveiled at a large public gathering in October 2019 a life-size statue of Eugene J. Bullard, with his family descendants in attendance. Eugene Bullard was finally honored and recognized posthumously on that warm autumn morning as the first African American fighter pilot in US history. This unveiling constituted the final public activity of the Georgia World War I Commission, which, like its national parent organization, was launched in 2015 and conducted its business thereafter with private funds. One hundred and four years after Bullard left the United States to fly and fight for the French in October 1914, the people of Georgia honored his unique trailblazing achievement. Of course, while that achievement was celebrated finally in 2019, the United States would have excoriated his activities and achievements back in 1914. A black American fighting for a foreign nation in a war in which the US was officially neutral would have been vilified and punished for his perceived racial insolence and public disobedience. But Bullard was a pioneer who changed the rules, and the people of Georgia one hundred years later were using the story of his war not only to illuminate the past, but, more importantly, to assert Georgia's current commitment to racial equality and justice. The state's commitment to a post-civil rights-era vision has been an unfolding pathway through history, and Bullard was honored as one of those Georgians who both laid and walked along that path. Bullard and his war are, in this sense, a heroic illustration of the past, present, and future. The Georgia Commission's statue and ceremony shows that America's twenty-first-century military might and its superpower status were forged not only by the military-industrial complex that World War I initiated, but also by quiet, heroic figures like Bullard. The life and work of such an individual turned history on its head, even if it took four generations and great struggle through the decades of segregation and then the civil rights era to appreciate the significance of World War I veteran Eugene J. Bullard.

Ironically, while the United States came belatedly to its First World War narratives, local American communities were quicker to define and memorialize the war for the very reason that they endured the war's legacy with such immediacy and personal suffering. In the 1920s, numerous local communities created memorials for the scores or hundreds of their lost local citizens, husbands, fathers, brothers, and sons. For them, the war had a sudden and tragic meaning. These memorials are scattered today in towns, cities, and villages throughout America, providing for subsequent generations a reminder and distant voice from the past. Some are evocative, powerful, creative, and artistic. The statue of the doughboy in Emmitsburg, Maryland, provides such an example. The bronze statue shows a doughboy, grenade held aloft, marching through barbed wire and looking eastward down Main Street, facing France some four thousand miles away. The statue is dedicated to 123 fallen men of Emmitsburg and lists separately the names of three additional "Colored Soldiers." Those black men's experiences of desegregation in France during the war could not change the segregated memorial that would await them in posterity. These memorials were places of grief long ago. Today, they certainly invite us to remember the pain and loss from a war one century ago, but more tellingly provide a focal point for each generation to consider the lives, outlooks, and habits of their own communities, in Emmitsburg, Maryland, and countless other places called home around the United States.

Today, the most demonstrated and publicly accessible memorial of the First World War, especially with the Commonwealth nations, is the red paper poppy, worn on lapels prior to the Remembrance Sunday closest to November 11th annually. In the millions, the citizens of Britain and the Commonwealth nations wear their poppies with pride, seemingly in larger numbers each year. This perennial memorial has one advantage over all the magnificent stone monuments built over the past century around the globe: the poppy is portable and can be worn by any individual who wishes to bear it as a personal emblem and statement of remembrance. John McRae's poem "In Flanders' Fields" gave us the poppy as the quintessential motif of beauty and suffering over the past century. Such a romanticized concept, expressed poetically by a Canadian doctor who worked and died on the front, has a power that both grounds us symbolically in the soil of Flanders and allows every successive generation to appropriate it as a statement of current identity and solidarity with those long gone. Although originally conceived by Molina Michael of the American YMCA in 1918 on hearing of McRae's death, the poppy emblem rapidly gained popularity in Britain and its Commonwealth. In 1921, the British Legion first used it as a symbol to help raise funds for the vast numbers of injured veterans, and by the 1930s the Women's Co-Operative Guild expanded its use henceforth as a symbol of aid to victims of war, originating from the casualties of the Great War. The centennial years in Britain and the Commonwealth breathed new life into its universal nature. It even evolved into a metal version manufactured from the endless shell casings still being exhumed from the Somme region, with the British Legion issuing shell-case metal poppies in 2016 as a fundraising device. Each purchased metal poppy was identified in honor of a specific fallen soldier of the British Empire under the title "Every One Remembered," with a brief account of the soldier issued with the memorial souvenir. This desire to identify and honor each fallen soldier was more personal than the grand monuments of the 1920s yet still reflected the significance of the war in a person and an event long gone. By the time the centennial concluded in Britain, poppies were adorning thousands of buildings. No more magnificent and extraordinary was the exhibition "Blood Swept Land and Seas of Red" described earlier, numbering one million handmade ceramic poppies placed by individuals in the moat around the Tower of London. The exhibition captured a distinctly British desire for grand symbolism, romanticized affectation, and over-whelming messaging that grabbed the attention of the world. Whether it helped explain the significance of the First World War any better is a matter of judgment. But its aesthetic power was une-qualled in the centennial years.

First World War memorials have, over the past one hundred years, worked to express the pain of the past and give meaning to the present. They have made us consider the loss of millions of dead and prompted us to make sense of the millions of living today. In doing so, there is something hauntingly recurrent and malleable, an almost dreamlike quality, in their interaction with each current generation. They enable the First World War to stay in the consciousness of each generation, but only in the way that a powerful dream may stay with us in the waking hours of our day. This dreamlike quality of the war and its remembrance has informed one scholar's recent analysis of the beginning of the war. In his study of the causes of the First World War, Christopher Clark[2] explored the much-examined issue of why the war occurred after such a long period of peace. His conclusion was novel and compelling, claiming that the metaphor of sleepwalking provides the clue. Whatever politics, alliances, policies, plans, and economics did to prompt the war, there is a still a puzzling gap, a sort of uncertain set of inexplicable actions, which turned the world on its head in the summer of 1914. Clark argued that the statesmen and leaders of Europe knew they were being reckless, but not fully; that they sensed ominously the anxious nature of that summer, but never fully believed it perilously dangerous; that they could see a possible emerging shape of conflict, but not discern its clarity nor its prompts; that they had feelings, fears, and emotions more than thoughts, strategies, and analyses that dictated the steps toward war. In short, Europe sleepwalked into the war, as a sleepwalking person is vaguely aware of their surroundings and their actions but unable to control them fully. Foreign Secretary

---

[2] Clark Christopher, The Sleepwalkers: How Europe Went to War in 1914 (New York: Harper, 2013).

Grey and his contemporaries woke up only when it was too late and realized that the lights had indeed gone out all over Europe, with no hope of them being rekindled.

This notion of sleepwalking provides a powerful insight that not only applies to the causes of World War I, but also to its conclusion and in the ways subsequent generations tried—and failed—to understand and explain what really happened in the 1914–1918 War. There is something elusive and cryptic about the First World War and its significance for humanity across the years. It was a riddle and remains a riddle, in part, even today. The Second World War lacks comparable ambiguity and uncertainty. It is perceived with clarity. We marched to war after Poland in 1939 and Pearl Harbor in 1941. But we sleepwalked to war after Sarajevo in 1914. That lack of certainty has provided four generations of descendants with the experience of a sleepwalker's perception of their environment, granting us a dim but incomplete picture of the reality that was the First World War. Yet like the environment is to the sleepwalker, it has shaped and guided the steps that we as a human family have taken for a century. The memorials that adorn the landscapes of the world's nations speak to this uncertainty and a deeper sense of our identity and our destiny. These awe-inspiring memorials invite us still to dream and to reflect on our possibilities, and to look back with great anxiety on a nightmare that consumed a generation between 1914 and 1918. The war at its core remains something of a conundrum, a mystery of sorts. Memorials across the world capture the mystery and invite each generation to ask what it meant and what it tells us today. Those memorials push us to consider more deeply our story and our identity. But to understand fully why the war happened remains elusive and would take the mind of God. In this sense, while the unidentifiable remains of anonymous corpses are truly "known unto God" alone, as the weathered epitaphs on the headstones remind us, the war in which these men perished still exhausts and confounds the human capacity to understand. That prerogative belongs to the divine; it is only known unto God.

A SILENT NIGHT, A DEAFENING CENTURY

By Christmas of 1914, the terrible mistake of the First World War was evident to all and was existentially devastating to the fighting men on the front lines and their loved ones back home. If Europe had "sleepwalked" into the war, its sudden opening had dramatically awoken and traumatized the peoples of Europe and their empires from their slumber, with shocking impact. On the first day of the war in August of that year, the British Army, highly respected and professionally elite, totaled only 250,00 regular men. For years, the Whitehall planners and the military chiefs had estimated that a quarter of a million men would be enough strength for engaging in a European war in the early decades of the twentieth century. By Christmas of that year, the British had suffered three hundred thousand casualties in combat. Britain's elite standing army had been wiped out. A new kind of war was to begin, with volunteer civilians from around the world marching into an unimaginable, unplanned, and inconceivable conflict.

It is therefore perhaps not surprising that quickly the fighting armies began to regret the course of events. What is perhaps more surprising is that in one astonishing but very human moment, they gave expression to a hope of something better, kinder, and more familiar in the world than the savagery they found themselves facing. Fittingly, Christmas was the moment that brought this hope to fruition. The Christmas Truce of 1914 is legend and has been recounted in many ways, including film, over the century. Its brief elements are worth revisiting, not for its tragic and haunting tale of hope against all odds, but because of its capacity to tell us what of significance we gained from the First World War.

What we know is that the Christmas Truce was illegal and unofficial and could have been deemed as treason by the headquarters of the combatant armies. Even so, by 8:30 P.M. on Christmas Eve, when snow began to fall and the ground froze as if to create a perfect Christmas atmosphere, British troops in the southern sector of Belgium observed makeshift trees, illuminated with candles, being placed on top of the German trenches. These were accompanied by the sounds of Christmas carols and greetings in English shouted from the German lines. This, in turn, led at first to verbal responses and songs from the British troops, and then, after some bantering back and forth, to the first tentative, timid forays out of the trenches and into no-man's-land, with the German troops taking the initiative. In response, with hands on guns and bayonets for caution, individual English troops similarly emerged nervously, and small groups of opposing soldiers approached each other. The viral nature of this unplanned, spontaneous outburst of vulnerable humanity rapidly spread. Soon several sectors of the Western Front were witnessing personal and social fraternization of enemy troops, with no eruptions of violence. The early awkward interactions appear to have been characterized by the exchange of alcohol, food, laughter, halting use of each other's languages, and displays of family photos. It is unclear specifically where and who began the Christmas Truce, aside from the display of German trees and singing of *"Heilige Nacht"* ("Silent Night"), but that is unimportant. What is clear is this informal truce was replicated quickly along many miles of the front and was welcomed by large swaths of troops from opposing sides. Estimates suggest that as much as one third of the front in the southern half of Belgium had quieted all weapons and were engaging socially across no-man's-land by Christmas morning.

Likely factoring into this eruption of peace was the nature of the troops on each side. Firstly, by Christmas, volunteer soldiers, not professionals alone, were filling the gaps that five months of war had created. Their patriotism was as strong as anyone's, but their militaristic training and instinct not as deep. Secondly, the British were facing Saxons in the opposite trenches, notoriously easygoing and different in reputation from more ideological and authoritarian troops, such as the Prussians. Indeed, legend recalls that initial German invitations to meet the British were accompanied by explanations such as, "We are Saxons, and you are Anglo-Saxons, so why are we fighting?!" The Christmas Truce legend also has often recounted a football (soccer) match between groups of Scottish soldiers and the 133rd Royal Saxon Regiment, which prized itself on its footballing skill prior to the war. Indeed, regimental photos and records exist of their Saxon team. Scant evidence exists, however, that such a game was played during the truce, but the story has persisted of a Saxon win by a score of 3–2 over the Scots. Much of the evidence is derived from a couple of British—but not German—letters back to loved ones, referring to a ball being kicked around. That story appears to have been embellished over the years. Rupert Graves, one of the surviving poets, wrote about the truce with added fictional elements including details of the football match in his 1962 short story, *The Christmas Truce.*[1] The likely scenario is that sporadic activities, such as a game of football, occurred along many miles of the lines, and that they morphed in their retelling into definitive events rather than simple examples of interaction.

Whatever the details, the extraordinary nature of the truce, and even its apocryphal football match, became quickly known across the Western Front and recounted back home to London, Paris, and Berlin. On January 1st, 1915, *The Times* of London[2] reported the truce and its football tale to the British public, and the truce was thus established forever as an object of uniqueness, fascination, anxiety, bewilderment, and hope. It was a legend that began resonating, and its mesmerizing nature has not diminished over the decades. Yet

---

[1] Originally published as "Wave No Banners," *Saturday Evening Post* 235/45 (15 December 1962): 34–41.
[2] "More Tales of the Truce." *London Times* (2 January 1915).

the truce itself died out within a few days. The soldiers of both sides began slowly to revert to the combative norm, and for those slow to do so, their officers persuaded or threatened them back literally into line. After several days of friendly forays into enemy trenches and half-hearted or fake versions of hostility, the impending return to a state of war became the inevitable order. The troops on both sides recognized the impossibility of this temporary peace, and so the return to hostilities was not solely because of the threat of court-martial or execution. They knew and recorded in their memoirs that the truce was a moment of light in the dark, a fleeting and ephemeral moment of human dignity, rather than an actual end to the war itself. It was individual agency at its finest and most noble, perhaps, but it had no chance of permanently changing the structure and destiny of the First World War. That force was too strong and universal, and individual acts of vulnerability and heroism were not going to change the inevitable. Such realism was expressed succinctly by one participant in the truce, George Eade of the Royal Irish Rifles. Eade had developed a friendship during the truce with an English-speaking German artilleryman. Most British soldiers struggled to speak German during the truce, but the situation was eased because many Germans had worked or traveled in Britain before the war, and Eade's new comrade was an English speaker. At the point when the truce began to deteriorate and mutual farewells seemed in order, Eade recalled in his memoirs that the German soldier remarked to him, "Today we have peace. Tomorrow, you fight for your country. I fight for mine. Good luck."[3]

The Christmas Truce was unique and never repeated or replicated. On the Eastern Front, the facing Prussian and Russian troops did not establish a truce, perhaps because of Prussian vigor in the pursuit of war and Russian Orthodox Christmas occurring on January 6th. The Prussians and the Russians were seemingly in the wrong place at the wrong time for a truce. Indeed, the Great War

---

[3] Mike Dash, "The Story of the WWI Christmas Truce," *Smithsonian Magazine* (23 December 2011): 5.

never again saw anything like it, except remotely in the French frontline mutinies of 1917, which were motivated by entirely different reasons. The Christmas Truce stands alone, and to the British, its romanticism was reestablished at the time of the centennial. In December of 2014, one hundred years after the truce, Prince William, heir to the British throne, unveiled the memorial "The World War One Christmas Truce," featuring a sculptural handshake suspended in air around a metal frame. This followed an earlier memorial to the truce in 2012, highlighting the legendary football match. Using the bombed-out ruins of St. Luke's Church, Liverpool, destroyed during the Second World War blitz, the memorial shows an English and a German soldier shaking hands above a football. Placing an artistic interpretation of a cherished memory from the first war within the devastated ruins of the second made for powerful commentary. In this respect, the British romantic review of the First World War still retains its strength and presence.

Does the Christmas Truce deliver a hopeful story of the human spirit, as its romanticized retelling suggests, or something of greater symbolism? Its persistence as a story over the past century indicates a perennial appeal and value. But what appeal and what value? This enduring fable illustrates a broader issue of how the First World War has been viewed and utilized retrospectively by successive generations to interpret the war and its meaning for their own times. That the truce occurred as an historical event is indisputable. The more important lesson lies, though, not in its sentimental notion of human courage and vulnerability in a brutal context, but in its prefacing and illustrating an enduring legacy that the war left to the future, for both good and bad. That message is the birth of popular agency in a world of structure, for the war is the event and point in modern history that triggered a new place and voice for the popular masses in the governance of nations. The rule of the people found unstoppable momentum because of the tragedy of World War I. The 1914 truce in this context was an eye-catching example or motif of a critical moment of popular advancement in global geopolitics, with all its associated promises, possibilities, and problems. Those risky, even reckless, fortunes found appeal and expression as early as the Christmas Eve of 1914, because as an act of defiance and its vain hope in the return to normalcy, the Christmas truce sent a shock wave through the military power structure. In so doing, it remains less a sentimental story and more of a fanfare to the common person. That cold and silent night of December 24, 1914, stood as a hushed symbolic entry of the ordinary people onto the stage of a deafening century that has sought, in ways both good and bad, to replace the powerful few with the rule of the masses. The men who left their trenches showed an autonomy and agency that was to grow in the fractious and anxious years ahead. Their small example of agency in no-man's-land has intrigued generations not only because it showed human courage, but more importantly, because it inspired the hopes of others in the face of poverty and powerlessness across the century.

That is also why tyrant and liberator alike could reach back to the violence of the First World War and the populist forces it unleashed and draw on that common source for their energy and agendas. Movements representing the will and the rights of the people had already gained foothold in the nineteenth and early twentieth centuries, such as in the British trade union movement and its emergent Labour Party, or Theodore Roosevelt's Square Deal program for the ordinary American. The forces underpinning these movements were magnified and catapulted onto the world stage because of the war and its aftermath. The debate thereafter, and indeed for much of the twentieth century, was how best to fulfill the rule and rights of the people and which political systems could best deliver that aspiration. The populist vision did not necessarily resemble the kind of liberal democracy that Woodrow Wilson had espoused as the justification for the war. As noted in previous chapters, the populist agenda took its legitimacy from the mass democratization that the First World War had delivered to the whole world in its experience of global suffering as the great equalizing moment in human history. By the 1930s, the Fascist and Communist responses confidently espoused the same honoring of the masses and saw their systems as the rightful expression of that populist vision and response

to the war. The tyranny, hypocrisy, and inability of those dictatorships to deliver on that claim, however, was exposed only through
the unfolding of subsequent events and history. But in 1932, Mussolini could garner support when he—much like his Communist adversaries might claim regarding Soviet Russia—asserted that "Italy
and Germany are the greatest and soundest democracies that exist
in the world today."[4]

This was the tightrope that democracies had to balance upon
for the rest of the century. Their claim to popular assent was challenged and disputed, and their efforts to realize democracy became
an ever-vigilant and difficult work in progress.

Making sense of the First World War is slightly more compre-
hensible when the conflict's messy outcomes appear to correspond
with equally messy inputs. This is to say the march *to* war in 1914 is
as unclear, bewildering, and incomplete an explanation as the march
from war in 1918. Clark's "sleepwalker" argument is persuasive in
this respect. The dialectic between events and stories is one that his
book has sought to portray in making sense of the Great War and
its consequences. And this same dynamic between event and story
was equally present in each European nation's march—or sleep-
walk—to war in 1914. If, as Clark proposes, London, Berlin, Paris,
and Moscow were all relying on subjective, anxious narratives to
shape their policies, relationships, and decisions in 1914, story and
event continued to shape the course of human events after the November 11th Armistice. Already in the period of 1900 to 1914 Germany had made up its mind—or maybe its heart—that the "ring of
steel" of other nations around its borders was threatening, rather
than neutral, and that those nations and their military steel sought
to diminish German power. We could call this German paranoia,
but maybe German vulnerability would be a kinder term. Similarly,
the ancient Austro-Hungarian dynasty had come to believe its own
nineteenth-century script about it being the essential, stable fulcrum

---

[4] Jill Lenore, "In Every Dark Hour," *New York Magazine* (4 February 2020): 20–25.

of Central Europe, so that anything that might shift that fulcrum would disrupt the entire continent. In this self-talk, the Sarajevo assassination in June of 1914 was symbolically demonic and dangerous, even if it was only an objective threat to Austro-Hungarian pride and not to its power.

The Allies, too, brought their nineteenth-century narratives to the new century even as those narratives increasingly ignored the changing context of geopolitics and the enormous threat to humanity from their new military technology. Great Britain, passionate for its empire and navy and unable to decide its relationship with Europe (fast-forward to Brexit), had no accurate measure of what German imperial growth and strength might mean, let alone German motivation. How could it? Germany itself was vacillating in its motivations and messages, other than displaying fearful, defensive anxiety. And so, London increasingly saw its navy and empire under threat, though German interest was primarily in an economic community where its industry might thrive, rather than in an arms race or a desire for British imperial territory. The French also believed too much in their own stories. After their defeat by Prussia in 1871, their borders, forts, and military were built defensively, even as their alliances with Russia indicated full-throated participation in the "ring of steel" around Germany. Meanwhile, Russia's inability to create a contemporary society with a reliable and responsible government that cared for its citizens meant that its weak and despotic czarist government appeared to Western friends and foes alike as a wild Russian bear about to wreak havoc. To the Central powers, the ludicrous and incongruous relationship between Russia and its Western democratic allies of Britain and France merely fed the line that the Allies were out to dominate Central Europe, even with the most unlikely of friendships and alliances. This was the fragile, unstable, and reactive environment in which event and story conspired to produce the conflagration that was World War I. It was not inevitable, but primed. It did not have to occur but was constructed piecemeal. It was reckless, not necessary. It was chosen, not required. When the conditions were right, and all the anxious participants satisfied that their own stories and the events around them were in perfect alignment, all it needed was one minor spark to detonate the whole arsenal that was the military might of Europe's nations. That detonation confirmed to each nation its own logic and reason for war, even while those reasons were antithetically incoherent and neutralizing of each other's case. As Clark put it regarding the Sarajevo assassination: "Russia and France thereby tied the fortunes of two of the world's greatest powers in highly asymmetrical fashion to the uncertain destiny of a turbulent and intermittently violent state of Austria-Hungary."[5]

This concept of the interaction of event and story provides a better way of understanding the evolution of events both into and out of the First World War. It also allows for a meaningful way of honoring cause and effect, confirming that choices by individuals and nations do indeed have consequence and culpability attached to them. In this way, the so-called Fischer thesis of the 1960s, when the East German academic Fritz Fischer[6] made the case for German guilt and aligned German militarism of 1914 with that of 1939, is not entirely inaccurate but is perhaps misused. The danger of the Fischer thesis and other causal arguments is that they lead too easily to a judicial concept of blame or guilt and interpret actions as born from conscious intent. But intent is often overshadowed by emotion in human action, and proponents of the Fischer thesis tend to look for a smoking German gun. A more nuanced argument would be that while Germany certainly held much responsibility for the war—perhaps the most responsibility—there was no conscious intent or plan for the unfolding of the events of that fateful summer of 1914. Even with its generation-old Schlieffen Plan in hand, Germany did not establish the conditions or the stories that abounded in 1914.

---

[5] Clark, *Sleepwalkers*, 559.

[6] Fritz Fischer, *Germany's Aims in the First World War* (New York: Norton, 1961).

All of Europe established those. No singular event, indeed, no smoking gun, identifies the solitary culprit of that calamitous war. As Clark put it, "Viewed in this light, the outbreak of War was a tragedy, not a crime."[7]

This should not be reassuring for those of us living one hundred years later. It should alarm us greatly. It tells us that the years leading to the war were reckless and full of misfortune. Additionally, they were full of misinformation. Fake news, we might say. It tells us that the years after the First World War continued this reckless and misguided way of cojoining event and narrative right through the twentieth century, now with the added fuel and accelerant of competing ideology and weapons of mass destruction thrown into the toxic mix. Our twenty-first-century world exhibits a similar comingling of thinking, emotion, mythology, and behavior that once led the world to a cataclysmic collapse in July of 1914. The consequences of that war then produced new narratives that would shape the twentieth century, with unimaginable suffering and humiliation added as potent elements to the future stories that nations would tell themselves. Perhaps the hand-wringing architects of Versailles were never right that this could be the "war to end all wars," and it could only ever be the war to raise to new heights the capacity of humankind to embrace new levels of cruelty and destruction, with reinvented narratives of hatred and loss providing just and righteous cause to march again shortly thereafter to the drum of war.

Today, we can still see how this mythical blending of event, history, and story abounds in our lives and our world, in our consciousness both as individuals and nations. At its best, this kind of mythology provides us with unifying symbols of identity and enjoyable celebrations and memorials, such as the July 4th Independence Day in the United States. At its worst, it gives us the ideology of a Hitler, a Stalin, a Pol Pot, and every other despotic nationalist or internationalist that has darkened history to today's Syrian Civil War. Those despotic foes are not far away from our democratic friends.

---

[7] Clark, *Sleepwalkers*, 561.

In 2011, the West welcomed the Arab Spring, once more echoing the distant voice of Woodrow Wilson championing the arrival of democracy in the Middle East. Ten years later, Syria stands as a tragic example of what happens when naïve hope in the raison d'etre of democracy is confounded by brutal resistance.

What is vital for our generation—the fourth descendant generation from the First World War—is that we recognize that today we are again experiencing an ingredient that was present in 1914 but absent for most of the twentieth century. Currently, not only is our understanding of democracy once again fluid and uncertain, but the checks and balances that held the nineteenth century and the second half of the twentieth century together have been eroded. They disappeared once before, in the years before the First World War. In 1914, the passionate stories and events that came into play effectively created a geopolitics of Europe where there was no grand strategy, no enduring framework, and no supra-national checks to provide clear guardrails for the policy initiatives of Europe. Instead, short-term expediencies ruled the day. Nations had their stories to tell themselves, and then effectively moved ahead with tactical decision-making as new problems arose that reinforced their own narratives. In that environment, stable relationships were hard to forge and even harder to sustain. Distrust and insecurity appeared to offer each nation a better chance for self-advancement than taking the vulnerable risk of suspending their disbelief. By 1914, the nations of Europe—and North America and Asia, too—were regularly oscillating in foreign and domestic policy, communicating unclear motives and messages, deciding major political and economic actions based on quick arrangements, and establishing at each step an atmosphere of confusion, distrust, and anxiety. In short, they were all being reckless and risking considerable misfortune.

Fast-forward one hundred years and our fourth-generation world exhibits the same blurring of lines, confusion in approaches, lack of overarching strategy, defensive nationalism, and attention to short-term expediencies at the risk to long-term improvement, as was evident in 1914. Our ancestors at Versailles would be astonished by much of the scientific, technological, and digital influences that pervade our lives, but would vividly recognize the political, international, and ideological world we inhabit in the third decade of our twenty-first century. That is not to say that we have fully abandoned strategic initiatives and policies over the past half century. Many organizations and mechanisms have endured the test of time, especially since the defeat of totalitarianism in 1945 and its Soviet collapse in 1989. The creation of an ideological and military alliance of democratic nations within NATO since the Cold War stands as a supreme example of that successful strategy. Elsewhere, democratic strategy has characterized much of our Western world for many decades. The European Union, for example, was and is an extraordinarily hopeful strategy, a phoenix rising from the literal ashes of the Second World War. Its longevity has been a hallmark of European democratic success in a century when nationalist hatred and war was the norm just two generations earlier. The eurozone crisis of 2011 to 2012 illustrates the difference well. One hundred years earlier, the economic volatility of Europe had no mechanism, other than German ambition, to create a strategic approach. One hundred years later, the European Union successfully navigated a strategic solution that exemplified the power, stability, and success of the European experiment. And then came Brexit. Europe's success is still very much a work in progress.

Indeed, Brexit is one compelling example of how potent and unpredictable an experiment democracy is, particularly in its relationship to populist expression. The United States, Europe, and Asian democracies today are all struggling in their own ways with managing this populist agenda. New stresses and fissions are appearing no longer simply at the margins, but increasingly in the mainstream of democratic parties and systems. Whether Brexit or the rise of nationalism or the Trump presidency are our best expressions of "the rule of the people" is a matter up for debate that history will answer. They may indeed be our "better angels," to use Lincoln's term. Or not. To those who cherish democracy, the challenge is to uncover and sustain our angels and conversely to expose and confound our demons, namely those dangerous persons and reckless stories that bring out the worst in ourselves and others and threaten the fabric of democracy from its fringes.

Democracy has obviously survived and thrived through these kinds of moments, and that is reason to be optimistic. We are not the first generation to have our values of governance challenged, and, indeed, without that challenge, our quality of governance could not grow. From the Treaty of Versailles onward, this question of the "rule of the people" has challenged democracies to their core throughout the century. The reckless nature of history requires the testing of ideas, even dangerous ones, for proper evaluation and for sounder ideas to prevail. So, for example, it is not surprising to find that in 1930 the American political commentator Walter Lippmann, addressing the students at Berkeley, claimed, "The present century is the century of authority, a century of the Right, a Fascist century."[8]

For the remainder of the century, the United States and Europe would, through great turmoil and renewed conflict, discover their true souls and retain the center ground where democratic values and ways of being could be forged. FDR's New Deal during the Great Depression and the civil rights legislation of the 1960s stand as examples of this journey to reinvent for each generation a democratic way of living, with its instinct for improvement of the human condition. It is a continual work in progress and one that each generation of democratically committed persons must undertake. Today, this undertaking is required for democracy to be guaranteed. The story of democracy may require foundational principles that underpin pillars of strength for its endurance, such as the Constitution of the United States, but its continuance is nevertheless an unfolding struggle that engages each generation anew if democracy is to survive, let alone thrive. For its longevity and sustenance, it must weather new storms. Without each generation actively ensuring the

[8] Lenore, *In Every Dark Hour*, 20–25.

continuation of democracy by refusing to be lulled into the mistaken belief of its inevitability, we are only one step away from complacency about its relevance or necessity. Our times today present us with reminders that complacency is a weak defense against alternative visions of "the rule of the people." This emergent challenge is not unique to one nation alone but is present and relevant across the globe wherever democracy is rooted. Authoritarian leadership is in vogue and continues to mesmerize many citizens of developed and modern nations. Whether Putin in Russia or Erdogan in Turkey or Orban in Hungary or Kaczynski in Poland, these leaders are prideful, even boastful, of the strength and success of strong-arm, strongman leadership. The same, of course, has been noted about Trump in the US. This does not mean that they are tyrants, but it does mean that they represent different views on how the rule of the people should feature and work in modern societies. In so doing, democracy is under strain today in the most unlikely of places.

In short, democracy needs defenders and fighters for it to thrive. It cannot make its case to the people without effort and legitimate defense. It needs to argue its case in order to survive. That was the role of the lauded greatest generation of the Second World War, who came to democracy's defense when the alternatives appeared to have won. As Dorothy Thompson, speaking in 1935 at the centennial celebration of Alexis de Tocqueville's work *Democracy in America*, noted, "The war against democracy begins by destruction of the democratic temper, the democratic method and the democratic heat."[9]

As the anxious decade of the 1930s neared its end, the World's Fair opened in New York in 1939. Titled "The World of Tomorrow," it featured a vast pavilion with all the nations of the world represented, fronted by a vast Court of Peace. The opening of the World's Fair coincided the same week Hitler's panzer divisions crossed the Polish border, thus forcing the Greatest Generation to take up the arms of war once again to ensure that a future Court of

---

[9] Ibid., 23.

205

Peace could exist in the world of tomorrow. That defense of democracy was a crisis moment in human history that was emphatically
settled to the benefit of the world by 1945, and for a long while
democracy was perceived as strong, successful, and broadly cherished, the Soviet Union and China aside. In recent years, though,
that confidence has waned, and the West has slowly returned, in
varying degrees and places, to a place of geopolitical instability and
strategic uncertainty. Additionally, our ideological fluidity is leading
us incrementally toward the contesting of many democratic instincts, traditions, and establishments. Those establishments are still
standing and have not been unearthed, but cracks have been appearing since the fall of the Berlin Wall. In the United States, those
cracks have lengthened since 9/11. We appear to have accepted, like
the leaders of Europe in 1914, crisis management, expedient relations, and confusing leadership as the norm for the governance of
society. We also appear to be replicating the economic trend that
existed at the time of the First World War regarding the distribution
of wealth. Today's increasing experience in the United States and
Europe of an "us versus them" culture, a disparity of income and
resources, and a stretching of the economic continuum to broader
extremes has parallels from one hundred years ago. Irving Fisher,
progressive economist and leading mind behind capital theory, addressed the American Economic Association in 1918 about economic disparity, as the First World War drew to its messy conclusion, warning "of a great peril, perverting the democracy for which
we have been fighting."[10]

Recent economic analysis, such as that by French economist
Thomas Piketty and American Anne Case, has identified the same
challenge facing us a hundred years later. Democracy appears not to
be working economically and effectively for the uneducated and un-
skilled. And if it is believed not to be working efficiently, it is easy
not to value its worth, so the argument might be made. Certainly,
the twentieth century showed that democracy could overcome those

---

[10] Idrees Kahloon, "The Leveller," *The New Yorker* (9 March 2020).

risks before, and so we have reason to assume it could do so again. Lyndon Johnson's Great Society and Barack Obama's Affordable Care Act stand as American examples of a grand strategy to reunite and reincorporate the fringes back into the main body. But today this sense of incorporation and unity is fractured once more. Forces of division and dissent are strong in Europe, displaying skepticism about the value of the principle of democracy. This may be part of the natural dialectic of democracy, and since the word "demos" means a crowd, it is only one emotion away from being a mob. Part of the messiness, frustration, and diversity of democracy might be its very willingness to embrace both the emotive mob as well as the thinking crowd. It may run the risk of being a victim of its own success. The democratic principle, though, has been fought for and sustained through a century of great grief. The world has determined in recent generations that the crowd is preferable to the mob, that union is greater than division, that listening is preferable to shouting, that family is better than tribe, and that leadership is honored over dictatorship.

The First World War thrust onto the stage of history the same conundrum and struggle that our fourth generation faces today. Outside of Winchester Cathedral, the ancient capital of Anglo-Saxon Wessex and the seat of King Alfred, who united the Anglo-Saxons against the Viking Danes, there is an unassuming concrete bench in a courtyard against the rear wall of the cathedral. It was placed there, with the poignancy the British have displayed well in recent years, to commemorate the centennial of the First World War. The bench has at one end of the seat a concrete helmet in the design of the British Army of the war, leaning against a concrete backpack in the fashion of a British infantryman's kit. On the front of the bench the words are engraved "A Promise Honoured."

This is an intriguing phrase, the complexity of which this book has sought to express. How could the war in any sense be a promise honored, as implied by the myriad of Allied centennial events and symbols, such as the Winchester bench? In a sense, the statement is better understood as a question. Did the war produce any honor, and

207

what promise was its effect? If it promised the end of war, it failed. If it honored national dignity, it did so at a tremendous cost to the fighting men and their families. Perhaps the only understanding of the bench outside Winchester cathedral is the chilling conclusion that it was an unnecessary war of a catastrophic nature. That it can only promise to us, the fourth generation, that the sacrifice of our ancestors was for our benefit, was for us to learn, was for us to cherish, and was for us to understand. The need for the war, in this explanation, lies with what we make of it now, not why they undertook it then. It calls on us to think anew about our world and our options, to avoid repeating prior mistakes, and, instead, to choose to live better as a human family.

In a sense, the task of each generation is to prepare the next to live well. What is living well? Democratic voices across peoples and times have answered that question differently, but those varied answers have shared the belief that the engagement of people with their destinies is intrinsic to living well. This democratic imperative has survived tyrannies of many kinds and faces, and it has affirmed across cultures the principle that being human at its core involves shared freedom and responsibility, history being the final judge of each generation's response to that democratic imperative, including our own. Critically, that democratic imperative also derives its enduring validity from the common assent of certain shared virtues, to be taught to each subsequent generation, such as peace, dignity, respect, prosperity, freedom, and justice, not solely for one's own benefit but also for the community at large. These virtues come from the spirit—or soul—of ethical and responsible communities. This is why democracy is more than a system of governance. It requires each generation not only to organize but also to aspire to a moral concept of what it means to be truly human.

Four generations ago the world lost sight of that aspiration. Instead, nations, first from Europe and then from across the world, chose hatred, fear, injustice, oppression, and total war as their legacy to the future. We have spent the last one hundred years living with the consequences, including considerable misfortunes, of a global war that started as a reckless gamble in 1914. If we wish to learn from that war, the task of each generation is to create a legacy where wisdom, not recklessness, and promises, not misfortunes, can be delivered to the future. Without that, our century ahead will resemble the pain of the preceding one. And even when we do embrace the virtues of living well, because we are all flawed beings, we people often do this poorly and falteringly. But do it we must, for as the First World War showed us, the alternative is far worse.

This might provide us a crumb of comfort for our generation, as well as a clue to the meaning of the war to its original participants. As the war came to an ominous end in 1918, the clues to the future were strewn around the battlefields. The German Army had sunk into disarray, as General Ludendorff and his military cronies increasingly became despotic and tyrannical, both in civilian and military affairs. Meantime, in those waning months of 1918, the Allied armies worked together and respectfully to full effect, and their military success was astonishing. At the "United States in World War I" symposium at the Georgia Institute of Technology's Ivan Allen College of Liberal Arts in October 2018, one of the presenters described a compelling and simple thesis. His argument was that by the end of the war, the Allied coalition of British, French, and American forces finally understood how to work together. They finally saw themselves as a coalition of equals. They held themselves and each other accountable for their military plans and actions. They respected each other to permit places of intellectual debate and dissent, believing debate was essential and would produce successful outcomes. In short, they behaved like armies and soldiers who believed in and lived out democracy. And it worked.

In the last stanza of "In Flanders Fields," John McCrae wrote, in 1915,

Take up our quarrel with the foe:
To you from failing hands we throw
The torch; be yours to hold it high.
If ye break faith with us who die
We shall not sleep, though poppies grow
In Flanders fields.

McCrae's poem of the war spoke to his generation with poignant and profound meaning. Continue the fight, for that is the only way to honor the dead. It still speaks today to us, to the fourth generation. Continue the fight, for that is the only way to honor the dead. For us, the foe is not the German front line yards across no-man's-land. This foe is harder to see, but just as dangerous. It takes shape every time we forget how we gained our voice, our agency, our rights, our responsibilities, and our freedoms. President Woodrow Wilson may ultimately have been right about seeking to "save the world for democracy," even if his idea of liberal democracy needed refining through the fire of the ensuing century. The enemies of freedom and democracy are as dangerous as any troops in opposing trenches, even if they do not wield gun, grenade, or cannon. McCrae warned us that the dead shall not sleep if this fight is not enjoined. It is time for us to let the dead of Flanders and of all the battlefields of the First World War to sleep and to lie in peace. They earned that peace forever, like the sacred silence of a Christmas Eve, even as the world that emerged from their experience delivered a deafening scream and cacophony of anguish—and of hope—across a century. It is our fourth generation's turn to give word, meaning, and voice to the long gone of the First World War. To honor them does not require the laying of wreaths or wearing of poppies, no matter how moving those ceremonies are. To honor them is to fight today, with the power of our words and actions, the same cause they fought with their arms of war a century ago, at a time of great mistake and confusion, to uphold the human spirit of freedom against the crushing blow of oppression. The First World War was a calamity, and it was recklessly chosen, not inevitable. There are better ways of living and relating as people. That is what the dead from the 1914–1918 War teach us. Their darkness and pain tell us to find brighter and more hopeful ways of choosing our destiny. That is the torch our fourth generation is still handed to hold high from the outstretched arms of the dying of Flanders.

BIBLIOGRAPHY

Arendt, Hannah. *The Origins of Totalitarianism.* New York: Schocken Books, 2004.

Attenborough, Richard, director. *Oh! What a Lovely War.* 1969. Los Angeles: Paramount Pictures.

Barker, Pat. *The Eye in the Door.* New York: Plume, 1991.

―――. *The Ghost Road.* New York: Plume, 1995.

―――. *Regeneration.* New York: Dutton, 1995.

Bell, Daniel. *The End of Ideology: On Exhaustion of Political Ideals in the Fifties.* New York: The Free Press, 1960.

Blake, Christopher. *And Half the Seed of Europe: A Genealogy of the Great War 1914–18.* Macon, GA: Mercer University Press, 2017.

Blake, William. "Jerusalem ["And did those feet in ancient times"]. 1810. *Poetry Foundation.* 2020. https://www.poetryfoundation.org/poems/54684/jerusalem-and-did-those-feet-in-ancient-time.

Boden, Richard, dir. *Blackadder Goes Forth.* London: BBC, 1989.

Bosch, Hieronymus. *Last Judgement.* 1482. Academy of Fine Arts, Vienna.

Boswell, James. *Life of Samuel Johnson, LL.D.* 1791. Oxford UK: Oxford University Press, 1953.

Bouverie, Tim. *Appeasement: Chamberlain, Hitler, Churchill, and the Road to War.* New York: Tim Duggan Books, 2019.

Bryson, Bill. *Neither Here nor There: Travels in Europe.* New York: Harper Perennial, 2001.

Churchill, Winston. *This Island Race.* London: Cassell & Company, 1964.

Clark, Alan. *The Donkeys.* New York: Random House, 1961.

Clark, Christopher. *The Sleepwalkers: How Europe Went to War in 1914.* New York: Harper Perennial, 2013.

Dash, Mike. "The Story of the WWI Christmas Truce." *Smithsonian Magazine* (23 December 2011): 5.

European Union. https://ec.europa.eu/commission/presscorner/detail/en/IP_12_1393.

Evans, Richard J. *The Pursuit of Power: Europe 1815–1914*. New York: Penguin, 2016.

Ferguson, Niall. *The Pity of War: Explaining World War I*. New York: Basic Books, 1998.

Fischer, Fritz. *Germany's Aims in the First World War*. New York: Norton, 1961.

Fukuyama, Francis. *The End of History and the Last Man*. New York: The Free Press, 1992.

Fussell, Paul. *The Great War and Modern Memory*. Oxford, UK: Oxford University Press, 1975.

Garton-Ash, Timothy. *The Magic Lantern: The Revolution of '89 as Witnessed in Warsaw, Budapest, Berlin, and Prague*. New York: Random House, 1990.

"Germans Agree to Sign." *The* (London) *Times* (24 June 1919): 13.

"Germany Submits." *The* (London) *Times* (24 June 1919): 1.

Gerwarth, Robert. *The Vanquished: Why the First World War Failed to End*. New York: Farrar, Straus and Giroux, 2016.

Goldhagen, Daniel Jonah. *Hitler's Willing Executioners: Ordinary Germans and the Holocaust*. New York: Knopf, 1996.

Graves, Robert. "Wave No Banners." *Saturday Evening Post* 235/45 (15 December 1962): 34–41.

The Great War. Documentary. 1964. London: BBC.

Grey, Edward. *Twenty-Five Years, 1892–1916*. New York: F. A. Stokes, Co., 1927.

Hughes-Hallett, Lucy. *Gabrielle D'Annunzio: Poet, Seducer and Preacher of War*. New York: Knopf Doubleday, 2013.

Hampton, Ellen. "How World War I Revolutionized Medicine." *Atlantic Magazine* (24 February 2017). https://www.theatlantic.com/health/archive/2017/02/world-war-i-medicine/517656/.

Hart, Peter. *The Great War: A Combat History of the First World War*. Oxford, UK: Oxford University Press, 2013.

————. *The Somme: The Darkest Hour on the Western Front*. Cambridge, UK: Pegasus, 2009.

Hastings, Max. *Catastrophe 1914: Europe Goes to War*. New York: First Vintage Books, 2013.

Hesse, Hermann. *If the War Goes On, Reflections on War and Politics*. Translated by Ralph Manheim. New York: Farrar, Straus and Giroux, 1970.

Huxley, Aldus. *Brave New World.* New York: Doubleday, 1932.

"'Journey's End' and the First World War." *Imperial War Museums.* December 2018. https://www.iwm.org.uk/history/journeys-end-and-the-first-world-war.

Kahloon, Idrees. "The Leveller." *The New Yorker* (9 March 2020).

Keegan, John. *The First World War.* New York: Vintage, Random House, 2018.

Klaas, Brian. "The Survival of Democracy in Eastern Europe, with Ivan Krastev, Timothy Garton Ash and Brian Klaas." Podcast episode. *Intelligence Squared* (12 November 2019). https://open.spotify.com/episode/43ZyZwGJmbmy3nGCPpQvKK.

Knight, Sam. "What Will Brexit Britain Be Like?" *The New Yorker* (31 January 2020).

Lang, Sean. *The First World War for Dummies.* Hoboken, NJ: Wiley, 2014.

Lenore, Jill. "In Every Dark Hour." *New York Magazine* (4 February 2020): 20–25.

Levitsky, Steven and Daniel Ziblatt. *How Democracies Die.* Portland, OR: Broadway Books, 2018.

Littlewood, Joan, director. *Oh! What a Lovely War.* Theatre Workshop. Theatre Royal, Stratford East, 1963.

MacMillan, Margaret. *The Road to 1914—The War That Ended Peace.* New York: Random House, 2014.

McRae, John. "'In Flanders Field' in Punch, 1915." *Punch* (8 December 1915). 2018. https://poets.org/text/flanders-fields-punch-1915.

Mcwhirter, Cameron. *Red Summer: The Summer of 1919 and the Awakening of Black America.* New York: Henry Holt & Co., 2011.

Mendes, Sam, director. *1917.* Universal City, CA: Universal Pictures, 2019.

Meyer, G. L. *A World Undone: The Story of the Great War, 1914–18.* New York: Random House, 2006.

———. *The World Remade: America in World War 1.* New York: Random House. 2016.

"More Tales of the Truce." *The* (London) *Times* (2 January 2015).

Murphy, Donald J. *World War I.* New York: Greenhaven Press, 2002.

Nash, Paul. *Outline: An Autobiography and Other Writings.* London: Faber and Faber, 1949.

O'Toole, Patricia. *The Moralist: Woodrow Wilson and the World He Made.* New York: Simon & Schuster, 2018.

Owen, Wilfred. "Exposure." 1918. Poetry Foundation (2020). https://www.poetryfoundation.org/poems/57261/exposure-56d23a961ef5a.

Postman, Andrew. "My dad predicted Trump in 1985—it's not Orwell, he warned, it's Brave New World." *The Guardian.* https://www.theguardian.com/media/2017/feb/02/amusing-our-selves-to-death-neil-postman-trump-orwell-huxley. Accessed 2 February 2017.

Postman, Neil. *Amusing Ourselves to Death: Public Discourse in the Age of Show Business.* New York: Viking Press, 1985.

———. *Building a Bridge to the 18th Century: How the Past Can Improve Our Future.* New York: Alfred A. Knopf, 1999.

Reynolds, David. *The Long Shadow: The Great War and the Twentieth Century.* New York: Simon & Schuster, 2013.

"Robert Cecil to the War Cabinet." October 1916. The National Archives, Kew. Memorandum on Proposals for Diminishing the Occasion of Future Wars. CAB 24/10/85.

Sassoon, Siegfried. "Survivors." *Counter-Attack and Other Poems.* 1918. The First World War Poetry Digital Archive. 2020. http://ww1lit.nsms.ox.ac.uk/ww1lit/collections/item/9686.

Shakespeare, William. *The Tempest.* New York: Simon & Schuster, 2009.

"Shell Shock." London: BBC. http://www.bbc.co.uk/insideout/extra/series-1/shell_shocked.shtml. Accessed 3 March 2004.

Spender, John Alfred. *Life, Journalism and Politics.* Vol.1. New York: F. A. Stokes, Co., 1927.

Swift, Daniel. "The Classic Book." *History Today,* 64/8 (August 2014): 61.

Jackson, Peter, director. *They Shall Not Grow Old.* 2018. Los Angeles: Warner Brothers.

Tuchman, Barbara. *The Guns of August.* New York: Macmillan, 1962.

Wells, H. G. *The War That Will End War.* New York: Duffield & Company, 1914.

"Wilson Leaves Paris; Sails Sunday; Germans Pledge to Act in Good Faith." Final Edition, Image 9. *The Evening World* (28 June 1919).

https://chroniclingamerica.loc.gov/lccn/sn83030193/1919-06-28/ed-1/seq-1/.

INDEX